P9-EDA-170

Erik Satie

Saint-Saëns and His Circle
Sacha Guitry, The Last Boulevardier
The Duke of Wellington
Massenet
Rossini
The Astonishing Adventure of General Boulanger
The Ox on The Roof
Gounod
Lost Illusions: Paul Léautaud and His World

Anthology
Lord Chesterfield's Letters to His Son

Erik Satie

JAMES HARDING

My brother was always difficult to understand.
He doesn't seem to have been quite normal.
Olga Satie

He was a knowing old card. He was full of
guile and intelligently mischievous. I liked
him from the start.
Igor Stravinsky

Praeger Publishers
New York

Published in the United States of America in 1975
by Praeger Publishers, Inc.
111 Fourth Avenue, New York, N.Y. 10003

Copyright © James Harding 1975

Library of Congress Cataloging in Publication Data

Harding, James.
  Erik Satie.

  Bibliography: p.
  Includes index.
  1. Satie, Erik, 1866–1925.
ML410.S196H3   786.1'092'4 [B]   75-5829
ISBN: 0–275–53720–X

Printed in Great Britain

For
ROLLO MYERS
descubridor and pioneer

Contents

List of Illustrations

Acknowledgements

Two kind people who helped me when I was preparing this book have, alas, died before its publication. One was Marcel Jouhandeau's wife, the exuberant Elise, who, though daunting to the end, camouflaged reserves of geniality behind her formidable legend. The other was the gentle Darius Milhaud, one of the rare friends with whom Satie never quarrelled.

I am also grateful to René Clair for his memories of *Entr'acte* and *Relâche*; to Yves Lescroart, curator of the Honfleur museum; to François Lesure, head of the Département de la musique, Bibliothèque Nationale; to Madame Martine Kahane, keeper of the Bibliothèque de l'Opéra; to Jacques Chailley, head of the Schola Cantorum; and to Monsieur R. Picot, deputy mayor of Arcueil.

Kenneth Thompson has generously given permission for the catalogue of Satie's works to be based on the list he compiled for his monumental *Dictionary of Twentieth-Century Composers*.

Once more I acknowledge my debt to the secretarial skills of Mrs D. L. Mackay and the accomplished photographic work of Mrs Stella Mayes Reed.

It should be recorded that the Phoenix Trust made a grant which helped to smooth the way of research.

Ouverture

Satie in his time was, except for a small band of loyal admirers, an obscure and ridiculed musician. Today, when the astringent nature of his music is recognised by an age which can appreciate its modernity and its refusal to strike romantic poses, he has become a cult figure. No other minor composer is the object of so many picturesque legends.

He was an original who loved animals, children and his art. He disliked women, conventions and accepted ideas. Religious feeling was strong in him. As a boy he responded eagerly to the charm of Gothic atmospheres and Gregorian modes. The grown man adopted mystical beliefs. The vague spell of the Rosicrucians held him for a time. Then he founded his own church. It had one member: himself.

Starting his career as a velvet-suited Bohemian piano player in Montmartre cabarets, he developed into what looked like a typical bourgeois clerk. The bowler hat, the pince-nez, the wing collar, the dark formal suit, became a uniform. His umbrella he cherished with a fetishistic compulsion. Despite his neat appearance he never took baths. It was his habit to clean his person, in little bits at a time, with pumice stone, which, he argued, was more effective than water.

His manuscripts were written in coloured inks with the elaborate hand of a calligrapher. This music he baptised with absurd titles – genuine flabby preludes (for a dog), things seen to right and left (without glasses), dried embryos – and loaded it with dotty commentaries. The visual fantasies he indulged in were no less bizarre. After his death thousands of scraps of paper were found carefully preserved in a cigar box. Upon them were drawn, in fine detail, imaginary maps, Gothic houses, incredible machines and mediaeval fancies.

He lived alone in suburban Arcueil, a dolorous outcrop of Paris. The landscape of factory chimneys and grimy workshops pleased him. His home was a room in a working-class tenement. No one else ever penetrated this sanctum while he remained alive. He was tenacious in defending his privacy.

On his father's side he descended from a long line of Norman seafarers. His mother was Scottish. The little port of Honfleur, where he "came very young into a world that was very old", to quote his own remark, is noted as the birthplace of stubborn-minded characters with a dry sense of humour all their own. Satie put up a smoke-screen of puns and facetious word-play that had a deal in common with the techniques of *Alice in Wonderland*. His other method of keeping the world at bay was drink. He turned into an alcoholic and shortened his life with the inevitable liver complaint. He was not a happy man.

Short-tempered and ultra-sensitive, he would flare up into violent rages that exhausted his friends. A slight was never forgotten. His anger burgeoned at trifles and expressed itself in cold, wounding gibes. Yet he could also be the most charming of companions.

Satie has been much abused for his manias. "His folly was so great that it is, perhaps, difficult to see whatever wisdom there was in him," a disapproving commentator has said. Another has condemned him for his 'intellectual salesmanship". Satie's reply was mild: "I quite agree with our opponents. It is regrettable to see artists making use of publicity. Yet Beethoven was no mean hand at advertising. That's what made him known, I think."

In many ways his personal behaviour resembled that of a spoilt child. At the same time, in Rollo Myers' perceptive phrase, he was the small boy who discerned that the Emperor wore no clothes. He pointed out the stupidities of a dying tradition and undermined it with parody and with satire. What was to replace it? Laboriously he produced music of a type that was inimitable, bare and serenely objective. He had found an individual solution. Others would have to find their own. Stravinsky exclaimed: "*Parade* confirmed me anew in my conviction about Satie's merit and the part he played in French music by confronting the dying wave of Impressionism with a musical language that was firm, clear-cut and stripped of all picturesque ornament."

It is true that Satie the hermit once called out the police when he suspected a woman of being anxious to press her attentions upon him. It is true that Satie the wit, after the first performance of Debussy's *La Mer*, remarked to his friend about the opening movement which is supposed to portray the sea between dawn and midday: "Old chap, there was a little bit in particular between half past ten and a quarter to eleven that I thought was terrific." But it is also true that, after a lifetime's self-imposed poverty inspired by his refusal to take the easy way out, he declared: "Capitulation is always a sign of weakness if not cowardice . . . The practice of an art bids us live in a state of the most complete renunciation . . . Music demands much of those who wish to serve it . . . A true musician must be obedient to his art, he must place it above all human wretchedness, he must draw his courage from within himself and himself alone."

J.H.

PART ONE

Reluctant Musician

I

Honfleur and Uncle Sea Bird

His birth certificate is firm on the point. "Eric Alfred Leslie", it says, and not "Erik" with a "k" as he was later, through a whim, to call himself. He arrived at nine o'clock in the morning of 17 May 1866. In the afternoon his father Alfred registered the birth at the town hall of Honfleur. A business acquaintance witnessed the formality. The town was in a fructuous mood that day, for the register shows that the deputy mayor was called on more than once to attest the births of infant Honfleurais.

The Satie family lived at No. 90 rue Haute. This street, where there are houses dating back to the sixteenth century, is traditionally the spot shipping men have chosen to inhabit. Alfred Satie, who was twenty-four years old when his son Erik came into the world, followed the profession, not with great enthusiasm it was later to appear, of shipbroker. Like Erik in later years, he contradicted the evidence of his birth certificate, which described him as Jules Alfred. He preferred to be known as Alfred only.

The rue Haute, by an agreeable paradox, is in fact the lowest street in Honfleur, having become so through the growth of the town upward to the hill. In the eighteen-sixties it was rarely frequented by traffic. Many children played across its desert expanse. Old ladies squatted on straw-bottomed chairs in the middle of the roadway and were indignant when the driver of a cart told them brusquely to move. The smell of seaweed and mud, the clack of gulls and the creak of boats could be sensed in the rue Haute and were among the earliest impressions Erik Satie knew. The street ended in a square with a lighthouse flashing out over the sea. Down by the quays the reek of fish lay pungent on the air. There is, properly speaking, no real beach at Honfleur. This has helped to preserve its singularity, to spare it from becoming just another overcrowded holiday resort. It remains a quiet fishing town with slate-roofed houses, an elm-fringed esplanade and a fifteenth-century Gothic church built of wood.

The painter Eugène Boudin, whose stone features gaze across one of the squares, was born here. His pictures of Honfleur, of crinolined Second Empire ladies walking with their tiny umbrellas on the jetty, of clouds streaking over the sky, of crystal sunshine, have captured the essence of the place as it was during Satie's childhood. Corot, Jongkind and Whistler also came often and painted it.

Charles Baudelaire, obstinately known in the district as Beaudelaire, is thought to have written "Le Voyage", one of the poems in the *Fleurs du mal*, at Honfleur. "Honfleur a toujours été le plus cher de mes rêves," he once said. His stepfather, the worthy General Aupick, had a six-roomed summer home in the square at the end of the rue Haute, now demolished and replaced with a modern building. This was, in fact, all the wealth her second husband left to Madame Baudelaire at his death, for the General, a high-minded public servant, believed it immoral to make money out of the country to which he was devoted. His wife found herself destitute. A statue commemorated the respect he enjoyed in the town. An item of local history that Satie enjoyed and often repeated later was the story of how Baudelaire, too, came to have his statue. A member of the town council put forward the idea. His colleagues were unresponsive. At last, in desperation, he cried: "After all, he was General Aupick's stepson!" This immediately decided the matter and the vote was successful. Although one old councillor was heard to grumble: "We should have asked how many stepsons General Aupick had. There might be no end to it!"

A year after Erik's birth the family in the rue Haute was

4

increased by the arrival of his sister Olga. In 1869 he was joined by a brother, Conrad. All three children were baptised in the Anglican faith. This roused disapproval among the elders of the Satie family. On his father's side Erik's ancestors were Norman and Catholic. "The origin of the Saties goes back perhaps to the remotest times," he would observe. "Yes. On this point I can confirm nothing – nor deny it, for that matter, yet I suppose that this family didn't belong to the nobility; that its members were modest and worthy toilers at their lords' pleasure." In a community where everyone numbered fishermen, sailors and ship-builders among their predecessors, where it was a commonplace to have had a great-uncle who fought at Trafalgar or a grand-father who worked on the ship that brought Napoleon's ashes back to France, the male Satie line was typical.

There was François Satie, Erik's great-grandfather, who captained one of Napoleon's vessels. None was more faithful to the Emperor's memory or detested the English with a sharper hatred. To his son Jules he bequeathed a seasoning of Norman stubbornness and a refusal to compromise which were to mark the great-grandson. Jules became a shipbroker, a sturdy citizen of Honfleur, a respected captain of the local fire brigade and member of the town council. The Légion d'honneur proclaimed his solid worth. His marriage to an Alsatian girl brought into the family another touch of hard-headedness that doubtless played its part in shaping Erik's character. There were three children: Alfred, Adrien and Marguerite.

The two brothers were quite different in personality. Adrien was little interested in his studies. Alfred, on the other hand, enjoyed going to school in the nearby town of Lisieux. There he attended classes with his exact contemporary and fellow Hon-fleurais Albert Sorel, later to be a distinguished historian of the French Revolution and to have a square named after him in his native town. Alfred worked well at school. It was here that he discovered intellectual tastes which afterwards clashed with the career his father chose for him.

When the Saties' hallowed dislike of the English is remembered, it is odd that the two brothers should have been sent for a time across the Channel. Perhaps Jules had reacted against his father's opinions. He may have found it tedious listening night after night to the old man's fulminations, to accounts which by then he must have known only too well of how the intrepid French had beaten the lackeys of treacherous Albion. Whatever the reason for this mildly surprising decision, Adrien and Alfred were lodged for a spell in the home of an English clergyman.

Within and without the parson's house, Alfred behaved immaculately. His wilder brother scandalised their host's flock. He played practical jokes during holy service and strove energetically to seduce the maids. When Alfred and Adrien returned to Honfleur their father decided it was time for them to settle down. Himself a shipbroker, he was able, with his connections and experience, to set them up in the same profession. Alfred quietly accepted his father's choice and applied himself to his new rôle. Adrien, unwilling and rebellious, only submitted out of respect for the heavy paternal authority which Jules was never afraid of exercising.

There came one day to Honfleur a lady called Mrs Anton and her daughter. Mrs Anton, who was Scottish, had been widowed early in marriage. She had little money and was reduced to acting as companion to her more fortunate sister. The latter had married a gentleman of affluence and high religious principles who, on his visits to the wicked town of Paris, was in the habit of distributing moral tracts. Mrs Anton left her daughter Jane to board at Honfleur. Soon Alfred Satie had made the girl's acquaintance. They liked each other. He then took the first of several steps that were to set him on a path that led away from the hallowed notions and customs of his family: he married her.

Jane Leslie Anton was twenty-two years old. Though born in London she was wholly Scottish through her parents. To Scotland the couple went for their honeymoon, and there, presumably, Jane showed her husband the places associated with her family. Next year their son Erik was born. There is a story that his godfather was a knight on his mother's side. Referred to as "sir Anton" – according to the French habit which produces a "sir Beecham" and a "sir Lipton" – the name of this legendary figure was ever afterwards given by his godson the full-throated French pronunciation: "sire Hâneton".

The births of Olga and Conrad which followed soon afterwards may have helped, as often happens, to soften the reluctance which Alfred's family showed towards the marriage. Even so, Jane and her husband did little to improve affairs by having all three

6

children raised in the Protestant faith. Here, perhaps, can be detected the hand of Jane's uncle, the distributor of tracts, and also the influence of her Scottish relatives as well as her own convictions. But Alfred's father and grandfather were staunchly Catholic, as had been previous generations of the family. His aunt Marguerite, indeed, was so devout that, not content with having a permanent place reserved for worship in her own parish church of Saint Catherine, she also kept one at Saint Leonard's church in another part of the town. The Saties could not look with anything but misgiving on the Protestants within their gates.

However loyal Alfred felt towards the clan, his first duty lay to Jane and himself. In 1871, as soon as the Franco-Prussian War had ended, he resolved the awkward situation by selling his shipbroking practice and moving to Paris. Next year Jane Satie died at the early age of twenty-nine. The widower sent his children back to their grandparents in Honfleur and remained in Paris. He had presumably convinced his father that he would do better there. In fact, he was now able to develop all the interests which the demands of business and the restrictive atmosphere of a small town had up to then prevented him from enjoying. He went to lectures at the Sorbonne and the Collège de France. Regularly each week he dined at Versailles with his old schoolfriend Albert Sorel, now working for the Senate and already launched on the first stages of a notable career. The study of foreign languages in particular occupied Alfred at this time. English he had probably acquired from Jane. His German and his Italian profited from long periods he spent in Lubeck and Milan. Through Albert Sorel he obtained a post as translator, and the new friends he was making in academic circles could also have provided him with commissions.

Erik was six when Jane Satie died. Back in Honfleur, living again at 90 rue Haute with his grandparents, he found the childhood memories of his mother quickly fading. He had known so little of her. His brother Conrad took after their father and was a thoughtful, well-behaved little boy whose interest in science was to make him a chemist. In later years he collaborated on a treatise about the chemistry of perfumes. Erik was already a solitary. At the local school, today known as the Lycée Albert Sorel, he once came top in Latin – for which he retained a taste throughout life – and in history. Apart from an honourable mention these were his only academic successes. Conrad, meanwhile, went on collecting, sagely and steadily, as did his cousin Louis, a row of distinctions.

Now that the children were safely back in the fold they were re-baptised as Catholics. Erik's grandmother was a pious woman, her husband less so. The Satie strain of fantasy had bypassed her and come to full flower in Erik's uncle Adrien. He had soon given up the life of a shipbroker. The hero of many a disgraceful scene in the English clergyman's household then took over a small printing works. This, again, he quickly tired of and handed over the management to his wife Marie. For the rest of his life he devoted himself entirely to his twin passions: horses and boats.

While Marie dealt with invoices and typefaces and bindings at the print-shop in the cours d'Orléans, Adrien, nicknamed "Sea Bird", was usually to be found sitting beside the inner port now known as the Vieux-Bassin. This curious eighteenth-century construction is surrounded by ancient houses, many built of wood. They have the characteristic slate roofs and are tall, sometimes as high as seven storeys, though often there may be only two windows in the whole of the front. Their jumbled shapes and crazy angles suggest that they have been dumped on the spot and left there by some absentminded giant. This faintly unreal setting provided an appropriate backdrop to Adrien's mild eccentricities.

He would sit by the water for hours, smoking his pipe and staring beatifically at the view before him. What he contemplated with such tenderness was a magnificent yacht, a vessel he had had built and named *The Wave*. So precious was it to him, so fearful was he of its being damaged, however slightly, that only on the very rarest of occasions did he take it to sea. Sometimes he would actually go aboard to feel the deck beneath his feet and touch the beloved object that he worshipped each day. When he was not absorbed in admiration of *The Wave*, he would be up on the Côte de Grâce, a lovely stretch of country high above the town looking out over the estuary and Le Havre in the distance. Here he appraised with a knowing eye the various points of the horses that were being exercised. Did he not own a superb carriage, as splendid in its fashion as *The Wave*? And it was in just as immaculate a condition, for no one dared get into it lest its glory be scratched or spoiled.

Erik gravitated naturally towards Uncle Adrien. Out of school he would often sit with him at the water's edge and listen to his talk about the boats they saw, his comments on the manoeuvres of the fishing smacks, the steamers that collected passengers for Rouen, the tall ships that lay by the quay and unloaded coal from England and timber from Norway and Russia. Once the incredulous boy was even allowed aboard *The Wave* for a trip around the harbour.

Adrien would also take him to the theatre which stood in the place Thiers opposite the bandstand. Naturally, his uncle was well known backstage, and Erik always awaited impatiently the interval when Adrien took him behind the scenes and into the dressing-rooms. The actresses patted him on the head. The actors joked with him. The little theatre, provincial though it was, a port of call for second-rate touring companies, gave him an exciting taste of raffishness. Yet its stage had known the famous of the day. Among them was the celebrated Madame Agar, who once played Honfleur at the time when she was a rising young actress of the Comédie-Française. Afterwards, as a leading lady, she was engaged again. But now, a star in her own right, she could not be troubled to make the journey from Paris. The Honfleurais were slighted and disappointed. A local journalist took his wry revenge. He wrote: "L'Agar demeure et ne s'y rend pas!"*

* A neat play on what is supposed to have been Cambronne's reply when called on to surrender at Waterloo: "La garde meurt mais ne se rend pas."

II

Anglican, Catholic . . . Gregorian

At the age of eight Erik was showing more interest in music than in the subjects he studied at school. On this account the family had already nicknamed him "Crincrin" (fiddler, scraper). Grandfather Jules decided that he should take music lessons.

In 1873 a new organist had been appointed to the church of St Leonard. His name was Vinot and he had but recently emerged from the school founded by the Swiss composer Louis Niedermeyer. A better teacher than composer – his one success was a very popular setting of Lamartine's poem "Le Lac" – Niedermeyer set up his establishment with the aim of training young musicians who would go out and improve the musical standards of French churches. While, of course, he did succeed in producing such ornaments of the organ loft as Eugène Gigout and Gustave Lefèvre, as well as one great musician, Gabriel Fauré, he also, to his surprise had he known it, was responsible for training that master of operetta André Messager. Other products of his school who went on to contradict his exalted aims by writing music so light that it has since been almost entirely blown away, included Edmond Audran, whose *Grand Mogol* and *Miss Helyett* delighted for a time the connoisseurs of opéra-bouffe and vaudeville, and Claude Terrasse, the composer of *Chonchette* and *Le Sire de Vergy*. It is possible that Vinot studied under Saint-Saëns, who, for a brief period, taught the piano at Niedermeyer's school. He certainly followed, in his off-duty hours, the tradition of light music that had attached itself irreverently to Niedermeyer's teaching. His name was prominent, as accompanist and composer, at concerts given by the Honfleur Philharmonic Society, or "Philar" as it was locally known. The Society had the use of a rehearsal room in the town hall which now does duty as a police station. If the weather was fine they gave their performance in the bandstand. If wet, they took refuge in the theatre.

At these concerts Vinot played the piano and accompanied, with tactful sympathy, the chairman of the Society when he gave a violin solo. Vinot's own compositions showed a resolute frivolity. His *Valse brillante* charmed subscribers to the autumn concerts. His *Valse des patineurs* was heard with pleasure. Like Parisians at café-concerts, the Honfleurais enjoyed the vigorous rhythm of a waltz.

These less austere activities did little to augment Vinot's slim stipend at St Leonard's. Soon after his arrival in the town he advertised for pupils. An issue of the *Echo Honfleurais* in October 1873 carried an announcement that M. Vinot, of 32 rue Bourdet, was prepared to give music lessons to the youth of the town.

For months this newspaper, doubtless with many others, lay about in the Satie home. Perhaps among the family obsessions was that of hoarding useless objects, a mania which Erik later displayed with his collections of virgin handkerchiefs and unworn corduroy suits. On a morning in the spring of the following year Jules Satie toiled up the steep incline of the rue Boudet that rises from the square and leads to the high countryside beyond. He was dressed, says one account of sober authority, in the full splendour of his uniform as captain of the Honfleur fire brigade.

Jules stopped at Vinot's door and knocked. When the organist appeared he explained the reason for his visit. He was well aware, he said, of Monsieur Vinot's talent, having often had the pleasure of hearing him play at "Philar" concerts. With Monsieur Vinot's performances at St Leonard's he was less familiar, since he did not often frequent holy service, though his wife, being very devout . . .

11

Unfolding his copy of the *Echo Honfleurais* which contained Vinot's announcement, Jules spoke of his grandson Erik, who, like his father, had shown signs of an interest in music. Would Monsieur Vinot take the boy on? The matter was agreed, and Erik henceforward left school in the afternoons to have his music lesson with Vinot.

St Leonard's church, where Vinot played the organ and trained the choir, is not the biggest of its kind in Honfleur. That title goes to St Catherine's, which was built of wood on stone foundations by the fifteenth-century ships' carpenters of the town. Across a little square and separated from it stands its ancient clock tower, a building also of wood and shored up with beams of chestnut covered in the omnipresent slates. The style is flamboyantly Gothic. Yet the smaller church of St Leonard's, built in the same order of architecture, seems more truly to express its spirit. The sixteenth-century portals are surmounted by a single turret, and just inside are large sea-shells which are used for sprinkling holy water. Here, as Vinot's pupil, Erik would have had his first and prolonged exposure to that Gothic atmosphere which was such an influence on his life and thought. Here, too, he probably attended mass, for the deeply religious Alsatian grandmother with whom he lived would have taken care, once he had been received into the Catholic faith, to make of him a regular church-goer.

Other influences began to work on him. The école Niedermeyer where Vinot had studied was no ordinary school. The teaching there was inspired not only by the wish to produce capable musicians but also by an ambition to perpetuate the ideas of Alexandre Choron, an early pioneer in the reform of church music and the man who gave Paris its first performances of major works by Palestrina, Bach and Handel. Niedermeyer himself wrote manuals on the art of accompanying plainchant and services. He founded a journal to publicise his ideas and introduce new religious music. He advocated a return to earlier, purer masters, and criticised the music, much of it trivial and unsuitable, which was then used for church purposes. Like all who studied under Niedermeyer's régime, Vinot would have been an adept of Palestrina, Lassus, Marcello and Bach. Once Erik had learned the basics of music he, too, would have inherited from Vinot something of the Niedermeyer tradition and its chosen composers. The visual and aural combined: the Gothic look of Vinot's church and the sound of the Gregorian mode which he heard there.

Regularly he made his way up the rue Bourdet, a street inhabited by artisans and small tradesmen, its peace disturbed by the chatter of women gossiping from door to door and the din of children playing at their feet. He does not seem to have been an outstanding pupil. His name is absent from the lists of Vinot's pupils who were selected to play at school concerts. Yet he must have paid more attention to his music lessons than to what went on in the classroom. His development as a mature composer proves it. From Vinot he received one of the most important elements of his art.

In July 1878 Vinot gave up his post in Honfleur and moved to Lyon. Although he continued from time to time to appear at "Philar" concerts, his link with the town, and with Erik, was broken. This was also the year when Erik's grandmother died with a strange suddenness on the little beach at Honfleur. The event distressed grandfather Jules and upset his ideas. With the coming of old age he had already resigned from the fire brigade and the town council. Now he turned for comfort to the religion of which, up to then, he had only been a tepid practitioner. Even so, a vein of originality persisted. The new convert took with him to mass not a conventional breviary but a work by that Rousseau-esque lover of nature Bernardin de Saint-Pierre. It was not even the famous *Paul et Virginie*. Jules' choice of reading during the sacred office fell upon the *Harmonies de la nature*, a confused and extravagant treatise which pleaded the beauties of nature as an effective argument against atheism.

And 1878, finally, was the year when Erik took his first communion and, at the age of twelve, left Honfleur for ever. His father, now well established in Paris, was about to marry again. Alfred once more could offer his children a home and a mother. Accompanied by his father and grandfather, Erik went to the little railway station which for the past twelve years or so had served Honfleur. The clumsy little building, made of red brick and yellow wood roofed with zinc, was the scene of his farewell to the town where he was born. As the train moved out he caught glimpses of sails and rigging and sometimes a funnel. Sea gulls clucked and swooped. The smell of salty air and tar came from a nearby inner port.

To the end of his life the resonance of Honfleur persisted. At the back of his mind when he wrote the early *Ogives* with their Gothic undertones could well have been the pointed arches of St Catherine's church. The rue de l'Homme de bois, down which he often scampered as a boy on his way to music lessons, may have come to the surface over thirty years later in the title *Croquis et agaceries d'un gros bonhomme en bois*. Certainly, when young, he would have heard the popular song "Maman, les p'tits bateaux . . . ont-ils des jambes?" which he quoted in the *Descriptions automatiques*. For the boats moving around the inner ports of Honfleur could appear, if viewed from certain angles, to be gliding over solid ground. His liking for waltz rhythms had been nurtured by those he heard in boyhood, including the ones composed by his teacher Vinot. And had not Vinot, trailing clouds of the Niedermeyer school, given him a permanent taste for liturgical music that was to influence most of his compositions to a greater or smaller extent?

Like everyone else, Satie was the prisoner of his childhood. Heredity had given him a vein of independence which, emerging in grandfather and father and blooming into eccentricity with his uncle "Sea Bird", was to achieve its fullest flower in the composer. Religion surrounded him from the earliest age, and argument about religion, for although he was too young to appreciate doctrinal subtleties he had known both the Anglican and the Catholic beliefs. As his later development showed, he was not a deeply religious man. Catholicism had been imposed upon him from without. He observed the forms and obediently went to church as his grandmother wished. The inner conviction was not strong. Yet if doctrine made little appeal to him, the picturesque trappings and the mysterious atmosphere of religion had an aesthetic appeal. For a long time the language and the architecture had power to move him. He preserved an admiration for the saints. They were, he wrote in maturity, "unsurpassed models. A man like Saint Joseph is superior by far to Napoleon, Copernicus and other geniuses."

So he left the Honfleur which had made him. We do not know if he ever visited the town again. That he did so, at least once, as a youth of eighteen, is suggested by the manuscript of the earliest piece of music he is known to have composed. It is entitled *Allegro* and is dated "Honfleur, 9 Sept. 1884". At No. 90 rue Haute, where he was born and spent his childhood, a plaque has been fixed to the wall. It reads: "Ici est né Erik Satie, musicien français, 1866–1925." Few of the hurrying passers-by have time to glance at it.

III

"Monsieur le Pauvre"

Alfred Satie was now installed in the rue de Constantinople, that long and, despite its romantic name, lugubrious street which runs towards the noisy and manifold railway tracks of the nearby Gare Saint-Lazare. At that time the unpromising district harboured, oddly, several poets. In the rue de Rome, which is crossed at one point by the rue de Constantinople, Mallarmé lived and held his now famous "evenings", distributing hot toddies to guests who included Oscar Wilde and Paul Valéry. At No. 9 in the rue de Constantinople itself, a few years later, the boy Guillaume Apollinaire used to stay on visits to Paris when his flighty mother, in between tours of the provincial casinos that were her usual beat, decided to give him the pleasure of her company for a while.

Erik's father led in Paris the sort of life that had been denied to him in Honfleur. At the home of his friend Albert Sorel he met a young music teacher called Mademoiselle Barnetche. He married her, not, it is thought, to Erik's great delight. Another unattractive aspect of the household in the rue de Constantinople was that it also included the bride's mother. During the months before the marriage – it took place in 1879 – Erik knew a brief period of liberation. His father took him away from school. Together they went to lectures at the Collège de France and elsewhere. Then came marriage, the women descended, and Erik may sometimes have longed for Honfleur. Even though church and school loomed large there, he had always been able to slip away for solitary wanderings around the port and gossip with Uncle "Sea Bird". Now there was no escape from Alfred's new wife and mother-in-law.

Worse still, from Erik's point of view, was the passion for music which inspired the happy couple. Doubtless at the urging of the Barnetche family, Alfred Satie started giving music classes at an address in the rue de Turbigo. The enterprise did not flourish. When grandfather Jules died and left a modest inheritance, it was used by Alfred to buy a stationery shop in the broad and bustling boulevard de Magenta. His mother-in-law presided behind the counter. Soon – dangerous omen – he added the sale of sheet music to his trade in pens and envelopes. From this to the act of publishing music was but a short and fatal step.

Both Alfred and his wife suffered from the urge to compose. Naturally he published his own works. His Opus 28 was a polka-mazurka for piano entitled *Souvenir de Honfleur!* The cover bore a nostalgic view of his native town. Another piece in the same genre had the English title *Connubial Bliss*, which, published as late as 1890, seems to show that his activities extended over several years. Drinking songs were a speciality – *Le Dévot buveur* and *Le Vin de Chablis* are there to prove it – and he was not too haughty to overlook the needs of young pianists for whom he wrote the easy waltz *Bulles de savon*. His Muse was equally at home with comic songs like *Y a vraiment d'quoi vous suffoquer!* and with stirring polkas like *A tous les diables*. This polka, indeed, came out in a second edition five years after its first appearance, so he cannot have been without admirers among the host of amateur pianists who in those days needed a constant supply of music for parlour recitals and home dances.

His bride was no less prolific. Between the date of her marriage and 1897, a year when her Opus numbers attained the respectable total of ninety-six, the name of "E. Satie-Barnetche" appeared frequently on items published by Alfred. She does not seem, like him, to have written songs. Her compositions were exclusively for the piano. She favoured brisk measures, the mazurka, the

17

bolero and the scherzo. Although in quieter moods she would produce a nocturne or a song without words, she expressed herself more gratefully, one feels, in the fiery witches' dance (Opus 85) and the exotic waltz *Las Estrellas!* (Both she and Alfred were fond of exclamation marks.) By 1897 her music was being published under the imprint of E. Baudoux. Had the establishment in the boulevard de Magenta closed down? In that year Alfred would have been fifty-five. The funds he inherited under his father's will would long ago have run out, and his publishing business was not a prosperous one. He probably did not mind. He had done what he wanted to do and enjoyed himself. That he had lost money rather than made it was of little importance compared with the pleasure he got out of his life.

A tone of strenuous musicality pervaded the home in the rue de Constantinople. Madame Satie-Barnetche had been a pupil of the famous organist Alexandre Guilmant, later to be a co-founder with Vincent d'Indy of the Schola Cantorum and a teacher at the Conservatoire, institutions that Erik in time knew well. He, whether it pleased him or not, was often taken under escort to the Church of the Trinity where Guilmant played regularly, or to the Trocadéro for the series of recitals given by the organist which had become a feature of musical life in Paris.

The talk was all of the latest productions at the Opéra and the Opéra-Comique. There was much concert-going. Alfred had a colleague who, like him, kept a stationer's shop round the corner in the rue de Rome. The stationery business, in Alfred's circle, seemed to be the favourite occupation of intellectuals, for this acquaintance had come to it from teaching Latin at a Jesuit school. He had a daughter. It was arranged that Erik should have tuition in Latin and Greek, subjects at which he had not done badly during his schooldays, while in exchange his stepmother would give piano lessons to the stationer's daughter. A ritual established itself. The Latinist and his pupil went into the drawing-room. Erik, of course, would have done no work at all since their last session. Telling the boy to recite his lesson, the teacher would doze off. Like the young Rossini, whose piano teacher was given to a convenient somnolence, Erik would sit in silence, fearful of waking him, until, at the old man's surfacing, he could claim to have done his lesson. His teacher was not in a position to contradict him.

18

In the time he could snatch for himself Erik read widely. He explored his father's library and plunged one after another into the romances of Alexandre Dumas. Other light reading was provided by the humorous works of Eugène Chavette, son of the man who founded the restaurant Vachette. When he grew a little older he was able to appreciate the astringent wit of the novelist Alphonse Karr, an attractive figure who, after producing the epigram for which he is best remembered – "Plus ça change," he said of the 1848 Revolution, "plus c'est la même chose" – settled in Nice and grew flowers for a living. Erik enjoyed, too, the adventure stories of Joseph Méry, a pamphleteer like Karr but also the author of popular books, and the poetry of Alfred de Musset. As a corrective there was always the healthy irony, the sense of the ridiculous, which Voltaire supplied. Of all the books he discovered at this period, the one that left the deepest impression on him was a volume of Hans Andersen's *Fairy Tales*. These he read and re-read throughout his life. The strange fancies of the unworldly Dane captured his imagination. As his career developed there were to be many parallels between himself and the tales told by the creator of the Ugly Duckling.

In 1879, when he was thirteen, his parents decided to send him to the Conservatoire. The skill he showed for the piano at his age convinced them that he should study the instrument seriously. He claimed later that a musical career had been thrust upon him, as had religion. With little enthusiasm he presented himself at the decrepit building which then housed the Conservatoire. From the outset he disliked the place. It reminded him of a prison: huge, grim, uncomfortable. The peeling walls enclosed dark corridors and ill-lit rooms. Through long disuse the windows, clamped shut with dust and grime, could rarely be opened. The furniture was clumsy and dilapidated. There was an air of decay. Against a background of heavy traffic rumbling outside, the narrow little courtyard was filled with the discordant noise of students practising in the rooms overlooking it. For some musicians who studied there during the nineteenth century its lack of modernity was endearing. For Satie it was depressing.

His piano teacher was Emile Decombes, whose memory survives faintly as the composer of once-acclaimed drawing-room music. For theory he may have attended the classes of Albert Lavignac, a distinguished authority and editor of the eleven-volume *Encyclopédie de la musique* which is still a valuable reference work. It is with something of a shock, knowing the generally sober tone of his publications, that one comes across a decidedly lighter work on the subject of *Les Gaietés du Conservatoire*. Little of this gaiety rubbed off on Erik during his time there. His years at the Conservatoire were a period of melancholy lightened only by his private reading.

His studies under Decombes ended on 15 June 1882. After an unexplained break he entered, in October 1885, the piano class of Georges Mathias, a former pupil of Chopin and once the teacher of Madame Satie. His certificate of admission was signed on 6 November by Ambroise Thomas, then Director of the Conservatoire. The long-lived composer of *Mignon* and *Hamlet* was still, at the age of seventy-four, writing the music which earned him many official honours and gained him the privilege of being the first musician to receive the Grand-Croix de la Légion d'honneur, the highest rank in that famous order. Only a few years later, at the age of seventy-eight, he produced one of his best-known ballets, a fantastic piece entitled *La Tempête*. Soon after he died, though, the great reputation he enjoyed during his life had dwindled away. A pillar of the Opéra and the Opéra-Comique, he represented all that was most fashionable and accepted, all, in fact, that Madame Satie adored. The young student whom he authorised to enter Mathias' class belonged to a generation whose mockery found a convenient target in his once popular music.

Satie spent only one more year at the Conservatoire. He used to say afterwards that Mathias, his piano teacher, told him he should take up composition. Whereas his harmony teacher advised him to concentrate on the piano ... He left Mathias' class on 9 December 1886.

His first published works, to appear in 1887, had already been composed. Apart from a whimsical ascription to "Opus 62", they contained little to disturb his father and stepmother. The titles, *Valse Ballet* and *Fantaisie Valse*, tell the whole story. They made their appearance in a publication called *La Musique des Familles* and were prefaced with a note showing evidence of his father's – or Erik's? – skill at public relations. The music, it declared, was "elegant in construction, graceful in rhythm and free of youthful awkwardness. All the composer's works, among which we would mention three songs, show a leaning towards reverie and a tendency to avoid the rigid laws of symmetry."

All the composer's works? The only others known at that date are five songs which presumably include the three mentioned. These are settings of poems by a young man called J. P. Contamine de Latour. He was a poet of Spanish origin and great ambitions. He also possessed a consummate ability for myth-making. Among his kinsmen, he declared, was Napoleon. Doubtless for this reason, Satie nicknamed him "le Vieux Modeste".

Satie one day was eating outside a café with "le Vieux Modeste". A dilapidated person hovered near them. What was his job, enquired Contamine in friendly tones. He had none, replied the tramp, and his efforts to find employment were unsuccessful.

"Why," remarked Satie, as if visited by an inspiration, "why not set up as a doctor?"

"A doctor?" came the astonished response. "You can't just become a doctor like that. You have to pass exams, get qualifications."

"Not a bit of it. Qualifications aren't necessary. They're harmful, even. It's a career open to everyone. It's the most liberal of professions and you can earn a jolly good living at it."

"Do you think so?"

"I'm sure of it. And the proof is that, here and now, I'm making you a present of my practice."

"And so am I," broke in Contamine.

"If that's how it is then, I'll try," said the tramp. "Thank you for your good advice."

"Bonjour," said Satie.

The relationship between Satie and Contamine was close and amical, probably to the extent of sharing girl friends. The *Trois Mélodies*, Opus 20, which Alfred Satie published, are charming period pieces well within the convention of drawing-room songs, though provided with a few tactful discords to add piquancy. The second, "Elégie", in particular has a melody with a shape and phrasing that owe a great deal to Massenet. "Sylvie", which is dedicated to sister Olga – she was similarly honoured by her father who wrote a waltz for her – follows the same line. "Ma Sylvie" is so beautiful, says the verse, that the angels are jealous of her. Her eyes are like stars, her mouth like rubies, her voice sweeter than honey . . . and so on. The short phrases, rising and falling in a predictable pattern, are obviously the work of a musician who had not been unimpressed by the recent triumph of *Manon*.

The other songs of this period, also to poems by Contamine de Latour, include a sprightly little "Chanson" that laments, in tones of folk-like simplicity, the shortness of life and love. With "Les Fleurs" we are back again to the Massenetic idiom.

Yet at the same time as he was writing in this traditional vein he was also evolving in the direction that eventually led him towards originality. The year of the *Trois Mélodies* is the year of *Ogives*. (An *ogive* is, in Gothic architecture, a special type of pointed arch. Victor Hugo was also fond of the word, using it in his poetry and drawing it in those eerie, contorted Gothic sketches that fill his notebooks.) These four piano pieces each follow a scheme of mathematical rigidity. The theme is given in its barest form. It then appears as block harmonies moving in unison and played very loudly. A slightly different harmonisation follows, to be played very softly. Finally, the second version is repeated.

Even at this early stage Satie dispenses with bar lines. The melody moves forward in those austere plainsong accents which he remembered from the church of St Catherine at Honfleur. Already you sense the atmosphere of timelessness, the unbroken meditative line that will characterise his mature writing.

He was twenty years old. With Contamine de Latour, who dedicated one of his short stories to him, he discussed art and poetry. Another acquaintance was Charles Levadé, only three years his senior and one of Massenet's star pupils at the Conservatoire. Like so many of Massenet's students he was to be awarded the Prix de Rome. His name is associated with the second of the *Ogives* as witness to Satie's friendship. The fourth is dedicated to brother Conrad, who, though he had decided on a scientific career, was still, for the moment, on good terms with Erik.

A mystical mood overtook him. His talks with Contamine de Latour, his long reading into the night and his studies of Gregorian music inspired him with a sort of religiosity. He affected an extreme and humble modesty. His friends nicknamed him "Monsieur le Pauvre". When he should have been attending lessons at the Conservatoire he was lurking reflectively in dark corners of Notre-Dame cathedral. At the Bibliothèque Nationale he pored extensively over books about Gothic art by Eugène Viollet-le-Duc, the protégé of Mérimée, a brilliant architect whose nineteenth-century "restorations" of some of France's greatest architectural glories caused as much praise as they did censure. The *Ogives*, clearly, were a personal as well as a musical statement.

After a year in Mathias' class he departed from the Conservatoire and began his military service. On 15 November 1886, delighted at having left behind him the tedium of the classroom, he joined an infantry regiment at Arras. But the military life, he soon found, was no better than the Conservatoire. He had only exchanged one variety of boredom for another. And the army was more difficult to escape from than the Conservatoire.

His solution of the problem was drastic but effective. One chilly night, in the depth of winter, he bared his chest at length to the glacial breeze. A sharp attack of bronchitis followed. For three months he was confined to bed. Throughout the peaceful days of convalescence he read voraciously. Among his books was Flaubert's *Salammbô*, that exotic romance of ancient Carthage. Laden with gorgeous description, stiff with historical detail and full of voluptuous evocation, the novel made heady reading. A work that had even more effect on him was a novel that had appeared two years before under the title of *Le Vice suprême*. The author was Joséphin Péladan.

Le Vice suprême was the first in a series of fourteen novels to be called eventually *La Décadence latine*. The theme of the work seems to be that the Latin races have gone into a decline as a result of neglecting religion. Religious practices have been allowed to wither away. What is needed, argues Péladan, is a revival of the mystical sense and a return to religion. He sets about pleading his case in an original fashion.

The heroine of this introductory novel is a princess of many talents. Having been corrupted during her education (which, inevitably, took place in a convent), she emerges into adult life as an accomplished linguist who, in between sessions of sadistic perversity, enjoys nothing better than studying the writings of the learned Boethius. After her husband's death (he was an effeminate

masochist), she is consumed with boredom. She knows everything and has done everything. What else is there for her, exclaims
the ineffable Péladan, but Sodom, Gomorrah and diabolism?
As a further refinement, she maddens her lovers by promising
all and, at the last moment, refusing her favours.

The leading male character here, as in all Péladan's novels, is
a magus. In this one it is the strong man called Merodack. He is
obviously Péladan himself, as the following description shows:
"His long, wavy hair veiled his forehead under its curls, like ivy
on the top of a tower, and formed a black halo around his head.
His eyes, huge and slow to focus, penetrated with an unpleasant
stare despite their gentleness. Beneath the nose with its softened
Jewish curve the blood-red mouth stood out in the sable jet of
his twin-pointed beard."

This disquieting apparition has had a troubled life. Merodack's
ambition has been to overcome the seven deadly sins. He has
forced himself to read pornography and to stay pure. He has been
loved by young women and has resisted them. He has acquired
a taste for exquisite food and rare wines and then submitted
himself to a diet of bread and water. After leading a life of
complete idleness, he has made himself work eighteen hours a
day and has written three hundred pages of metaphysics in a
month. Now, master of himself, he will be the master of others.
Merodack, we are gravely told, has known the tortures of the
damned and come through triumphant: for he has had the dread-
ful experience of giving up smoking, the worst of the sufferings
any man can endure.

Such is Péladan's masterpiece. Whether Satie persevered with
the remainder of the interminable series – novels went on appearing for years and only ceased in 1925, the date of Péladan's death
– we do not know. He was, though, deeply impressed at this
period by what he read. The atmosphere of incense, of lubricious
mysticism, of exotic perversion and of hermaphrodite frolics,
stirred him as potently as had the Gothic interiors of churches.
Tucked up in bed in the bleak surroundings of the military
hospital, he wandered in the imagination through the colossal
halls of Chaldean temples and assisted at elaborate ceremonies
of the cult.

Péladan represents a very minor branch of that movement in
French literature which produced at least one classic, the novel

Là-Bas of Huysmans. As a writer he offers little of worth. His most glaring fault is a total lack of humour. He goes on turning out page after page of excruciating claptrap without the glimmer of a smile. He is of interest only to the literary historian – and to anyone concerned with Satie.

For we must remember that, however ludicrous Péladan may seem today, in the last few decades of the nineteenth century he expressed some of the ideas that excited artistic and literary circles of the time. There was a new interest in Satanism and in psychopathology that fertilised literature and art. Péladan had, in fact, greater importance as an impresario of Symbolist art than as a writer. When Satie actually met him a few years later the spell increased even further. He was ready for the cult of Rosicrucianism which Péladan advocated as a way of arresting the decline of the Latin race. In the meantime, swaddled in army blankets, he followed, enthralled, the adventures of Princess Leonora d'Este, of the boyish courtesan La Nine, of the holy man Nebo, and of all the lascivious pasteboard creations with which Péladan eked out his absurd epics.

PART TWO

Pagan Mystic, Café Pianist

IV

Gymnopédies

Within a short time of leaving to join the army Satie was back once again at the family home in the rue de Constantinople. At the age of twenty-one he still showed no signs of wanting to embark on some obvious career or to make plans for the future. His father and stepmother had cause for alarm. Olga Satie appears to have been a quiet girl and to have given no trouble. Conrad worked diligently at his studies and was clearly destined to be a responsible professional man. But Erik?

From what has been said so far about Alfred Satie and his wife it might seem that they were a dim and slightly absurd couple. This view of them would be unjust. Parenthood is not the easiest of occupations. Children rarely do what is expected of them. Not always does the brilliant pupil turn out to be a success in adult life. The dunce will not inevitably follow the road to perdition. As for ambition, if children themselves do not know what they want to do, parents can hardly be expected to tell them.

When Satie showed signs of musical talent it was an obvious step to arrange lessons for him, to take him to concerts, to enrol him at the Conservatoire which was the most suitable place for higher education in the art. None of this pleased him. His parents had done what they could. They did not know what else to suggest for their ugly duckling – an ugly duckling who, since demobilisation from the army, had grown a beard and started wearing an expansive Lavallière bow tie.

The adoption of these picturesque Bohemian affectations was followed by a more disturbing incident. There was a maid in the Satie household, a pretty maid, or one at least whose charms were enough to tempt Erik. The atmosphere became heavy. It was thought best that he establish himself elsewhere. In any case, he was of an age when he could not continue to live at home. It is true that both father and son were intellectuals of a sort. But Alfred's intellectualism revolved around the universities, celebrity lectures and academic drawing-rooms. Erik's leaned towards the raffish areas of Montmartre. And the episode with the maid confirmed a strain inherited from his disreputable Uncle Adrien, who, during his youthful stay in England, had been caught up – or out – in just such an adventure.

He took a room in the rue Condorcet, which was on the edge of Montmartre and not far from the Cirque Médrano with its brassy blare and the roar of performing animals. He was free, free to do what he liked in his own way and, like his father before him, to follow his own interests without being cramped by family convention. These included a new opera by Emmanuel Chabrier, the exuberant composer whose music, witty and original, was to influence both Debussy and Ravel. *Le Roi malgré lui* was first performed at the Opéra-Comique on 18 May 1887. Satie could well have heard it then, though despite its success the run was cut short after three performances by a fire which destroyed the theatre.

The novel harmonies and fresh inspiration of *Le Roi malgré lui* excited him. He showed his admiration by delivering to Chabrier's home the manuscript of some of his own music. It was beautifully written and bore a personal dedication in exquisite calligraphy. No acknowledgement came in return. The genial Chabrier was doubtless too upset by the disappointment of his hopes for the opera, or else too busy to appreciate what had been offered to him.

This music probably consisted of the *Trois Sarabandes*. The third of these grave but unquiet pieces features a progression that occurs for the first time, at least in French music, during the early sections of the overture to *Le Roi malgré lui*. The Sarabandes in general have a restless atmosphere. Though cloaked in a Gregorian mood, as are the *Ogives*, they move forward in great chunky chords of a feverishness not usually associated with this solemn measure.

More serene are the *Trois Gymnopédies*. The name was derived by Satie from the adjective "gymnopaedic" which became current in the mid-nineteenth century. It refers to the dances and exercises ritually performed by naked boys at public festivals in ancient Greece. Although he claimed that the *Gymnopédies* were inspired by his reading of *Salammbô*, their style is the opposite of Flaubert's elaborate exoticism. A closer parallel, it has been suggested, is with Puvis de Chavannes, an artist to whom Satie was partial. The cut of the melodies, in fact, does echo the clear lines of a fresco by Puvis, its unforgiving simplicity and its statuesque groupings.

Even today the *Gymnopédies* create the impression of being either very archaic or very modern. Their unforgettably haunting tone has put them among Satie's best-known works. Although they are complete in themselves, the line they follow extends to infinity. They are not heard, they are overheard. The melody floats unhurriedly over a misty bass and creates an illusion of movement while, at the same time, it never travels very far. The *Gymnopédies*, in short, which Satie wrote at the age of twenty-two, are the first expression of his originality.

Two years later he wrote the *Trois Gnossiennes*. Like the *Ogives* they are without bar lines or time signatures, though since the rhythm of the music falls naturally into place there is no need for them. Presumably the title refers to Knossos in Crete, where the Minotaur of Attic legend held monstrous sway – or perhaps it had been coined from the word *gnostique*, in a reference to the esoteric knowledge Satie had read of in his studies of Péladan. His music was decked out with literary embroidery which took the shape of serio-comic directions to the performer. "Questionnez", runs one of the injunctions. "Without pride", says another. The player of the third *Gnossienne* is advised: "Fit yourself with clear sightedness."

Like the *Gymnopédies*, the *Gnossiennes* are uncompromising in the stubborn regularity of their rhythm. The melodic line is more fluid, but though, on occasion, it may rise in a hopeful curve, at the end it comes down again, eternally dissatisfied and unresolved. The listener is kept at arm's-length. Elusive and withdrawn, these enigmas never yield up their mystery. That Satie was aware of this is probably shown by one of his mocking instructions to the player of No. 3: "Conseillez-vous soigneusement."

V

Black Cat and Nail Inn

The remarks he attached to the *Gnossiennes* have a flavour of that
dry humour which was the speciality of Alphonse Allais, a fellow
native of Honfleur. Allais was twelve years older than Satie. His
father ran the chemist's shop in the little place Hamelin, and no
doubt the Satie family, who lived near by, would have been
among the customers. Like Satie, Allais has a plaque recording his
birth in the town, although he has been promoted one step higher
in the ranks of celebrity by having a street named after him.

Satie made the acquaintance of "Alphi", as he was known to
his friends, in the bars and cafés of Montmartre which he had
come to frequent regularly. Allais was already a well-established
figure there. He usually wrote his newspaper articles at a café
table, undisturbed by the chatter and the shouts of hard-pressed
waiters rushing to the counter for trays of glasses. Always he left
his writing to the last minute. When the deadline approached he
would quickly scribble out his piece and, without troubling to
re-read it, would hand it to a waiter to post. In this way he wrote
thousands of articles and stories full of incongruous comedy and
that deadpan humour which is associated with the "pince-sans-
rire".

Although he soon gave up the early training as a chemist which was supposed to prepare him to follow in his father's footsteps, he continued to be fascinated by science. Among its fruits was his account of the explodable mother-in-law. He told of a man who detested his wife's mother. Having observed that this lady wore cotton garments, the son-in-law one day contrived to make away with a set of her clothes. These he soaked in a chemical solution which turned the material into gun-cotton. Then he dried them and put them back into her wardrobe. Next day the sun was very hot. While his mother-in-law sat peacefully reading in the garden, he trained a magnifying glass on her. Suddenly, with a tremendous explosion, she went up in flames. The coroner decided that she had been an alcoholic. It was, he added, a very interesting case of spontaneous combustion.

In his writing Allais proposed many wonderful inventions. Why not, he suggested, cover the roads with cardboard? This would at once preserve them from wear, keep the dust down and leave plenty of room for advertising slogans. Another idea was to lay sheets of cork over all seas and lakes – think, for example, of the time you could save travelling all the way by train to New York! Yet his ideas did not seem all that far-fetched when compared with the inventions which he found had been registered with the Ministry of Trade. These included a gadget for removing mustard from the insides of mustard-pots; ventilated shoes; a luminous hat; a fan worked by pedals; and a combined pipe and alarm whistle.

Such bizarre notions appealed to Satie. He wrote a description of a phonometer for weighing music which could have come from Allais. He claimed to have weighed the whole of Beethoven and Verdi. His researches showed, he reported, that an ordinary F sharp could weigh up to ninety-three kilogrammes. With a phonoscope he examined a B flat. It was, he concluded, a repugnant sight. His sketches of steel gliders, dirigibles, streamlined railway engines and polar navigation boats translate into minutely detailed graphics the type of literary conceits with which Allais filled his columns.

Not content with expressing himself on paper, Allais joked his way through life as well. A drinking companion of his once stood at a parliamentary election. The programme Allais supplied included "the revival of licentiousness in the streets with a view to re-population", the suppression of bureaucracy, and the levelling of the Butte Montmartre. If the last project were too costly, it was proposed, then the rest of Paris could be raised to the height of the Butte for the sake of regularity. His candidate obtained a hundred and seventy-six votes.

When a waiter offered him new potatoes in a restaurant he waved them away: "There's nothing new under the sun." He set his readers problems in arithmetic: "If a company of a hundred and twenty-five men takes six hours to get from Caen to Falaise, how long will it take a regiment of one thousand two hundred men to cover the same distance?" His answer to the Shakespeare/Bacon controversy was: "The proof that Shakespeare didn't write his plays himself is that his name was Willy." (A reference to Colette's first husband, who, under the name of "Willy", employed a team of ghost-writers to produce his books and articles.)

Like most professional humorists Allais was basically a sad man. His lugubrious and inscrutable expression rarely changed. He took refuge in practical jokes and heavy drinking – though never noticeably drunk, he was never quite sober – and he had a compulsive neurosis where puns were concerned. To the seven towns which disputed the birth of Homer, he added an eighth: Alaure. Alaure? Yes, he went on, wasn't Homer known also as "Homère d'Alaure"? (A neat play on the crude French oath.)

He was timid as well, like Satie, which helps to explain why he surrounded himself with a cloud of relentless pleasantry. Women terrified him. His wife, who was seventeen years younger, liked a grander mode of existence than the one he preferred. They travelled ceaselessly. "My home is my luggage," he explained drily. On 27 October 1905 he said to a friend: "I shall die tomorrow." And on the 28th that is what he did, of an embolism, at the age of fifty-one.

Impressed by the mystic leanings of his fellow-exile from Honfleur, Allais nicknamed him "Esoterik Satie", and, on account of his compositions so far, described him as "ogival and gymnopaedic". They spent a lot of time together. Besides their Norman origins they had in common an oblique approach to life and a refusal to take it seriously. Allais was to do Satie at least one good turn. As a well-known figure at the Chat Noir "Alphi" had influence with Rodolphe Salis, the proprietor of that famous cabaret. The pianist who supplied the music there had just been sacked. He was a composer called Dynam-Victor Fumet, a young man of uncompromising ideals who, outraged at a request to play some more than usually inane popular tune, had refused indignantly. Allais introduced Satie to the Chat Noir, where he was taken on as pianist.

Satie came to the Chat Noir during its great days. Rodolphe Salis had been an artist of sorts and the moving spirit of a short-lived "École vibrante". His talents were better suited to organisation, and a few years previously he set up a cabaret in the Latin Quarter that soon became a favourite spot with artists and writers. The presence of a stray black cat on the premises, thin and undernourished, gave him the name of his establishment. The proceedings there were noisy and unruly – so much so, in fact, that when one of his staff had his skull cracked open during one of the frequent skirmishes, the proprietor decided to move elsewhere. He chose a large house which formerly belonged to the painter Alfred Stevens. A procession of habitués accompanied by a laden wheelbarrow and Salis in the unauthorised uniform of a Préfet set out one night for the rue Victor Massé, where the new Chat Noir was to be set up. In the flickering torchlight a banner proclaimed the strange device "Montjoye-Montmartre' and fife and drum resounded through the darkened streets.

The Chat Noir already had its resident literary clique. They were called Les Hydropathes. Allais was a prominent member. The leader was Emile Goudeau. One day his curiosity had been roused by a waltz – the *Hydropatenwalze*, the best-known work of the irrepressible Gung'l – and he enquired into the origin of the name. This waltz, redolent of last year at Marienbad, evoked those wealthy invalids who took the waters at Spa and elsewhere. Goudeau found, to his delight, that the Greek origin of the phrase had an analogy with his name: "goût d'eau". Since the taste of water was repellent both to him and his friends, out of defiance they adopted the phrase for themselves.

The Hydropathes wrote most of the material for the journal also called *Le Chat Noir*, for it was Salis' ambition to run a literary magazine as well as a cabaret. Goudeau's fee as editor was a monthly packet of tobacco. A notoriously sharp businessman,

Salis always tried to avoid paying both his contributors and those who entertained his customers in the evening. He could reply that he had made his protégés famous. What more did they want? At one time Guy de Maupassant worked for him on the paper.

Nearly everyone of any repute in the arts came at one time or another to the Chat Noir. Poets recited their verse, famous actors gave monologues, and a certain type of song became famous there. Sometimes macabre, sometimes fantasist, and often inspired by cruelly realistic observation of the life of the poor, they were the songs that Yvette Guilbert introduced to a wider audience than the one that frequented the Chat Noir. In many ways Salis' establishment was an influence on literature.

In the vestibule, at the foot of the grand staircase, Houdon's statue of Venus displayed her marble charms. Beside her stood the usher, a splendid personage in full uniform bearing a halberd. He announced new arrivals in a thunderous voice. Pewter, stained glass and heavy oak furniture created a seventeenth-century atmosphere. (Somewhere in the house, rumour said, were bones of François Villon and a glass that had belonged to Voltaire.) To the left was the Salle des Gardes, a long room dominated by a huge picture, the work of Willette who was Salis' accredited artist. Entitled *Parce Domine*, it showed Pierrot rushing to the grave followed by a line of frenzied revellers. Willette's Pierrots and Columbines decorated many of the Montmartre night places. He embodied the spirit of the neighbourhood, its careless humour and Bohemian urge to live in the present. Then he got religion, lamented his misspent life and raged at his twin abominations, Rodolphe Salis and the Salvation Army, as the work of Satan. In the 1889 elections he stood as an official anti-Jewish candidate.

On the first floor was the bar where Allais liked to entertain his cronies. On the second was the Chat Noir's most famous attraction, the "Ombres Chinoises", or shadow-show. This was the work of Emmanuel Poiré, another of Salis' discoveries. Better known as Caran d'Ache (the Russian, it appears, for pencil), the dandified artist produced many cartoons and sketches for humorous papers. For the shadow-shows he designed and cut out all the figures in zinc. Across the illuminated screen, a circle framed in elaborate woodwork and lit by gas lamps, passed the outlines of Napoleon and his marshals, the battle of Austerlitz, the troops retreating from Moscow.

The commentary boomed out in Salis' loud tones: "Now here we are, my Lords, with the Grande Armée at the camp in Boulogne . . . A grenadier presents arms." And Caran d'Ache, behind the screen, would operate the ingenious mechanism that did the trick and executed the manoeuvre. During the battle scenes Allais hammered on a kettledrum to produce the sound of musketry, and Caran d'Ache, equipped with a bass drum, joyfully imitated the roar of the cannon. At the piano Satie tinkled out folk-songs to accompany the epic of Napoleon, marches and patriotic choruses. Other productions included a Temptation of St Anthony, perhaps based on Flaubert, a Carnival of Venice, an episode about St Genevieve, patron saint of Paris, a Conquest of Algeria, and a nativity play which mingled silhouette, words and music with genuine artistry.

For a decade or so the Chat Noir flourished as the most notable of the "cabarets artistiques". During the early years the black cat, "Maigriou", which gave its name to the place and was immortalised in Willette's design, could still be seen there, thin and bony as ever. The waiters sported, by a whim of Salis, the green ceremonial uniforms of the Académie Française. One of the rooms was even called the "Institut", and here favoured customers retired to drink absinthe while other patrons had to be content with beer at double the price. Here came Verlaine, Sarah Bernhardt, Maupassant and Anatole France.

Salis, the inimitable "gentilhomme-cabaretier" as he liked to be called, dominated everything with his commanding voice and stocky figure. He was celebrated for the elaborately humorous insults he threw at his customers. Habitués were given pompous titles and courtesies were exchanged with ironic politeness. When Salis died at the age of forty-five there was no one to replace him. The mantle passed to Aristide Bruant, who had begun his career at the Chat Noir as one of Salis' performers.

Among the singers whom Satie had to accompany was Vincent Hyspa. He came from Narbonne, and it was inevitable that, having a strong Southern accent, he should be introduced by Salis as a Belgian. To begin with he specialised in parodies of sentimental songs. He wore floppy Turkish trousers, had the benign mocking face of a bearded Chinese mandarin, and delivered his numbers in a cavernous voice. His commentaries on topical events were ingeniously satirical, though he could on occasion be gentle: his poem about the fountain in the place Pigalle and its effort, pathetically doomed, to rise higher still, has a certain tender philosophy. One of his successes was the punning *Ver solitaire*:

Mon verre n'est pas grand, mais je bois dans mon verre,
Je suis le pauvre ver, le ver solitaire . . .

Hyspa was fond of Satie, who had by then moved to a new address at No. 6 rue Cortot, which is higher up the slope of Montmartre. The quarterly rent was thirty-five francs. He must have had difficulty in finding even this modest sum. Hyspa himself, a leading draw at the Chat Noir, received no more by way of payment than his dinner three times a week and a two-franc piece. What the frugal Salis allowed his pianist as wages can be imagined. Yet Satie treated his poverty with good humour. In the depths of winter he never had a fire in the room he called his "cupboard". When he left the Chat Noir to go home at night, he would rub his hands gaily and joke to Hyspa: "Well, I must go back to my cupboard and sit beside my cold."

During his long nights and early mornings at the Chat Noir Satie had become a hard drinker. It was difficult in those surroundings to stay aloof from the trays of absinthe that circulated continuously. He drank because the customers often pressed a hospitable glass on him. He drank to stay awake and to keep himself pounding at the keyboard. It began to affect the quality of his playing and even his punctuality. Salis, who remained the clear-headed businessman when he was at his most flamboyant and the atmosphere was at its gayest, soon noticed his employee's behaviour. He gave him the sack. Pianists were two a penny and easy to find.

Satie was then taken on as pianist at the Auberge du Clou, a tavern in the rue Lepic conveniently near his new home. Here the owner, le père Tomaschet, was unlikely to object to his drinking habits, for he himself spent all his time slumped in an alcoholic haze, vacantly smoking his pipe beside the bar. It was the favourite resort of the humorist Georges Courteline, who came there regularly to play interminable games of cards with his drinking companions. Several of the comedies in which he lovingly explored the recesses of human stupidity take place among the card-players in just such a place as this and, no doubt, reproduce the setting of the Auberge du Clou which he frequented over some thirty years.

Courteline would order a mixture of Pernod and anisette which he called a "précipité" to give himself the illusion that he wasn't drinking absinthe. Between correcting proofs and cursing the bad hands his partners played, he set up practical jokes. One of these he called the "Idiotometer". This was a glass tube marked in segments from one to fifty and half filled with red liquid. A hidden rubber pipe ran down to the cellar below where a friend was stationed. His task, at a given signal, was to blow along the pipe, hard or soft according to instructions. The victim in the bar was told to grasp the tube, which would then register the degree of his stupidity.

Le père Tomaschet was invited once to test it out. He held the tube as advised and the joker in the cellar blew hard. The liquid rose to the forty mark, forty-five, fifty, and then shot right up towards the ceiling and sprinkled the customers.

"Tomaschet," shouted Courteline, "you've won the booby-prize!"

The old man blinked a glaucous eye, and, not understanding at all what was going on, relapsed into his usual stupor.

With such an easy-going employer as Tomaschet even Satie could not do wrong. The piano he played was elderly and a little out of tune. It somehow typified the spirit of the place. There was sawdust on the floor. The benches were covered in fawn imitation leather. The tables had white marble tops. Waiters padded slowly about, and the lady cashier, cut off at the waist by her desk, meditated dreamily over her accounts. In the heat of summer it was peacefully cool. In winter a rumbling stove threw out a friendly warmth.

At about ten o'clock each evening Courteline would appear. Manille was his favourite card game, and soon epic battles were being fought. If things were going his way he would order drinks all round and remark: "Alcohol is a slow killer, so they say. That's all right, we aren't in a hurry."

One of his regular partners at Manille was a young Spaniard called Miguel Utrillo. He had studied art and architecture at home and now was following an engineering course in Paris. At that time he was the lover of the artist Suzanne Valadon. In fact, he may well have been responsible for introducing Satie to the only woman with whom the composer is known to have had an affair.

VI

Bohemian Lover

Or else Satie may have met her at the Chat Noir, where everyone knew her, as they did by now throughout the whole of Montmartre. Her mother was a peasant woman from Limoges who had come to Paris just before the years of the Commune. Montmartre, in those days very much a rural community with its trees and windmills perched on the hill, reminded Madeleine Valadon of her country home. She settled there and worked as a seamstress, more often as a charwoman. The terrible events of the Commune bemused and disillusioned her. She sank into apathy. Alcohol was all that kept her going.

Her illegitimate daughter, Suzanne, whom she had brought with her to the capital, was educated by nuns. The quick-witted child became an inveterate truant. She learned more in the streets of Montmartre. The bare-footed urchin preferred boys to girls, for with them she could play strenuous games and do acrobatics. She had a ready tongue and was never at a loss for a sharp retort. There was no time for dressing up dolls or reading fairy-stories in her life. Instead, she was already trying to draw pictures.

At the age of nine she was put to work reluctantly at a dress-maker's. After three years of this sweatshop she ran away and washed dishes in a restaurant. Then she sold vegetables from a cart in les Halles. Her next job was as a stable lad, and her tiny but wiry figure was occasionally to be seen performing somersaults on the broad back of a trotting horse. She even, so she said, did a turn in circuses. Of this she was particularly proud, although her imagination was liable, when she looked back on her past, to colour her exploits with a certain romanticism.

When she was sixteen she became an artists' model. An early mentor was Puvis de Chavannes, the painter of those large and ambitious murals which now decorate various provincial town halls, the Panthéon and the Sorbonne. He made a lot of money from these commissions and gave the impression of a successful professional man – yet at the same time he was admired by, and influenced, the younger Symbolist painters. His life-style resembled the tone of his pictures: cool, serene, unhurried. The turbulent Suzanne was puzzled and impressed by this strange tranquillity. She moved into his Neuilly flat and for several months lived with the artist, who was nearing sixty, as his mistress.

When the idyll with Puvis had evaporated she found another lover in Miguel Utrillo. It is thought that he was the father of the child she bore, the one later to be known as Maurice Utrillo. The putative father returned to Spain and Suzanne presumably received financial support from somewhere, for now she lived in a proper flat of her own with the baby and a nurse to look after it.

Motherhood did not interfere with her usual train of life. A short time afterwards she had an affair with Renoir and claimed that he painted her in several of his best-known pictures. Unfortunately he was also at this period using as a model the girl whom he later married. Suzanne's opinion of the future Madame Renoir was distinctly uncharitable to the extent of claiming that the figure of the wife in certain paintings was in fact her own. Her pride was hurt.

By now she was sketching in her own right. An early customer was Toulouse-Lautrec, who admired her drawings so much that he hung some of them at home and discussed them with his friends. She posed for him often. He advised her on how to look after her little boy – an intractable child given to outbursts of violent rage – and how to cope with her difficult old mother.

43

He even helped her choose clothes. A portrait he painted of her shows her big round eyes and wide mouth surmounted by an elaborate hat, the peak of eighteen-eighties fashion, which he had bought for her.

Her next lover was the morose and secretive Degas. Women of his own social class made him uneasy. Suzanne gave him a frank and forthright companionship in which he could relax. Her drawings pleased him. They satisfied his high standards of draughtsmanship. He led a solitary existence guarded by a fearsome housekeeper, and Suzanne brought into his sombre home a spark of the outside world, its gaiety and its gossip. Her earliest engravings were made in his studio, and it was Degas who helped to arrange her first exhibition. Though he nicknamed her "terrible Marie" (Toulouse-Lautrec had persuaded her to change her baptismal Marie-Clémentine into Suzanne), she was the only woman with whom the gruff old hermit never quarrelled.

Her next lover (she adored variety) was a rich young man who, generous in standing rounds of drinks, soon won acceptance by the artists of Montmartre. He asked her to marry him. She refused but agreed to be his mistress. Though his bourgeois instinct did not approve of the irregular situation, his feelings impelled him to accept it. No sooner had he done so than he was faced with another affront to his conventional beliefs: Satie also became her lover.

The first time Satie met Suzanne Valadon he proposed marriage. After which, it seems, they were so busy, so preoccupied with each other, that there was no time left to mention the subject again. Despite her wide experience she had never met a man like him before. They were both of an age, in their mid-twenties and he a year younger than she was. His bizarre wit amused her. The fantasies he conjured up with a straight face and only a small glint in his eye both intrigued and entertained her.

The difference between her two lovers was piquant. She wished to retain both of these interesting specimens, the well-off banker and the penniless musician. The former protested. Ah yes, she told him, she loved the two of them with an equal passion. Hopelessly captivated by her, he believed what she said. And so, for the time, did she. Was she not loving enough for two?

Satie took an endearing interest in her eight-year-old son

44

Maurice Utrillo. He gave the boy flowers and encouraged him to learn more about them. One evening he took Suzanne and the third partner in the odd triangle to the theatre. A pair of black boys, engaged for the purpose, went before them beating on drums.

It would be pleasant to think that the rue Cortot where Satie lived had been named after the famous pianist who played and wrote about Satie's music so well. Unfortunately this seventeenth-century thoroughfare was re-christened two years before Satie's birth in honour of the sculptor whose work decorates a number of solid Parisian monuments. Some wisps of old Montmartre still cling to the street and its raised pavement and steep ascent. In one direction lies the famous sloping vineyard, the only one of its kind to be maintained in a capital. Its annual harvesting is an event in the Montmartre calendar. At the top of the slope is the old house, once the property of an actor in Molière's troop, which now contains the enchanting Montmartre museum. A little way off lies what must be one of the shortest streets in Paris, the rue Lucien Gaulard, which, after six numbers only, leads into what must be the smallest cemetery in the town. Here lie for ever Satie's acquaintance, the "Hydropathe" Emile Goudeau, and the son of his mistress, Maurice Utrillo.

The rue Cortot was very much the haunt of painters. Number 12 has a distinguished ancestry. Renoir lived here for a time and painted, among others, his *Bal au Moulin de la Galette*. One of his youngest and prettiest models was, when not posing, to be glimpsed delivering milk around the streets. As a condition of the girl being kept by a wealthy lover, her mother had insisted on her retaining her job. After Renoir that same house accommodated at one period or another the artists Raoul Dufy and Othon Friesz, and the theatre producer André Antoine.

The love affair with Suzanne appears to have flourished for two years or so. It was chiefly conducted on the bare cold floor of Satie's little room at No. 6. She painted his portrait, her first in oils, which immortalised his pallid features, the curling moustache and silky little beard, the rather prim mouth, the pince-nez and the soft hat.

At one point Satie himself began to show bourgeois tendencies and remonstrated with Suzanne about his unwanted partner in the enjoyment of her affections. She laughed at his pleading. He flounced off and tried to find consolation elsewhere. When he returned, several months later, he offered, by way of reconciliation, a little drawing of "Biqui" as he called her. Done on music paper, it showed a dolly-like head in black pen-and-ink lines which capture the wide mouth and large eyes. The words "Bonjour Biqui, Bonjour!" are set to a plaintive snatch of music. Underneath he wrote: "Authentic portrait of Biqui, drawn in the old town of Paris, 2 April (Easter Sunday) of '93."

The new mood of peace did not last long. She annoyed him so much that he displayed in his window, for all passers-by to see, a trenchant statement about his volatile mistress. Doubtless executed in his usual ornate lettering, this document assailed her virtue with robust language and proclaimed her worthlessness to the universe.

The end soon came. There was a row, so noisy and violent that the neighbours overheard and often spoke of it in the years to come. Suzanne departed for ever. Satie, according to her recent biographer,* was in despair. He wrote letters pleading for her return. She replied by moving in to No. 2 rue Cortot, two doors away from him, and setting up home there with her other lover. Often she drove out in her own smart donkey and trap, with, we are told, two wolfhounds nuzzling up to her feet, and, at her side, a parrot in a cage.

In the mid-nineteen-thirties, some forty years later, the novelist Peter de Polnay met her. He saw "a small, vivacious, ageing woman who wore spectacles, thick stockings and invariably the same raincoat, and seemed to talk most of the time . . ."

* John Storm, whose *The Valadon Story*, Longman, 1959, is a vivid and sympathetic account of the artist.

VII

The Lure of the Rosy Cross

The end of the affair with Suzanne drove Satie deeper into religiosity. His tendency to mysticism and his taste for the Gothic made him very receptive to a new vogue for the Rosicrucian faith which just then had arisen. "Faith", perhaps, is too precise a word to define the jumble of fancies and superstition which over the centuries has gathered around the order supposed to have been founded in the fifteenth century by Christian Rosenkreuz. Early members claimed to have the power of extending life, of turning metal into gold and of commanding spirits. No less extravagant were the claims of Joséphin Péladan, who, in the eighteen-nineties, was the most prominent of all the Rosicrucian revivalists. He arrogated to himself the ancient Babylonian style of "Sâr".

Satie had admired Péladan's writing, notably his novel *Le Vice suprême*, for several years. When he met the Sâr in person he was not disappointed. The sage of Rosicrucianism wore a silver waistcoat and fine lace at his wrists. His black hair and beard were exquisitely ringleted. Soft buckskin slippers encased his feet, and upon his head there perched a necromancer's bonnet. At his home in Passy he put on a red dressing-gown to conduct exotic ceremonies among a band of select disciples. He had started his career as a bank clerk with the Crédit Français.

Péladan's father was a citizen of Lyon who took much interest in oriental antiquities and the philosophies of the East. His salon was frequented by cardinals and mystics. He edited several magazines, one of them notorious for its attacks on Baudelaire. His elder son Adrien, a doctor, wrote at the age of twelve an *Histoire poétique des fleurs*. Adrien also evolved a theory – it concerned the evolution of bones in the fore-arm – which became a standard part of anatomical studies. He was an early pioneer of homeopathy and founded a journal to spread the gospel. His greatest ambition was to bring together occult theories and the latest advances in science. Before he could complete this undertaking he died, accidentally, of a preparation too liberally dosed with strychnine by an inexpert chemist.

Adrien left behind him a mass of occult material which he bequeathed to his younger brother. Joseph, who soon began to call himself Joséphin, based the greater part of his own literary work upon it. His earliest production, written at the age of twenty-three, was *Le Vice suprême*. It went, strange to say, through no less than twenty impressions. Although it is the French habit to print in very small editions, this must even so be accounted a success. Other works followed, among them a helpful treatise on how to become a magus ("Magic is the art of sublimating man"), and one containing useful hints on how to turn into a fairy.

The message was that which we have already encountered in discussing Satie's reading of *Le Vice suprême*. The magus should rise above common appetites. He must renounce the invitations to sin which Péladan thoughtfully enumerates: cafés, clubs, newspapers, gambling, sport, the haunts of light women and café-concerts. Once he has conquered these temptations, the wise man is fitted to exercise his powers.

Péladan himself did not hesitate to use magic. On his travels he once had a brush with a French customs officer who impounded some foreign cigarettes which the Sâr attempted to smuggle through in his luggage. "I swore an oath," wrote Péladan, "a terrible oath, in that little railway station where I was a prisoner of the French customs: I put into it all the strength of my thought, all my power as a Magus; it shall be recognised by its effects . . .

I shall reveal all that I was hiding of the mysteries of individuality; I shall leave thee, O egalitarian society, O dungheap race, a posterity of tigers: these shall not be made prisoners at frontier railway stations on account of a few foreign cigarettes . . ."

On another occasion the Sâr was deeply offended by Rodolphe Salis. The cat, as we all know, is a sacred animal, and Salis had committed blasphemy by adopting it as the mascot of his cabaret. Péladan wrote articles in which he "excommunicated" Salis and insulted him as a philistine and a bourgeois. Annoyed most of all, perhaps, by that last epithet, the "gentilhomme-cabaretier" sent Alphonse Allais and a friend as his seconds to demand satisfaction.

When first they called a maid turned them away. The "Mage d'Epinay", as Allais neatly described him, was taking luncheon and could not be disturbed. At their second visit they were granted an audience. The Sâr outlined his reasons for not wishing to engage in a duel. First, since he was not on good terms with Rome, having threatened to excommunicate the Pope, he would risk, if he fought a duel, being excommunicated himself. Then, his occult powers made it certain that he would kill Salis, and he did not wish to commit murder. Finally, such a murder would bring upon him an impurity which, there being no Magical College to lift it, would leave him with an indelible flaw. So, concluded Allais in his report of the post-prandial interview with the "Sâr-dînapâle", their mission was completed.

There were, too, some undignified passages with the novelist J-K Huysmans, whose interest in black magic was, it must be said, expressed with immeasurably greater artistry than Péladan's. Huysmans believed, at one point, that the marquis Stanislas de Gauïta, a close friend of Péladan, was trying to kill him with magic. Had not some occult power struck blows at him? Had not a chunky mirror suddenly collapsed on his desk? For a time he credited both Guaïta and Péladan with murderous intent. When he recovered from this mood he was able to dismiss Péladan in *Là-Bas* as a mountebank.

The Sâr believed himself to have descended from a line of seers and magicians. He was convinced of his extra-terrestrial powers. From time to time he issued "mandements" or decrees, in which he rebuked those who had displeased him and called for submission to his authority. Neither the sacred nor the profane

49

escaped him. The Archbishop of Paris received a warning against the moral dangers implicit in a proposal to arrange a bull-fight in Paris. Women at the spectacle, thundered the Sâr, would risk impurity. A member of the Rothschild family was bitterly anathematised for having demolished a chapel in her country house. The Sâr excommunicated her forthwith and commanded all writers and artists to cut her dead.

It is recorded that Péladan had been touched by grace in 1888 at Bayreuth. *Parsifal* gave him a vision of the future and inspired him to found the three knightly orders of the Rose + Croix, the Temple and the Grail. In the operas and writings of Richard Wagner he discovered a kindred spirit and one who shared his own taste for grandiose obscurity. When he returned to Paris he decided to establish his own Bayreuth there. His Théâtre de la Rose + Croix would perform dramas in which he outlined his theories of salvation for misguided humanity. The project was to be financed by Lady Caithness, herself the author of theosophical works.* She was not the only Anglo-Saxon to come under his spell. On his visits to France the poet W. B. Yeats, who dreamed of founding on the Irish coast a druidic settlement, paid his respects to the Sâr while making the rounds of occultist writers.

The Sâr's play *Babylone* was not unsuccessful in avant-garde circles. As did his novels, it featured our old friend the Sâr Merodack, though now his ideas had a Wagnerian touch about them. Earlier still, in March 1892, his first play *Le Fils des Etoiles* caused a small stir and was revived in the following year. His other projects included an *Oedipe et le Sphinx* and a *Mystère du Graal*.

Le Fils des Etoiles was accompanied with incidental music by Satie. The latter had been appointed by the Sâr as official composer to the Rose + Croix. While he continued to play the piano in Montmartre cabarets to earn a living, what gave him a sense of fulfilment was composing music dedicated to the service of a philosophy which, for the moment at least, offered him spiritual comfort. An early piece, the *Première pensée Rose + Croix*, written in January 1891, sets the tone of this period. A single theme,

* She was Marie, second wife to the fourteenth Earl whom she married in 1872; she was created Duchess of Pomár in her own right by Pope Leo XIII in 1879.

repeated a dozen or so times in various disguises, creates with its upward movement a feeling of plaintive aspiration.

Of the music which he provided for *Le Fils des Etoiles*, only the three preludes have been published, together with a "Gnossienne" later incorporated in the *Trois Morceaux en forme de poire*. The prelude to Act I of this "Chaldean pastoral", set in an epoch three thousand years ago, introduces the story of a shepherd poet and how he succeeds in his vocation for the priesthood. Again, the musical thought is static and does not develop. Yet in a darkened theatre it would probably make an effect by its simple repetition of hieratic figures.

The hero, whose destiny is governed by the stars, meets temptation and overcomes it. In the end, having preserved his faith, he attains to the priesthood and is rewarded with marriage to the girl he has loved since they were children together. The third act, subtitled "Incantation", is preceded by music which, though stately as before, hints at restrained jubilation with distant fanfares.

If, on the whole, Satie's contribution has a distinctly subdued dramatic character, it is not unsuited to the nature of the play. Péladan's blank verse is concerned to express philosophical ideas, to invest his erudite analyses of Chaldean thought with a Christian flavour, rather than to excite an audience with stirring events. This is emphasised by the fact that, at the eight performances of the original production, a Palestrina mass was included among the music.

Another of Péladan's texts, this time the anthem *Salut au drapeau*, involved Satie. It must, again, indicate a degree of sincerity on his part that he was ready to set words which, a few years later, would have aroused his most ironic scorn. The flag, shroud of heroes, stained with the blood of the people, is saluted as the support of the race. Should it fall, then the nation dies. Satie's accompaniment, though tricked out with novel harmonies, slavishly duplicates the vocal line.

He had, by now, absorbed the literary style of the Sâr Péladan. The printed score of *Le Fils des Etoiles* bears a "dédicatoire" to his companions which invokes "the mercy of God, creator of things visible and invisible; the protection of the Redeemer's August Mother and Queen of the Angels; and the prayers of the glorious choir of the Apostles and Holy Orders of the blessed

Spirits." May the just anger of God, it ends, crush the proud and the immodest. The composer's signature and the mark of the Rose + Croix are appended. On the original manuscript the phrase "Wagnérie Kaldéenne" does not appear. It must have been inserted by Péladan himself, for assuredly, even at the height of his Rosicrucian fervour, Satie had little tenderness for Wagner.

Péladan was not the only occultist figure whose work he adorned with music. Almost as controversial a personality was Jules Bois, the author of a book on Satanism and magic which, prefaced by Huysmans, catered for a wide public interest in the devilish arts. His sensational career included several duels which invariably were attended by odd circumstances: carriages overturned, bullets stuck in pistols . . . No one was ever hurt. His play, *Les Noces de Sathan*, a Wagnerian epic, ends appropriately with "an ineffable voice" speaking the words: "Be united in pain and you shall have the greatest glory because you are the most mad!"

Debussy once considered writing incidental music for *Les Noces de Sathan*. Then he finally decided against it, not liking, perhaps, the atmosphere in which the author moved. Satie proved more receptive. For the story *La Porte héroïque du ciel*, which, like Bois' play, is described as an "esoteric drama", he composed a prelude. It is among the more successful of his Rosicrucian ventures. Although the manner is not very assured and the style is often clumsy, the music keeps moving with something of the impulse shown in the *Gnossiennes*. "I dedicate this work to myself," reads an inscription on the *Prélude de la Porte héroïque du ciel*.

Finally, there were the *Sonneries de la Rose + Croix* that Satie wrote for the famous series of art exhibitions which Péladan organised each year from 1892 to 1897. Financial help was provided by comte Antoine de la Rochefoucauld, who had been an early collaborator with Péladan in the Rosicrucian movement. He was himself a painter, and his *Sainte Lucie* shows an agreeably naïf representation of the saint. The Pointillist influence may have contributed to disagreements with the Sâr, who, in art as in everything else, had strong views. The two men parted, and Rochefoucauld switched his funds to supporting an occultist magazine run by Jules Bois. Early this century he disappeared from view. He is thought to have died round about 1960, by which time he would have been nearly a hundred years old.

Rather in the manner of Edmond de Goncourt launching his own Académie in opposition to the Académie Française, the Sâr introduced his annual exhibitions as a counterblast to the official Salon which every year presented all that was approved by the art establishment. The Sâr announced that he wished to reform Latin taste and create a school of idealism. He laid down in great detail those subjects he would not accept. These included rustic scenes and, a significant ban, anything at all humorous. As for the subjects he welcomed, these could be sure of acceptance, even if faultily executed. Such things as allegory in the style of Puvis de Chavannes or nudes sublime like Correggio's were favoured. A hint of the sponsor's political views peeped out of his interdiction against architecture: this was an art, he declared, which had been killed in 1789.

"Artists of every art, come to the Rose + Croix!" trumpeted the Sâr, having compiled a list that was harshly rigorous in its exclusions. All who believed in the Parthenon, Leonardo, the *Victory* of Samothrace, Beethoven and Parsifal would be admitted through the blessed portals of the Rose + Croix. His bag was not undistinguished. Among the believers in the Parthenon whom he assembled were some important disciples of Gauguin, the sculptor Bourdelle, a young Georges Roualt and several leading Belgian Symbolists. Although he had specifically excluded portraits, the Sâr was broadminded enough to allow one of himself to be exhibited. It was the work of Marcellin Desboutin, an artist patronised by Degas who painted him in *L'Absinthe*. The Sâr claimed it as the equal of Titian and pointed out, modestly, that no other living person could have provided the material for such a work of art. So pleased was he with this glowering picture of himself that in the catalogue he ennobled the artist as "Des Boutin (marquis Marcellin)". It is not a very good portrait.

The three Satie fanfares for harps and flutes were played at the first of the Salons de la Rose + Croix held in 1892. The work of sixty-nine contributors hung on the walls of the Galerie Durand-Ruel in the rue Le Peletier. At the opening ceremony visitors heard three *Sonneries de la Rose + Croix*. The first, a slow and meandering "Air de l'ordre", is typical of the Rosicrucian music in using disjointed blocks of chords. The "Air du grand maître", dedicated to the Sâr, and the "Air du grand prieur", which is linked with the name of Rochefoucauld who presumably

53

held this post in the movement, continue the method. The piano version, which is all that remains, features on the printed cover a motif from a Puvis de Chavannes picture. The *Sonneries* were to be performed at Rosicrucian ceremonies alone, and the Sâr would not allow them to be played elsewhere unless by consent. Such a precaution, one feels, was unnecessary.

After his last Salon de la Rose + Croix in 1897 Péladan adopted a quieter tone. In the final decades of his life he gave up his violet robes in favour of a soft hat and conventional dark clothes. He contributed, punctually and in a clear style, regular art criticisms which carried a sober authority among readers of the *Revue Hebdomadaire*. Having foresworn the extravagances of his earlier career he emerged as a writer who could support his judgements with massive erudition. One of his chroniclers goes so far as to discern his influence on d'Annunzio, who is said to have borrowed from Péladan's analyses of Wagner. Still more impressively, it is claimed that when Paul Valéry set about writing his *Introduction à la Méthode de Léonard de Vinci* he did so with knowledge of the Sâr's *Dernière leçon de Léonard de Vinci*.

VIII

Master of the Metropolitan Art Church of Jesus the Conductor

For a time Satie's attachment to Rosicrucianism was sincere. It could not have been long, though, before his sense of the ridiculous started to betray his religious aspirations. The total lack of humour in the Sâr's entourage must also have had a stifling effect. Satie would have noticed, moreover, that the Sâr's flamboyant dress, his sensational announcements (usually directed at well-known people) and his noisy "excommunications" paid good dividends in publicity. The Sâr could always be relied upon to supply useful "copy" when journalists found themselves short of a story.

On 14 August 1892, quite soon after he had been involved with *Le Fils des Etoiles* and the Salon de la Rose + Croix, the paper *Gil-Blas* published a letter in which Satie disclaimed the Sâr's influence. Written in mock archaic style, it was partly a reaction against the solemn Rosicrucian atmosphere, partly an assertion of independence, and partly an attempt to garner publicity for himself. Satie wrote:

'Tis cause for astonishment, that I, a poor fellow with no care but for my art alone, should be ever claimed as the initiator in music of Master Péladan's disciples. This causeth me much grief and pain, for were I to be the pupil of whomsoever, I think right to say that that whomsoever would be me; even more so inasmuch as I believe that Master Péladan, for all his great learning, could not make disciples either in music or in painting or in much else besides. Wherefore the good Master Péladan, for whom I have great respect and deference, has never had empire over the independence of my aesthetic; and stands in relation to me not as my Director but as my collaborator, just such as my old friends Gentles J. P. Contamine and Albert Tinchant. Before Holy Mary, mother of Our Lord Jesus Christ, Third Person of the Blessed Trinity: thus have I spoken, without hate or evil intention, that which mine heart feels anent this thing; and an oath I make before the Fathers of the Holy Catholic Church that in this matter I have not thought to injure nor dispute with my friend Master Péladan.

Kindly accept, Master Editor, the humble greetings of a poor fellow that hath no other thought than for his art and feeleth dolour at having to treat of a matter that paineth him so.

With Albert Tinchant, the friend mentioned in his letter to *Gil-Blas*, Satie planned to write an opera. Indeed, the newspapers referred to a libretto by Tinchant and music by Satie for a production of *Le Bâtard de Tristan* at the Grand Théâtre de Bordeaux. The project never went beyond the joke of the title.

Another collaboration, with Contamine de Latour, his partner in earlier enterprises, actually materialised. Suzanne Valadon designed a medallion for the cover whereon the heads of Satie and Contamine de Latour were shown in profile, their names lettered around the edge and the dates 1892–1893 inscribed at the base. In 1895 the two collaborators published a small booklet containing the libretto and some musical extracts. Other works in hand, it was announced, included *Onotrance*, a ballet in one act, and, "God willing", the ballets *Corcleru*, *Irnebizolle* and *Tumisrudebude*.

The cover of the work in question also mentioned that it had been "présenté au Théâtre National de l'Opéra le 20 décembre 1892". This was, to a certain extent, true. The score of *Uspud*, as they had named the ballet, was in fact presented to the Opéra –

and duly rejected. The director of the Opéra did not even bother to acknowledge receipt of the small black notebook which arrived on his desk. The outraged composer sent his seconds to discuss the affair. And the director, somewhat alarmed, received him in person to tell him, with courteous regret, that the Opéra could not perform his work.

The reaction of authority was not surprising. *Uspud*, a "Christian ballet in three acts", features a single character supported by various "spiritualities", demons and assorted wild animals. Uspud wanders across a deserted beach on his return from martyring Christians. He burns a few holy relics at the foot of a statue. A clap of thunder shatters the statue into fragments, at which point the sky whitens and a woman of great beauty in a golden tunic, her bosom pierced with a dagger, appears to Uspud and holds out her arms. She personifies the Christian Church. In his fury Uspud throws stones at her. They change into globes of fire. Stars and flames burst out. The first act ends with what the scenario calls "a great convulsion of nature".

In the second act Uspud is surrounded by demons in the shape of men with animals' heads: dogs, jackals, goats, sheep, baboons, crabs, boars, ostriches, crocodiles, oxen, unicorns . . . They torment him. The Christian Church materialises, this time white as snow and transparent as crystal with lotus growing at its feet. The dagger is plucked from its breast and buried in Uspud's. He falls into ecstasy while a gigantic crucifix rises from the ground carrying with it the Church to an accompaniment of singing from angels and archangels.

Uspud is converted. The third act finds him on a mountain peak stretched in prayer before a crucifix. A vision of Christ fills him with the Holy Spirit. Martyred saints process across the Dali-esque landscape bearing their afflicted remains. Despite the attempts of a legion of demons in monstrous form – black dogs with a golden horn on the forehead, fish with birds' heads and wings – Uspud remains faithful to the Lord. The demons tear him to pieces. Two angels carrying palms and wreaths escort the Christian Church as the soul of Uspud is transported to Heaven.

A feature of Satie's contribution to this Surreal work is that at no point does it reflect or coincide with the nature of what is supposed to be happening on the stage. Music and libretto are like two trains which pass in opposite directions. The passage relating to Uspud's consternation when the statue has been destroyed is used also to accompany the animal-headed demons' furious attack upon him. The great cataclysm at the end of Act I takes place to the same anodyne measures which depicted smoke turning into seraphims. The music consists of small disjointed fragments which are to be played "very slowly" throughout. There is no development and no attempt at a coherent follow through. The brief themes, some of them taken from piano pieces, are repeated at various points as if by hazard. Boredom is the overall effect, a boredom intensified by the listener's inability to identify with either the plot or the music which creeps remorselessly on in a drone of repetitions. It is not surprising that the Director of the Opéra should have felt that he was dealing with practical jokers or madmen.

But *Uspud* is not unimportant in showing the way Satie's thought was developing. The motifs he used are those with which he experimented, endlessly, in his notebooks. His method was to work over a theme and try out new, unexpected harmonies until, after long searching, he had reached something that approximated to what he sought. He was not easily satisfied. In this, his first work of any length, he sketched out the technique of building up small cells of music which later resulted in *Parade*. The disparity between music and action shown so glaringly in *Uspud* can be seen as an early protest, however clumsy, against nineteenth-century stage concepts. As he was afterwards to argue, there was no need for the orchestra to grimace when a character makes his entry on stage. Did the trees in the scenery grimace? What he wanted to create was an atmosphere, without the obvious "couplets" or Wagnerian "leitmotiv", that suggested Puvis de Chavannes.

On a more personal level *Uspud* demonstrated both his tendency to religion and his extreme naïveté. Although the effect of Rosicrucianism soon palled he never lost his interest in spiritual things, and even if the plot of this incongruous ballet may appear to be more the private fantasy of two young aesthetes of the Nineties than a serious project for the stage, it is typical of the sympathy for mysticism which remained with him for the rest of his life. As for simplicity of mind, this is shown by his obvious belief that *Uspud* had a chance of being accepted for performance at the

Opéra. When he challenged the Director to a duel for failing even to acknowledge delivery of the masterpiece, he displayed that touchiness which, as the years went by, was to make him so awkward a friend and so deadly an enemy.

Further evidence of his naïveté was given in 1892, the year of *Uspud*, when he presented himself as a candidate for election to the Académie des Beaux-Arts in the place of Ernest Guiraud who had just died. Guiraud had been typical Institut material. He was born in New Orleans where his father, also a composer, had settled after attempting without success to conquer the Paris stage. His son was luckier. Ernest wrote his first opera at the age of fifteen and saw it performed. He brought out several unpretentious ballets and comic operas – among them *Gretna Green* and *Piccolino* – which pleased their audiences. As teacher of harmony and then composition at the Conservatoire he proved an agreeable mentor to young musicians like Dukas and Debussy. For a time Satie himself attended his classes. He is best known today for having orchestrated Offenbach's *Contes d'Hoffmann* and having composed the recitations for *Carmen*. His experience as composer and teacher enabled him to bridge the gap between the theatre and the academic world, and his personal charm eased his passage through the fashionable drawing-rooms where reputations were made. Having reached the top of his profession with a chair at the Institut, he only lived another year or so to enjoy his triumph and died in his mid-fifties.

This was the man Satie hoped to succeed. He mounted his campaign with the utmost seriousness. A list of his compositions was carefully prepared – it included the *Gymnopédies*, each of which figures as an orchestral suite – and he made the traditional round of calls on existing members. Only the Symbolist painter Gustave Moreau, it seems, went so far as to receive him. The composer members of the Institut would have nothing to do with him. Their attitude was to be expected. Even if they had heard of him already, they were unlikely to favour a young musician with so little, either published or performed, to his credit. In the end, after the customary intrigues and jockeyings which make elections to the Institut such lively affairs, they chose Emile Paladilhe, composer of a once very popular song *Mandolinata* and a number of light works for the stage.

Satie was unabashed. Two years later, in 1894, he again

proposed himself, on this occasion to follow Gounod. Once more he was passed over. The successful candidate emerged as Théodore Dubois, an amiable pedagogue and sometime composer. There appears to have been some unpleasantness with the vinegary Saint-Saëns. This provoked an open letter to the venerable master which Satie published in the music paper *Le Ménestrel*.

Saint-Saëns was informed that Satie had presented himself not through presumptuousness but from a sense of duty. His candidature, he added, had been accepted by God, whence the affliction and surprise felt by Satie at his rejection. "You can reproach me with only one thing," he went on, "that of not knowing me as I know you ... By judging me at a distance and making your decision, you have behaved like one cast out by God and you have run the risk of Hell. Your aberration can only spring from poor understanding of the ideas of this century and from your ingratitude towards God, the direct cause of Aesthetic abasement. I forgive You in Jesus Christ and embrace You in the mercy of God." This novel rebuke must have confirmed Saint-Saëns' impression that Satie was a lunatic.

His third and final time of asking came in 1896 with the death of Ambroise Thomas, director of the Conservatoire at the time Satie entered it as a student, a pillar of the French operatic establishment and a member for forty-five years of the Institut to which he had been elected as Spontini's successor. Again Satie failed. The coveted chair went to Charles Lenepveu who had been Thomas' pupil. He taught at the Conservatoire and had composed, in addition to several operas, the forbidding *Cent Leçons d'harmonie*.

Although in later years Satie wrote with ironic humour about his campaigns for election to the Institut, membership of which represented for most professional composers the crown of an honourable career, he was at the start entirely serious in his aims. Then he must have realised, however hopeless his cause, that there was publicity to be made out of his activities. It is significant that his notorious letter was addressed to Saint-Saëns, then the most celebrated French composer of the day and one whose name was familiar even to the non-musical.

This letter was headed: "Erik Satie, Master of the Chapel of the Metropolitan Art Church of Jesus the Conductor ..." In 1892, on the death of his father, he had inherited a small legacy. With the aid of this money he decided to emulate the Sâr Péladan by founding his own religious movement. He announced, through pamphlets and a shortlived magazine, that the "Eglise Métropolitaine d'Art de Jésus Conducteur" would do battle with "those who have neither conviction, belief nor thought in the soul, nor principle in the heart". Satie himself, as "Parcier" and "Maître de Chapelle", would lead the struggle against "the aesthetic and moral decadence of our age".

The headquarters of the church were at Satie's little room in the rue Cortot. This modest lair, furnished only with bed, chair, bookshelf and chest (it lacked, typically, a piano), became "Our Abbatial". Here, where an intricate arrangement of shutters and blinds ensured the tenant's fanatical need for privacy, were to be conducted the rites and ceremonies of the newly established church. It called, with interesting precision, for 1,600,000,000 officiants in black robes and grey hoods, and many millions of other ranks in the carefully graded hierarchy prepared by its creator.

The *Cartulaire de l'Eglise Métropolitaine d'Art de Jésus Conducteur* appeared in the May and June of 1895. It served as a useful means of venting Satie's annoyance with those who had crossed him and those of whose ideas he disapproved. Among the latter was that distinguished theatrical pioneer Lugné-Poe. At the Théâtre de l'Oeuvre he specialised in the then avant-garde symbolist drama. He introduced Paris to the dramas of Maeterlinck, Ibsen, Alfred Jarry and of hitherto unknown foreign playwrights such as d'Annunzio and Bernard Shaw. For some reason one of his productions mortally offended Satie. He was therefore excommunicated by a document dated 24 January 1895, which he found one morning in his post. It was written in red ink and emanated from the "Parcier" of the rue Cortot.

Lugné-Poe stood accused of profaning art, of passing off base things in the guise of genius, of deceiving those whom he should have enlightened. "God who sees us and judges us will ask a terrible account of you for your harmful action: but, in the meantime, we, who are conscious of our mission and who suffer and fight to accomplish it, deny you the right to speak in the name of Art, which you and those around you have trampled underfoot ... In any case, I shall always be here to observe you and judge you. Do not forget it." Lugné-Poe, who had a sense of humour, was amused by the missive.

In the following March the Parcier widened his net to accommodate "le Tout-Paris". He included this time in his denunciation not only Lugné-Poe but also the editors of leading Parisian literary journals. Alfred Vallette, Alexandre Natanson and Léon Deschamps all came under the weight of his indignation. They were taxed with hypocrisy and abomination. The Parcier, he exclaimed, trembled before the crimes they had committed. "By Saint Mary, mother of Our Lord Jesus, who is the second person of the Divine Trinity, being in communion with Our Holy Mother the Church, the venerable host of Prophets, the glorious choir of the Apostles and in concert with the Holy Archangels, I forbid you all apology and thrust you far from me. I command you to silence and humiliation. My wish is that you submit to my Authority without murmur." Christians who had complaints about Lugné-Poe were invited to hand them in at the Abbatial, 6 rue Cortot.

Again following the shrewd example of the Sâr, his disciple had chosen as his targets men in the public eye and therefore most likely to attract attention as subjects of controversy. More sincere, more deeply felt, were Satie's outbursts against Henry Gauthier-Villars, the critic who, under the name of "Willy", relied on friends and colleagues, among them Debussy and Vincent d'Indy, to provide the material for criticisms and novels to which he added his wit and his name. His most famous though not his most amusing creation was Colette, whom he married when she was very young.

Willy's music criticism, which appeared under the pseudonym of "L'ouvreuse du Cirque d'Eté" – a device which allowed him much liberty of persiflage – is the most entertaining of its kind and highly readable. The tone displeased Satie. He was irritated by some of Willy's remarks about Wagner – which is odd, since Willy was an early and generous champion of that composer at a time when he needed it. The Cartulary for May 1895 positively boiled with virulence directed at Willy. He was told that he debased the critic's function by his lack of respect and incompetence. He had committed blasphemy in his judgement of Wagner. He was swollen-headed and presumptuous.

Satie's letter to Willy had been dated 2 May. In his newspaper article of 5 May, the object of the attack replied sharply. "A person called Erik Satie (6 rue Cortot), who some time ago made even

worse with his putrid music some trashy Chaldean play or other
by Péladan, busies himself with excommunicating folk from time
to time. It's better than going out boozing, I suppose. Recently
Teodor de Wyzewa [a writer on music] and Lugné-Poe copped
it; today it's my turn." For Willy, Satie's chords were "as sour
as vinegar". The composer was a charlatan, a loony and a complete idiot.

The reference to Péladan's *Le Fils des Etoiles* opened an old
wound. Satie had not forgotten Willy's mocking review of four
years ago. Ever since then his resentment had been quietly
stewing. Having demolished the pretensions of the Sâr – which
was not a difficult thing to do – Willy passed on to the music.
He made great fun of the Sâr's solemn announcement that Satie's
three preludes could only be played after due authorisation was
obtained from the Order. "As far as I'm concerned," wrote
Willy, "this ironmonger's music only gave me middling satisfaction. If, however, you want to hear it, just for a bit of a laugh,
all you need do is obtain the Grand Master's licence . . ."

After Willy gave his answer and effectively stirred up all the
rancour that Satie had been nurturing over the years, the Parcier
of the rue Cortot riposted with a furious letter dated 14 May. This,
too, was reprinted in the Cartulary with an irate note protesting
at Willy's quoting the original letter in his newspaper article and
distorting it with irreverent comments. The catalogue of Willy's
turpitude lengthened: falsehood, immodesty and boorishness
had made him the object of scorn. He was a repulsive oppressor
of Church and Art, a paid hack, a clown, a buffoon. Altogether
he was a monument of abject ignominy.

The French laws of libel being, happily, more relaxed than
those in England, no ill came to Satie as a result of these violent
remarks. Willy went on using his name as a convenient epithet
for stupidity whenever he heard a piece of music he thought
particularly inane. And "Our Dear and Venerated Parcier", as
Satie called himself, nourished his venom in silence. The rotund
little critic, who wore a famous stovepipe hat and a hugely curved
moustache and beard, who attended concerts and the racecourse
with Colette on one arm and on the other the notorious music-
hall singer Polaire, was a far greater master of publicity than Satie.
He encouraged leading cartoonists to caricature him. The stock
of postcards which he printed for dispatch to his correspondents

even included – a touch of the Sâr here – a representation of his head aureoled with sunbeams and the motto "St Willy, patron of Claudines" in a reference to his successful launching of Colette and her "Claudine" series of novels. Probably he welcomed Satie's attentions for, like Barnum, he favoured all publicity provided that his name was spelt correctly.

On one occasion the vendetta between critic and composer went beyond words. At a concert they fell upon each other with blows. In a whirl of clenched fists and walking-sticks they fought to settle an argument that could never be resolved.

IX

Pear-shaped Music

All Satie's attempts to make himself known, to gain the recognition he felt he deserved, had so far been unsuccessful. Yet if the public continued to ignore him, there were young musicians who found his ideas and his music both interesting and worthwhile.

An early friend and supporter was Debussy. He, too, had played the piano at the Chat Noir and frequented the taverns of Montmartre where he perhaps made Satie's acquaintance. Some time before 1890 they met each other at the Auberge du Clou, as Satie himself always declared, or at the Chat Noir. A third possibility is that they came within orbit at the Conservatoire. Debussy was four years older than his new friend. Impressed by Satie's gifts, he may have arranged for him to be present as *auditeur* (a student who attends but does not take part) at the classes directed by his own teacher Ernest Guiraud – the amiable Guiraud whom Satie later attempted to succeed at the Académie des Beaux-Arts.

Another member of these classes was the composer Henri Busser. He, the last pupil to have studied under Gounod, died at the age of a hundred and one in 1973. Among his recollections was that of a "rather mysterious character" named Satie whom Debussy had introduced and recommended to Guiraud. The new arrival, Busser remembered, showed little promise, and "had to work extremely hard just to write a simple counter-subject for a fugue which Ernest Guiraud asked of him, the sort of thing we others could all do on the spot without the aid of a piano".

One day, Busser goes on, there occurred a lively incident. Satie was already known as the composer of music to which he had given odd, even barmy titles. He brought with him to class a new piece of music for piano duet which he called *Trois Morceaux en forme de poire*. These he played with a fellow-student. In charge of the proceedings that day was Guiraud's assistant André Gédalge, an erstwhile bookseller turned musician who had already begun the career that made him a teacher noted for the severity of his discipline. He was disgusted and angered by what he took for a practical joke. The situation became so unpleasant, says Busser, that Satie never appeared at the Conservatoire again.

It has been suggested, not improbably, that the *Trois Morceaux en forme de poire* were written and baptised thus as an impudent gesture at Guiraud.* The latter, maybe, had given Satie some well-intentioned advice about paying more attention to form, whereupon the young musician produced these bizarre pieces and, moreover, included in the title a saucy reference to Guiraud as a *poire* (slang for "mug"). It is the conduct of a naughty child who, insecure and therefore rebellious, thinks to justify himself by impertinence. For Satie, deep down, was horribly sensitive about his lack of technique.

In any case, even without the offensive title, the *Trois Morceaux* would have been enough to discomfit his teacher. They sum up the two aspects of the peculiarly divided musical life Satie had led up to now. On the one hand there is the grave, religious side to his nature and the flavour of the *Gnossiennes*. On the other is the Montmartre cabaret influence, abrupt and mocking. The music evolves, aloofly, and just at the point where Satie appears to be loosening up, the mood suddenly changes, the listener is pushed away and held at arm's length again. The first piece ends with a typically derisive flourish. The complete set is an ironic mixture

* Edward Lockspeiser in *Debussy: His Life and Mind*, vol. I, Cassell, 1962. It may also be recalled that when W. C. Fields encountered Mae West for the first time, his unforgettable line of dialogue ran: "Come, my phlox, my flower, I have some pear-shaped ideas I would like to discuss with you." (*My Little Chickadee*.)

of counterpoint and music-hall tunes which marks a clear stage in his development. It looks back to the tranquil inspiration of the early *Gymnopédies* and at the same time peers forward beyond the clumsy stirrings of the Rosicrucian music.

Debussy perceived in the composer certain reflections of his own character, most of all that child-like quality which makes life so difficult in a rough and materialistic world. On a presentation copy of his Baudelaire settings he wrote: "For Erik Satie, a gentle mediaeval musician who has strayed into this century for the joy of Claude Debussy, his friend. 27 Oct. '92." There was, at the beginning, affection on both sides. "The moment I saw him," Satie remarked, "I felt attracted towards him and wanted to live beside him for ever. And for thirty years I was lucky enough to see my wish fulfilled."

Although he claimed not to be an enemy of Wagner, as the Willy episode proved, Satie told Debussy he thought it was time to break away from the Wagnerian influence which ran counter to national aspirations. Frenchmen should write their own music, "without *choucroute*". Why not follow the example of painters like Monet, Cézanne, Toulouse-Lautrec?

Both composers were interested in Maeterlinck plays as subjects for opera. Satie at one time thought of adapting *La Princesse Maleine* which Debussy had already obtained permission from the author to use as the basis of a musical work. The misty symbolism of Maeterlinck and the simplicity of his characters moved them equally. When Debussy's *Pelléas et Mélisande* was completed, Satie wrote: "There's no more to be done in that direction: I'll have to look for something else if I'm not to be outclassed."

Satie's medievalism and his basic innocence played a large part in the sympathy Debussy felt for him. The older musician stood towards Satie in the relationship of an uncle, a benevolent elder whose home was always open to him. Each week Satie appeared at Debussy's house. Here he was able to try out his latest compositions at the piano. He often stayed to dinner. The host, while he drank finer wines himself, allocated the more commonplace ones to his guest. The latter did not seem to mind. Only in later years did Satie allow, with some bitterness, the resentment he must have felt at his inferior part in this strange relationship to colour his attitude towards Debussy.

They often met, too, at the home of the Swiss conductor

Gustave Doret. Satie played there his *Trois Gymnopédies*. He was never an accomplished pianist. When Debussy saw that even these simple pieces gave him difficulty, he took over and played them himself. Why not orchestrate them, suggested Doret. The idea was taken up, and Doret conducted Debussy's orchestrations of the first and third *Gymnopédies*. Though not entirely true to the spirit of the originals, Debussy's version, which is a shade lusher than it ought to be, is nonetheless an interesting compliment to his friend.

If Satie was, to Debussy, something of a poor relation, with the young Maurice Ravel he acted as an avuncular guide and adviser. Ravel was nine years his junior. They met over a café table at the Nouvelle Athènes, a favourite haunt of Marcellin Desboutin, portraitist, it will be remembered, to the Sâr Péladan who ennobled him for his services. Desboutin was probably an acquaintance of Ravel's father, an engineer by profession whose cultural interests extended not only to music but also to painting. Through his younger brother Edouard, an artist, he had the entrée to painterly circles.

At Desboutin's table Ravel senior and his eighteen-year-old son were joined by Satie. It was an important meeting for Ravel. Satie and Chabrier were to be early influences on his music. Ravel himself acknowledged the traces of Satie in his unpublished *Ballade de la Reine morte d'aimer*. Those who have seen the manuscript of *Un grand sommeil noir*, a Verlaine setting, claim to detect a similar imprint. The most obvious example is provided by "la Belle et la bête" in *Ma Mère l'oye*, a sort of latter-day *Gymnopédie*. Other echoes of the composer whom Ravel described as "an awkward and inspired forerunner" may be discerned in *Sainte*.

Ravel was the first of those young musicians who, as the years passed, were to gather round Satie and to look on him as a mentor. "Ravel," Satie wrote, "is a very talented Prix de Rome. A more astonishing Debussy. He swears to me – each time I meet him – that he owes me a great deal. Well, that's alright by me . . ."

In the meantime, his music continued to show sudden and disconcerting switches between the genuine and the exhibitionistic. Among the latter were the *Vexations*, a brief piece covering half a page which is to be played eight hundred and forty times straight off. The performer is advised to prepare himself in advance, "and in the greatest silence", with complete immobility.

In some quarters, needless to say, this laboured joke has been taken seriously. (Mr John Cage estimates, gravely, that the complete performance, as specified, would last twenty-four hours.)

At the same time he was writing work of the calibre of the *Pièces froides*, also for piano. These two sets, each comprising a trinity of items, are labelled respectively "Airs à faire fuir" and "Danses de travers". Despite the humorous titles, there is not much here to put off the listener. The first group has an endearing lilt in the style of the *Gnossiennes* and the *Gymnopédies*, though with a brisker rhythm and greater melodic freedom. The second trio of pieces takes a series of broken chords and modulates restlessly until the end. Both airs and dances have a simplicity and a "rightness" that give them an important place in Satie's output.

These delicate and neatly wrought pieces are to be contrasted with the granitic *Messe des pauvres* of 1895. Written for organ or piano and voices, it has a genuinely antique ring, a resonance of François Villon and the bleak midwinter of mediaeval poverty when the only hope of happiness lay in the promise of an afterlife. The mass ends with a "Prayer for travellers and sailors in danger of death, to the very worthy and very august Virgin Mary, mother of Jesus", and a "Prayer for the salvation of my soul". The music is sparse and unforgivingly disjunct.

Extracts from it were published in the issue for June 1895 of *Le Coeur*, a magazine that existed to spread the ideas of the Satanist Jules Bois whose *Porte héroïque du ciel* Satie had illustrated with a prelude. An article by his faithful brother Conrad stressed that the *Messe des pauvres* was an essentially Catholic work. Satie was presented as one who had renounced the world and all its vanities. He had chosen poverty, knowing full well that mockery and indifference would be his lot. He was, said Conrad, a "pagan mystic".

The *Messe des pauvres* was the last of his consciously religious works. His farewell to the years of mysticism was symbolised by a change of address. In 1898, at the age of thirty-two, he left "Our Abbatial" in the rue Cortot and moved out to the distant suburb of Arcueil.

PART THREE

The Velvet Gentleman

X

Saint Erik of Arcueil

Of course, his personality did not alter overnight. He had not overlooked his old enemy the critic Willy. In the early months of 1898, five years after they'd been locked in physical combat, he addressed to him yet another insulting letter. This rebuke, dated 31 March, excoriated Willy in the usual magniloquent terms.

By October Satie had established himself in Arcueil, the suburb which lies four miles or so outside the boundaries of Paris. He now jocularly signed his letters: "Moi, Saint Erik d'Arcueil." In those days the place still had a touch of the provinces about it, though even then a pall of industrialisation hung over its shabby buildings. Four centuries ago the poet Ronsard and his friends came there for rustic jaunts beside the river Bièvre and the fountains that agreeably played. A thirteenth-century church, very Gothic, very Notre-Dame-de-Paris, still commemorates Saint Denis. Otherwise the meadows and spinneys where Ronsard loved to stroll have been covered long since by forbidding rows of warehouses, factories and narrow streets. A few traces of the Roman aqueduct that once crossed high over the valley of the Bièvre may be seen in the characteristically named rue du Chemin de Fer.

There was no reason for Satie to choose Arcueil. It was cheaper to live there than in Montmartre, but he could equally well have settled in districts just as economical yet more attractive. His austere taste for poverty may have urged him to light on this place of drab aspect and melancholy atmosphere, this prospect of sombre brick yards and mean lodgings. The rue Cauchy, now a one-way thoroughfare, takes over from the rue de Stalingrad and leads to the place de la République. In this street, at No. 22, in an angle formed by its junction with the avenue Raspail, stands a gaunt block known as "aux Quatre cheminées". It was named presumably after the factory chimneys that decorate the surrounding landscape. On the ground-floor there was a dark and dusty café frequented by workmen. At the weekend its patrons danced to the clatter of an accordion. The remainder of the four-storey block was inhabited by working-class families.

Here Satie took a room on the second floor. He did not move in immediately. The first few nights he spent there were troubled by mosquitoes which, he swore, must have been sent by the accursed Freemasons. Then he took the decision to settle there for good. The meagre furnishings of his lair in the rue Cortot were heaped onto a barrow which he pushed through the streets to his new dwelling. The room was large, too large for the hammock, the bench, the cupboard and the few planks that made up his chattels. During cold weather he placed, in a neat row beneath the hammock, bottles filled with hot water – rather like a marimba, somebody said.

At 22 rue Cauchy, in the building which still exists though re-numbered 34, he stayed for the rest of his life. His next-door neighbour was a mason. Through his window he could see the trees of school playing fields. He did all his own housework, dusting and cleaning, polishing the floor, and drawing each night water from the fountain in the place des Écoles to bring back home in a stone jug. Soon he wearied of these chores. The dust accumulated. Windows grew dim and bleary. The once-bright floor shaded over with grease and footmarks. The curtains, thin and faded, were seen from outside to have steadily rotted into grimy shreds. Yet if his room was neglected, his clothes certainly were not. He always looked neat. His laundry list, inscribed on a spare sheet of music paper in elegant writing and signed with his monogram, would include anything up to sixteen handkerchiefs in a week. His toilette was simple but laborious. "I never take a bath," he told a friend. "You can only wash properly in little bits! I use pumice stone on my skin. It goes further than soap, dear lady."

No one ever entered his lodging in the rue Cauchy. When he realised that neighbours, intrigued by the mystery, were attempting to peer into his room with binoculars, he took care not to open the window very wide. Since at this time he was always dressed in grey velvet from head to toe, the folk of Arcueil took him for an artist. This explained a lot, they said to themselves. His velvet suit and broad-brimmed felt hat became a familiar sight. Often he would go round the corner and down the boulevard Raspail to have a meal at No. 15, the restaurant run by "La mère Tulard" whose regular customer he became. The building was demolished in 1962.

Soon "The Velvet Gentleman" as he was nicknamed knew intimately all the cafés in the district. To one he became especially attached. The atmosphere was easy-going and congenial. Then the proprietress became over-friendly. Like a cat that repels familiarity, he abruptly moved off elsewhere. He at last came to rest in a café opposite the church of Saint Denis only a few minutes' walk from the rue Cauchy. From the terrace he could see the bulbous capitals on its Gothic façade. No one troubled him here. Customers sympathised with his wish for privacy and waited for him to speak first before starting a conversation. He sat at his table writing letters, composing music or designing little sketches. In between times he stopped to roll cigarettes from unusually large sheets of paper.

In Arcueil he was completely alone. There were no callers at 22 rue Cauchy except for the postman. Women did not go there. His love-life seemed non-existent. In Montmartre, where he still went to earn a living, he may have frequented brothels, though he could not have afforded even the cheapest rates available. As fellow professionals – he was, after all, like them in the entertainment business, though on the musical side – the girls might have taken pity on him and granted an occasional favour. It is equally possible that he lived a chaste existence. He did not care very much for women. His manner, a compound of cynicism and shyness, was not designed to encourage even those who were attracted by him. Through choice and circumstance he had little to do with females. His mother he had scarcely known. And experience with Suzanne Valadon was enough to have given him a jaundiced view of her sex. He had suffered once, through her, and he probably did not want to suffer again.

Amid the dreary surroundings of Arcueil he came to know a sort of peace. In this dim backwater he once remarked that he sensed the mysterious dwelling-place of "Notre Dame de Bassesse", the "Our Lady of Lowliness" who is sought out by the mystic in his eternal quest for humility. With the middle class, with the moneyed and the successful, he felt ill at ease. Even his professional colleagues, musicians of superior training and background, gave him, with a few exceptions, a feeling of inferiority. Like a grand seigneur who can only relax in the company of his groom and his serving wenches, Satie was most truly at home with the masons, the clerks, the dustmen, the mechanics, who were his daily acquaintances in Arcueil. He had, moreover, an Orwellian impulse to identify with the working class. As time went on, for psychological and political reasons this impulse strengthened.

Once they had become accustomed to his secretive ways, the local people grew to like and respect him. The few who gathered regularly with him at his café table looked forward to their reunions. They found him, once his initial reserve was breached, a genial and witty companion. His lack of self-seeking and disdain for money impressed them. They relished their long discussions which ended, usually, in loud bursts of laughter from Satie, so loud and so violent that his pince-nez flew from his nose and clattered onto the table.

Yet those early years in Arcueil were hard and grim. He had very little money. In the first quarter of 1903 his music earned him a royalty of seventy-six centimes. (As an added reminder of his penniless obscurity, his name was spelt "Erick" on the royalty return.) Not for the first nor for the last time he knew real poverty. When the Montmartre cabarets where he played shut down early in the morning, he could not afford the cab fare home. So he walked, a distance of many miles, right across Paris from the Butte to Arcueil. It took him hours and often he did not arrive until long after dawn. There were cafés on the way, some of them open, and he would drink there among the porters, the carters and others whose jobs involved nocturnal hours. For protection on his lonely walk he carried with him a large and fearsome hammer.

He felt discouraged and frustrated. The letters he wrote to his brother at this time are bare of his usual humour and fantasy. Conrad was told:

I'm so fed up that I could die of sorrow; everything I start on so humbly fails with a consistency I've never known till now.

What can I do, except turn towards God and point to Him? I end up by thinking that the old chap is more stupid than powerful.

What are you up to that's new? Tell me, dear old fellow; your future isn't the same as mine, happily for you; you'll have a horse and one of those grand carriages that's open in summer and closed in winter; you'll be dashing about all over the place as well-off people do.

At this period of discouragement he took comfort in his friendship with Debussy. Yet even here the consolation he received had a flaw in it. For Debussy had now completed *Pelléas et Mélisande* and Satie could recognise its greatness. "Since you ask me for news of *Pelléas et Mélisande*," wrote Satie to his brother, "I'll tell you quite simply this: it's terrific, absolutely fantastic."

While Debussy had been working on a masterpiece, what had Satie been doing? All he could offer, by comparison, was a handful of songs intended for the café-concert and the music-hall. He dismissed them as "rudes saloperies" and felt ashamed of such hack-work. They did not even earn him a great deal of the money which had been his chief reason for writing them.

Trash they may well have seemed to the composer of the *Gymnopédies* and of the austere *Gnossiennes*. One side of his character, however, took pleasure in them. They were "popular" music, the sort of things his worker-friends at Arcueil enjoyed dancing to on Saturday nights and liked to hear when sung by their music-hall favourites. One of the songs was called *Tendrement* and resulted from Satie's partnership with Vincent Hyspa at the Chat Noir. Though better known for his satire and his lampoons, Hyspa wrote a lyric that brimmed over with sentimentality. It spoke of a pure and tender love and of roses blooming in the garden of the heart. Satie, with complete seriousness, put it to music that was simple and made an immediate effect.

77

Other Montmartre acquaintances gave him words to set. Dominique Bonnaud was of Corsican origin and had begun his career as secretary to Prince Roland Bonapaite. After a period in journalism, when he published a new song every week, he quickly became a successful entertainer at the Chat Noir, often singing there and at several other cabarets in an evening. He specialised in political satire with a touch of Rabelaisian humour. In between his cabaret engagements this versatile performer worked for a spell as secretary to the Prefect of Nancy.

With his friend Numa Blès he founded the notable "Logiz de la Lune Rousse", a "cabaret artistique" like the one Salis established, which survived for many years up to the nineteen-sixties. Blès came from Marseille where he had studied for a teaching career. Early success as a chansonnier changed his ambitions and soon he was off on a world tour with the famous Lucien Boyer, joint-author of that hit of the 1914–18 war, *La Madelon*. An over-fondness for absinthe plunged Blès into madness and an early death.

His partnership with Bonnaud was fertile. Among the numerous songs they wrote was *La Diva de l'Empire*. The words are brisk and snappy. They portray a beauty in her "big Greenaway hat" with the laugh of a "baby étonné", a "Little girl aux yeux vel-outés" who enchants all the gentlemen and "tous les dandys de Piccadilly". This is the Queen of the Empire music-hall to whom the song pays homage in amusing Anglo-French. Satie provided a march tune in jaunty ragtime. The rhythms match the saucy verse and picture in music the arch expression on the singer's face.

La Diva de l'Empire was sung, to acclamations, in a revue called *Dévidons la Bobine*, which was first played at the seaside resort of Berck-Plage in 1904. The singer was Paulette Darty. She kept the number in her repertoire for some years afterwards. For her Satie also wrote *Je te veux*, a slow waltz of the type she made famous, compact of lilting nostalgia and artless romanticism. Indeed, her billing always described her, in large capitals, as "Queen of the Slow Waltz". She had dazzling blonde hair, a capacious bosom, and a statuesque presence that dominated the most unruly Saturday night audience. She sang sweetly and spoke with a clarity of diction that was essential to her craft before the age of the amplifier. In between verses and at the end of her number she waltzed round the stage in graceful circles. Mademoiselle Darty outlived her songwriter by many years and did not die until 1940 after a lengthy retirement. Satie dedicated *Je te veux* to her. They kept in touch for some time afterwards, long after he had deserted the cabarets of Montmartre and devoted himself to more serious music. In 1913 she was flattered with the dedication of one of the *Descriptions automatiques*. More to her taste, one suspects, would have been that languorous waltz *Poudre d'or* which also figures among his café-concert music.

Another Montmartre friend was Jules Depaquit, who gave him the scenario of *Jack in the Box*. Depaquit in his prime was a distinguished comic artist. With deft economy, said an admirer, he pared down his drawings until a head was reduced to a simple triangle. Within that triangle an eye was condensed into a small circle. Within that circle the pupil became a marble. Yet the whole presented an intense impression of life, of a mood caught and recorded in all its fullness. His own drawings of himself show a face with the profile of a depressed but irascible hawk and the eye of an alert owl. A friend always remembered him in a tall top hat that lurched forward at an angle, as did the hat of the demented dancer in Toulouse-Lautrec's pictures, and a lugubrious overcoat like a priest's robe. Then somebody reminded the friend that he must be mistaken: he was confusing with the real man his memories of so many grotesques whom Depaquit had pictured just like that. Life had come to imitate art.

Depaquit was a native of Sedan, that town close to the Belgian frontier which owes the bleak undertone of its name to Louis-Napoleon's tragic defeat during the Franco-Prussian War. Every two years the artist went back to Sedan to stay with his mother. When he returned to Paris he left behind his worn-out brown suit and took with him a new one intended to last another couple of years until his next visit. As soon as he left school he had begun to draw. He quickly became a star contributor to *Le Rire* and other humorous publications. One of his earliest inventions was a pair of skates for crossing water. When he tried them out in a nearby mill-race he almost drowned and had to be rescued, with difficulty, from entanglement in the mill-wheel. He once fought a duel on novel principles. Each adversary, his chest armoured with a piece of wood inches thick, had for weapon a bit and brace. At the command "Allez!" he started drilling into his opponent's breastplate. The first man to draw blood was acclaimed the winner.

By the nineteen-twenties Depaquit had lost his touch. He could no longer sell his drawings, public taste had changed, and he drifted into alcoholism, shuffling in floppy slippers from *bistrot* to *bistrot* and cadging drinks whenever the chance arose. One of his favourite tricks was to appear in a bar carrying a suitcase. Acquaintances gathered to ask where he was going. Home to Sedan, replied Depaquit mournfully, because he'd had enough of Montmartre. Touched, they stood him a farewell drink. More drinks followed and the leave-taking extended late into the night. Next evening Depaquit turned up at another bar and the performance was repeated. There are many bars in Montmartre.

The old clown, for whom affection persisted, was elected mayor of the "free commune" of Montmartre. He took the honour seriously and appointed his own captain of firemen and his own policeman. They accompanied him on picturesque occasions rigged out in fancy uniform and breeches. He travelled France with his "demoiselles d'honneur" and presided solemnly at "twinning" ceremonies between Montmartre and other towns. Tourists admired the spectacle without realising its commercial motive.

But in the nineteen-hundreds Depaquit, some thirty years old, was still an admired cartoonist whose work editors were eager to publish. He had met Satie at the Auberge du Clou where he often held court. For a time he lived in the place du Tertre, not far from his particular friend the caricaturist Delaw. Self-appointed "imagier de la reine" (which queen?) Delaw inhabited a house without a door. Entrances and exits were made through the window. He was from Sedan too, and brought a gentle fantasy to the humour of his drawings. Depaquit, Satie and Delaw spent hours together over their drinks, building elaborate fancies and hatching out preposterous notions. While Depaquit, birdlike and voluble, chattered excitedly, Satie puffed at a cigarette and added an incongruous remark sotto voce. Delaw, an eternal pipe in his mouth, beamed silently.

Delaw belonged to the "Club de la Clay Pipe". It had no members – but three chairmen: himself, Georges Auriol and Satie. They met at a café in the place du Tertre to smoke the long English pipes, with a carving of two chained slaves and tipped with vermilion, that Auriol discovered in mysterious suburban shops. When the last ashes were shaken out they all, except for Satie, tapped out these handsome pieces of craftsmanship and carefully put them away in a rack. But the composer had become attached to his and he carried it away in his pocket, the long delicate stem reaching nearly up to his ear.

Sometimes Depaquit would accompany Satie on his marathon walks from Montmartre to Arcueil. They set off at two in the morning through the sinister neighbourhoods of the Glacière and the Santé, the composer fingering nervously the hammer in his pocket. Usually the sun had risen by the time they arrived in Arcueil. So, after a quick refreshment, they would turn round and go back to Montmartre which they reached about midday. The sun! How Satie hated it. "It's a bully! If only my leg were long enough to give it a good kick up the eye-lash! It's a bully and an evildoer. Not content with roasting the windows of our prisons it amuses itself in wickedly burning the peasants' harvest. What a rascal!"

The letters Depaquit wrote were the joy of his friends. Illustrated with lively drawings, they told a complete story and could have been published as they stood. One of them, addressed to the editor of *Le Rire*, explained why he had been unable to deliver his drawings in time. He was writing from prison, he explained, having overlooked his obligation for military service and forgotten that "I had to devote to My Country (France) the best three years of my precious existence." For two representatives of authority, "vulgarly called policemen", had arrived to enlighten him at the very moment when "j'Alphonse Allais exécuter pour *Le Rire*" (the pun cannot be translated).

Depaquit infiltrated Satie's correspondence as well. On the back of a letter to Conrad he presented himself as "one of the unworthiest members of Christianity to touch his hat and introduce himself to you without the slightest modesty. The photograph enclosed will show you the physical aspect of the person who signs himself Depaquit and greets you." The "photograph" consisted of a rebus drawn with his usual love of intricate detail. A neat reference to the Dufayel delivery service ("paquet") accounted for most of his name.

Jack in the Box was intended as a ballet. Depaquit's scenario has not survived. It was probably mislaid, stained with absinthe and spotted with tobacco droppings, on some café table. The music also disappeared for many years, and Satie always thought he had left it on a bus. Only after his death was it discovered. The crumpled notebook in which he had written it was found stuffed behind the ancient piano in his room at Arcueil. Darius Milhaud orchestrated the ballet with finesse and sympathy for a performance later organised by Diaghilev as a tribute to Satie. The settings were by André Derain.

This little divertissement lasts in performance no more than seven minutes. There are three items, Prelude, Entr'acte and Finale, each of them written to jerky rhythms that reflect the title. The movements of Jack in the Box are further suggested by sudden time changes. Harmonies are cunningly blurred. These charming pieces are everywhere good-humoured and attractively naïf – though the impression of naïveté is fostered with knowing care. Why *Jack in the Box* rather than "Boîte à surprise" or "Diablotin"? Because, presumably as with *La Diva de l'Empire*, use of English phrases was then considered humorous, chic and "très snob" – just as Anglo-Saxon composers, seeking to give their compositions an air of mystery or glamour, once had a habit of calling their Studies "Études" and their concert pieces "Morceaux de bravoure". But whatever it is called, *Jack in the Box* remains a delightful little triptych and a pleasing memorial to the pawky humour of two friends who had more in common than the bars of Montmartre alone.

Lighter still than *Jack in the Box* was the operetta *Pousse l'Amour*. The actor Maurice de Féraudy wrote the words of this extravaganza and Satie provided a handful of musical numbers. Féraudy was the son of a physical training instructor, a circumstance which perhaps accounted for his suppleness and fine presence on stage. He had been a prize student at the Conservatoire and, when Satie knew him, was a distinguished ornament of the Comédie-Française where he played leading classical parts. A very famous theatrical figure indeed, he also starred in the first performances of important contemporary dramas.

Féraudy himself wrote poetry and a number of plays. *Pousse l'Amour* was his first venture into operetta. The collaboration with Satie did not run easily. At rehearsals the composer raised his voice in angry disagreement. He could not approve of the slick devices proposed by the deft but conventional man of the theatre. He made his exit and slammed the door behind him. But Féraudy was a thrifty man. For nearly a decade *Pousse l'Amour* slept in his bottom drawer. Then, much revised, it popped up in 1913 at Monte Carlo under the vaudeville title of *Coco chéri*. The whereabouts of the manuscript are unknown, if it exists at all. And that is how Satie would have wished it.

XI

Geneviève of Brabant

A more sympathetic collaborator was Satie's old friend Contamine de Latour. Their last project together was a puppet play called *Geneviève de Brabant*, which they had completed in 1899. The heroine, not to be confused with that Geneviève who is the patron saint of Paris, figures in legends dating back to the sixth century. She was the wife of Siegfried, count of Treves, whose villainous steward had designs upon her. When rebuffed by the virtuous lady, the steward told Siegfried that they had committed adultery together. Wherefore Geneviève endured much persecution until her innocence was proved and her calumniator punished.

The theme is a common one in mediaeval literature. A similar story, that of the patient Grisélidis who was sorely tried by her husband's suspicion of deceit, is recounted by Chaucer. He took it from Boccaccio. Many operas have been written around the story, and as late as 1901 Massenet brought out a version entitled *Grisélidis*.

The text Latour wrote was certainly the best he ever gave to Satie. Geneviève is left at home by her husband Sifroy, lord of the Palatine, who, called away to the wars, confides her to the care of his seneschal Golo. She is one month pregnant. In her lord's absence Golo tries to seduce her but is indignantly repulsed. At Sifroy's return Golo accuses her of adultery and she is thrown into prison. There she gives birth to a boy. The executioners drag her out to the forest. Touched by her plight, however, they release both mother and child. Geneviève lives in a pit in the depths of the forest, "without bread nor fire, light nor company save that of her dear son". A doe comes and gives milk to the child, while all around the birds sing and wild animals gather to comfort her.

Meanwhile Sifroy is stung with remorse. Out hunting one day he follows the track of the doe which has been looking after Geneviève. She leads him to the pit where he finds a pathetic and bedraggled figure.

"Geneviève is my name, i'faith, born of Brabant where is my family," says the apparition. "A great lord wed me for sure, and carried me to his country. I am a lady highly born, but my husband doth hold me in great contempt."

Sifroy, repentant and tearful, takes his wife and the boy home. The birds and the animals watch sorrowfully as they depart. The perfidious Golo is sentenced and skinned alive. Yet despite the loving care of her husband, Geneviève is only interested now in the greater love of Jesus, whom she had come to know in the vast solitude of the forest. She lives simply, eating nothing but the roots that sustained her during her long exile. Soon she dies in blessedness. A great light pierces out of the sky and turns night into day. Her corpse is followed to the tomb by rich and poor, by the animals of the forest and by the doe that succoured Geneviève and her child.

There was much in this scenario to please Satie: an age remote from his own, simplicity of feeling and a gracious martyrdom. The tone is that of an *image d'Épinal*, one of those folk pictures in bright colours that depict, for the benefit of an unsophisticated populace, an incident or message that points a homely moral. The short prelude contains a theme of nursery-tune flavour that returns in various keys throughout the play as an entr'acte and as an accompaniment to the entry of soldiers.

The most striking effect is the sense of alienation as a stage device. The play is, to begin with, acted by puppets. The chorus in Act I sing:

> Nous sommes la foule compacte
> Qu'on met toujours au premier acte

and remind the audience that they are made of cardboard. In Act II, Geneviève's aria pleading her innocence observes that no one wants to be killed in the prime of life and adds: "It is, I confess, harmful to one's health. Ah! cutting off your head can hurt a lot, and I'm not keen on it at all, not one little bit." When Sifroy has gone off to war, Golo childishly tries out his throne for size and exclaims: "Supreme power will be mine – I'll have my own civil list, my own fire brigade and policemen and honours by the thousand." And at the end of the play a final chorus sums up by telling the audience that the matter has passed off well, that virtue has been rewarded and crime duly punished, and that everything's over and done with.

All this would be merely flippant were it not that both words and music aptly re-create the atmosphere of mystery plays, of those mediaeval spectacles which mingled the crudest fooling and commonplace with true aspiration and reverence for the saints. The canticle in honour of Sainte Geneviève has the sweetness of an illuminated figure in a missal where the colours gleam straightforwardly and the proportions, lacking perspective, have an endearing clumsiness. The music is cool and made up of short, simple phrases. Geneviève contemplates beheading to a melody that unites folk tune with a Debussyist line. Golo plans his wicked scheme in measures that echo the tone of an old peasant round.

As with *Jack in the Box*, the rhythms generally are abrupt, suggesting the motion of the puppets which were to act the drama. And again like *Jack in the Box*, the manuscript of *Geneviève de Brabant* disappeared from view almost as soon as it had been composed. The ten items which make up this "complainte" nestled for many years in the same place as the earlier work: behind Satie's piano. Publication did not come until 1930.

XII

D'Indy and Roussel

In 1900 yet another Exposition Universelle had been held in Paris. It was the most brilliant and successful event of its kind to date. As if to add to the country's prestige, the African potentate Rabah, an old enemy of the French, was obliging enough to die and troops were able to capture a strategic oasis. Even the rumblings of the Dreyfus affair were muffled for a brief space.

The Exposition was celebrated in various ways. Among them figured the publication of a large and lavish album in several volumes devoted to contemporary musicians. Each composer was allotted a page or two on which his photograph appeared together with some music written for the occasion. These massy volumes were bound in ornately embellished leatherwork. Each page had the stiffness and consistency of cardboard. Therein featured every composer throughout the land, metropolitan and provincial, young and old, known and unknown, and many, it must be so, whose manuscripts remained obstinately unpublished. Monsieur Erik Satie is there, sandwiched between his equally eminent colleagues Messieurs G. de Saint-Quentin, G. Salvayre, Charles Silver and Georges Sporck. His contribution to the festive volume was a "Verset laïque et somptueux".

This was the nearest he had come to official recognition. Ever since then, in Arcueil, he had suffered growing depression about his ability, as the letters to his brother Conrad show. He was sensitive about the gaps in his knowledge of musical technique. Gibes at his ignorance wounded him, for he knew they were well founded. He took a courageous decision: he would go back to school and learn all those things which in youth he had scorned as pedantry.

Debussy warned him against the idea. Satie was approaching his fortieth year in 1905. "At your age," said Debussy, "you don't change your ways so easily."

Satie did not waver. If he failed, he explained simply, it would show that he was unfitted to be a composer. There was a desperation about his resolve that fitted in with his character. Humility, self-abasement, renunciation were his ideas. By submitting at his age to a strict discipline he would be fulfilling something of himself.

Obviously he could not return to the Conservatoire which he had left in disgust years ago. His choice fell upon the recently established Schola Cantorum, an institution which then stood in much the same relation to the Conservatoire as the Académie Goncourt does to the Académie Française. It was, in other words, a youthful rival to a body which, over many years, had become stiff in the joints, ultra-conservative and embalmed in tradition. At the Schola Cantorum he would be studying under the forceful Vincent d'Indy and his disciple Albert Roussel.

It was easy enough to make the decision. How he could afford it meanwhile posed a different question. Full-time study of the sort he planned called for a regular income. He drafted a letter appealing for funds.

"Monsieur le Président," he began. "I, the undersigned, have the honour to address to the benevolent board of management of the [blank] a request for a grant enabling me to follow the course in counterpoint taught by Mr R[oussel]. I am an artist ['poor' added in red ink], at grips with the difficulties of life; it is therefore quite impossible for me to pay the fees demanded of pupils following this course at your fine school. Please accept, M. le Président, my respectful greetings." On second thoughts he added: "In the confidence that you will be kind enough to take my request into consideration, I ask you to accept . . ."

This letter presumably came into the hands of Vincent d'Indy. It is probable that he was sympathetic. However odd, however alien to d'Indy's world Satie may have appeared, his poverty and his sincerity were undeniable. D'Indy would not have been so closely identified with the Schola had he not shared Satie's view of the Conservatoire. Whatever the result of the letter, Satie must have been able to come to some kind of financial arrangement, and in 1905 he duly enrolled as a student at the Schola Cantorum.

The school began its existence in the rue Stanislas, off the boulevard du Montparnasse and not far from the Collège Stanislas, that other temple to education. It had been founded in 1894 by Charles Bordes, a young enthusiast for sixteenth- and seventeenth-century music, with the aid of d'Indy and the organist Alexandre Guilmant. Originally intended as a society for the improvement of religious music, the Schola two years later became a teaching establishment. It was soon to flourish under d'Indy's vigorous leadership, a centre for the revival of old, neglected music and a vivifying aesthetic force.

D'Indy was a viscount, the heir to a noble family with a long tradition of diplomacy and soldiering. His mother having died in childbirth, he was brought up by his fearsome and autocratic grandmother the comtesse d'Indy. Daily routine was strict and never deviated by a minute from a rigid timetable. The principles of morality, duty, religion, patriotism, courage and self-discipline were branded for ever in his soul. He never forgot them. Music was prominent in the family circle. His uncle played the violin and knew Berlioz. Rossini often came to dinner. The young d'Indy, initiated by his grandmother, studied the art industriously under excellent teachers. He enlisted at the age of nineteen during the Franco-Prussian War and, while on sentry-go one night, conceived the idea for the scherzo in his *Symphonie italienne*.

His energy was formidable. When in 1931 he died at the age of eighty, he had led many lives: as composer, conductor, musicologist, teacher, editor and even biographer. Nearly every year he went on long concert tours throughout Europe, to Russia, to the USA and to Canada. He composed a great deal of music as well as immersing himself in every detail of the Schola's administration. His taste was for the grand fresco, solid and well-proportioned. Much of his inspiration came from Germany and the north. Himself he wrote the libretti of his grand operas

Fervaal, a subject based on Swedish legend, and of *L'Etranger* which he took from an Ibsen play. Schiller was the source of his *Chant de la Cloche*. Yet he was proud of his Frenchness and used effectively the traditional folk tunes of his native Vivarais in the *Poème des Montagnes*. For the bracing *Symphonie cévenole*, his most popular work, he drew on a folk theme from the Cévennes.

He had been a pupil of César Franck. Of all the young musicians who gathered round that influential figure, d'Indy was later the most active in perpetuating the ideals of disinterestedness and service to art which Franck personified. His biography of the master he revered was an act of devotion. He also wrote books on Wagner and Beethoven. The largest of his publications was the *Cours de composition musicale* which appeared in three stout volumes over a period of several decades. It traces with much erudition the history of the art throughout the centuries and contains ideas he expounded at the Schola Cantorum. There he revived many of the works he had analysed in his book, works that for long had been ignored in France. They included Bach cantatas and masses by Palestrina. He brought back to the stage operas of Monteverdi, Rameau and Gluck. His concerts at the Schola attracted commercial theatre managers eager to see the new talent he was training and the unfamiliar works his enterprise had rescued from oblivion.

One of his most distinguished pupils was Albert Roussel. This swarthy, black-bearded young man had, like Rimsky-Korsakov, been a professional sailor. Having passed his naval exams brilliantly as sixteenth out of six hundred competitors, he went to sea in the cruiser *Dévastation*. Later he joined the three-masted frigate *Melpomène*, the last French sailing ship of war, for a tour of duty in the Atlantic. There was a piano on board. Since childhood a keen amateur player, Midshipman Roussel was allowed to accompany the occasional religious service. In Madeira, one of their ports of call, he gave selections from operetta.

But now his twin passions, the sea and music, were conflicting within him. In a room he rented at Cherbourg, his home port, he played Beethoven trios with friends. At last he opted for music. He enrolled at the Schola Cantorum and deepened his knowledge of form and orchestration under the guidance of Vincent d'Indy. Yet he never lost his early love of the sea. Throughout the rest of his life he went on many voyages, storing up impressions and ideas afterwards to be elaborated in music that splices the Impressionism of Debussy with the techniques of firm construction which d'Indy passed on to him from Franck. A journey to India and Cambodia gave him inspiration for both the colourful *Evocations* and for the exotic opera–ballet *Padmâvati*. Even in his more formal music, the sonatas and the symphonies, the trace of Hindu, Greek and Chinese modes is unmistakable.

He had a fine country home near Varengeville, not far from Dieppe on the coast of Normandy. "Vasterival", as he called it, was surrounded by thick woods and crossed by salt sea breezes. Often he went down to the beach and, at low tide, sat beside the rock-pools to contemplate what Valéry called "La mer, la mer, toujours recommencée." Towards the end of his life he fell ill. Soon after he recovered a fire sprang up in the dense woods around Vasterival and the house was ringed by flame. With his wife he had to escape through burning undergrowth. Although no damage eventually was done to the property, the shock affected his health. He died in 1937, six years after d'Indy, at the age of sixty-eight.

So impressed was d'Indy by Roussel that, while the latter was still a pupil at the Schola, he put him in charge of teaching counterpoint there. This unusual move was fully justified. Roussel's technical mastery was equalled by his gift for teaching. One of his students, the Czech composer Bohuslav Martinu, remembered him affectionately. "With modesty, kindness, nobility, and also with a delicate and friendly irony," said Martinu, Roussel helped him put his ideas in order and find the path to be followed. "When I look now at all he taught me I'm astonished. What there was of the unconscious, hidden, unknown within me, he sensed it and revealed it to me, confirmed it, and in a way that was always friendly and almost tender ... What I had come to seek with him was order, clarity, proportion, taste, and direct, precise and sensitive expression: all those qualities of French art which I've always admired and wanted to know more closely. He possessed these qualities and shared his knowledge with me generously, very simply and very naturally, like the great artist he was."

For three years Roussel was also to be Satie's teacher. Their relations were to be as informal and friendly as had been the case with Martinu. By the time Satie joined the Schola it had moved from the rue Stanislas to an address at No. 269 rue Saint-Jacques.

This long and ancient street, which runs parallel with the boulevard Saint-Michel down to the river Seine, took its name from the thirteenth-century convent chapel that used to stand at No. 156. As lately as the seventeenth century the prospect was mainly of convents set in the midst of fields. The building at No. 269, where the Schola came to rest and has remained ever since, was itself a convent. The place was owned by Benedictine friars who fled from persecution in England. They built the convent in 1674. Although controlled by the French government, it belongs now to the Catholic bishops of England. Here died James II, deposed king of England. The chapel where his body lay has been turned into a concert room. It is a part of tradition that his ghost appears there at All Hallow's Eve.

Satie must have enjoyed the atmosphere of the building. Its conventual past was designed to charm his monkish sensibilities. The presence of a ghost suited his taste for the occult and the Gothic. The people, too, were congenial. In spite of d'Indy's haughty manner, his formal dress, the well-cut overcoat, the cigarette in the elegant holder, the neat silvery moustache and Imperial beard, the walking stick and the air of a retired military man, he had, beneath the aloof appearance, a kindly, even humorous personality. He shared with Satie an intransigence over matters of principle that could make them equally stubborn should the occasion arise. They had, it would seem, no arguments during Satie's course at the Schola. They were united in a love of the music which they analysed and worked on together. Roussel, the third member of the trio, became an even greater friend to Satie. And not the least remarkable aspect of this unusual episode in Satie's life was that he, a keen supporter of the Socialist party, should work in such complete harmony with a musician who was a typical representative of the upper middle class and with another who was a true-born aristocrat.

PART FOUR

Back to School

XIII

Counterpoint and Fugue

Satie joined the Schola Cantorum during its heroic period when d'Indy had been guiding its fortunes long enough to impress upon it his own ideas and high-minded conceptions. A few years earlier, at the new premises in the rue Saint-Jacques, d'Indy welcomed over a hundred and fifty students. "A superb start to the term," he wrote. "If they all paid their fees we could do some fine concerts; but we shall certainly have to give charity to those in need of it." D'Indy paid, out of his own pocket, many of the Schola's expenses, so that in the end he could almost, though he never did, claim that it was his creation twice over, materially as well as spiritually.

On the opening day of the new session in autumn 1905, Satie presented himself, a middle-aged gentleman among the fresh-faced pupils who streamed into classes. Roussel was incredulous still. His new student was three years his senior and, unlike the others, had behind him a record of work done.

"Satie knew his craft," Roussel observed. "The works he'd already published proved to me that he had nothing to learn. I couldn't see the advantages he hoped to get from theoretical and scholastic studies. However, he was obstinate. He was a very willing and diligent student. He was punctilious in handing over to me the homework he'd written out so beautifully, with such care, and embellished with annotations in red ink. He was tremendously musical."

During 1905 and 1906 Satie attended the classes given by Auguste Sérieyx, who at the Schola taught rhythm, melody and harmony to first-year students. Sérieyx, who had abandoned his law studies for music, was another of d'Indy's pupils and, like Roussel, showed such promise that he was allowed to teach others before he himself had properly graduated. He studied composition with d'Indy and was closely associated with the *Cours de composition musicale*, parts of which he assembled from d'Indy's lectures after his master's death. His compositions include church music and songs. After leaving the Schola at the outbreak of war in 1914, he settled in Switzerland where he died in 1949.

Satie's closest relationship at the Schola was, however, with Roussel. They got on well together and their friendship went beyond the formal student–teacher situation. The letters Satie wrote to him, full of gossip and opinion, were signed: "Your affectionate pupil." Even after he left the Schola he kept in touch with Roussel. "A young man, very musical . . . wants to follow your lectures at the Schola . . ." he wrote in 1911. "Do you think that, because he's Jewish, entry to the Schola would be forbidden him? This would be unfortunate . . ." The reference was obviously to d'Indy's fierce anti-semitism. Yet probably the young man would have been admitted. D'Indy did not allow prejudice to hamper him where artistic talent was concerned, as witness the sympathy and encouragement he gave to Paul Abraham Dukas, composer of not only the omnipresent *L'Apprenti-sorcier* but also of much else that a restless spirit of self criticism urged him to destroy.

Satie wrote out his Schola exercises in small oblong music notebooks, some of them of the kind used by children. It was amusing that he, so often accused of technical ignorance, should be using books on whose covers were printed in simple terms, for the sake of the little ones, the "Notes and signs of music". He also jotted down details of accounts – lists of pathetic little sums he had spent during the week on bus fares, laundry, meals – drafts of letters, times and dates of appointments, reminders about meetings, and sketches for lectures. Sometimes he tried out a title for music he planned. "Impressions Parisiennes" was a projected suite to include items depicting Paris at its morning waking, the bus, the avenue du Bois and the races. Another proposed a "Dance for a burial". Passing thoughts were caught on the wing: "The sea is full of water: it's beyond all understanding," or "Whoever drinks absinthe kills himself by mouthfuls."

Chiefly, though, the notebooks contain exercises in counterpoint and fugue which he laboured at with care and persistence. The different sections were scrupulously identified: subject, counter-subject, stretta and so forth. Unisons were labelled "good" or "bad". There were notes on orchestration and very detailed observations about the characteristics of individual instruments. The impression is of a painstaking student determined to get it all right from the very beginning.

His analysis of an extract from Bach's *Art of Fugue* was elaborately lettered in red and black ink with, at the bottom of the page, a courteous inscription: "Please turn over, Cher Maître." He would write: "I am happy to have had to analyse such a perfect work, a true and gentle artistic treasure filled with simple and tender logic, a treasure brimming over with steady and abundant inspiration." A study of the adagio in Beethoven's fourth symphony brought a comment from d'Indy: "There are excellent things here and it is very musical . . ." An exercise for Sérieyx earned the remark: "An interesting piece of work but not brought out enough."

The tone of his masters' comments did not change much. "There are some very good things here . . ." was d'Indy's refrain. A Palestrina motet aroused Satie's greatest enthusiasm. In the course of his analysis he wrote: "The religious feeling in this passage is immense. Yet the musical inspiration of each part is very simple. I feel that the ecstatic charm shown here results from the vocal inter-crossings. In any case I can see here one of the characteristics of Palestrina's transparent style, a heavenly style. The angelic musician must have been one of the greatest believers who ever existed. He is always close to God; his manner is holy; his genius is benevolent.

"Here truly is the charming son of our sweet religion, of that wonderful and imperishable Catholicism. Here is the brother of our dear cathedrals, of our Roman Christian Art, of all we love, of all we worship."

97

He singled out the "Benedicunt Dominum". He dwelt at length on the melody to which the word "corde" was set. "This analysis began very well," noted d'Indy, "and it's a pity it's not finished."

His essays in composition included a "Petite sonate". Ironically . . . more slowly (with good nature) . . . flowing . . . are among the directions to the player. "This miniature sonata is not at all disagreeable," commented his teacher, "and the first idea – whatever you may think of it – isn't at all bad. It has personality, and that's what I like . . . *It's good.*"

It was counterpoint at which he toiled most arduously. The notebooks for 1906 and 1907 were filled with exercises. "Quite good work," Roussel decided, "but still a little academic . . ." Such a judgement on Satie, of all people, was the richest of ironies. Another set of exercises impelled Roussel to observe: "These pieces of counterpoint are good, but you have found – and in the future you will find – *better* things certainly."

Throughout his studies at the Schola Satie proved to be a hard-working pupil eager to perfect his technique and to enlarge his knowledge. Though at first the incongruity of his presence made for a certain uneasiness, his sincerity and determination won the sympathy of the staff. It was all so different from his rebellious days at the Conservatoire. Even when he analysed for homework a piece by Ravel, the *Noël des jouets*, he did so with complete seriousness and avoided the temptation to make obvious sallies about the young composer who always spoke gratefully of the debt he owed to Satie.

His reward came in 1908 when he emerged from the Schola with his formal Diploma. Dated 15 June, it declared that "Monsieur Satie, Erik, a pupil on the course in counterpoint, has passed the end-of-year examinations with distinction and that he fulfils the conditions required for devoting himself exclusively to the study of composition." The document was signed flamboyantly by Vincent d'Indy, artistically by Roussel, and modestly by the Secretary of the Schola.

Satie's triumph, and a triumph with honours at that, delighted Roussel. But he still worried a little. Might not Satie's wholehearted immersion in the rigours of counterpoint, wondered Roussel, tend to sterilise the untutored inspiration which had given his early works their novelty and freshness?

XIV

Pied Piper of Arcueil

He was by now a well-known citizen of Arcueil. During the ten years he lived there the "velvet gentleman" had become accepted for his harmless eccentricities and cherished for his amiability. His interest in politics grew. He joined the local branch of the Socialist party and was elected to the committee. At meetings, which he attended faithfully, he would sit in a corner, smoking reflectively and examining the speakers with a close but enigmatic look.

Suddenly the arty velvet suits were discarded. By 1910 he had adopted the sober garments which, by a curious chance, emphasised his singularity more than the most outlandish raiment would have done. There may still be Arcueillais who can remember the black bowler, the black overcoat, the dark suit, the high wing collar whitely starched, the sober tie and the waistcoat tightly buttoned. Only the beard, the prim pince-nez and the ironical look remained to link him with the "velvet gentleman" of his youth. Everywhere he went, and at every time, he carried an umbrella, tautly furled. He enjoyed, in fact, bad weather. If rain threatened, the shopkeepers smiled at each other in the knowledge that they'd be sure to see Monsieur Satie that morning.

For one who preferred an eremitical way of life he showed himself to be oddly sociable once he was among his Arcueil friends. Although he did not appear to be the sort of man to join movements or establish societies, his membership of the Socialist committee gave evidence of an unsuspected gregariousness. So did his decision to found a regional group which he denominated by the names of the provinces involved: "Normandy, Maine, Anjou and Poitou." Every fortnight he contributed to a column reserved in the local paper for news of societies. Readers looking for the latest detail of what scouts or chess-players or anglers were up to would be confronted with droll paragraphs bearing the mark of a copywriter who knew the value of an arresting headline. "NO MORE BALDIES," said one, "if only everybody would take the trouble to join the new Aqueduct Savings Society. With what you save you could buy hair lotion." Another read:

BEING BITTEN BY A MONKEY
isn't as pleasant as going to No. 60 rue Emile-Raspail – at Friend Jacobs' place – where the "La Marguerite" dancing classes are held

or:

YOU'RE BEING DECEIVED
if you don't know that M. Ollinger-Jacob, the famous manager of The Greatest Cinematograph in the whole world, awaits you every Saturday, at half-past eight, in his superb rooms. M. Ollinger-Jacob holds decorations in several fictitious orders of knighthood; he is supplier to the Imperial Saharan Court, His Greatness the Doge of Manchester and His Heightiness the Sultan of Livarot. A magnificent show; tremendous enjoyment. People always enjoy themselves there.

An affection for animals and children began to show itself. He did not, like that other notorious solitary the writer Paul Léautaud, surround himself in his suburban home with dozens of cats, dogs, a monkey and a goose. He had, nonetheless, much in common with Léautaud. They both lived in near-poverty, were fiercely devoted to their respective arts, were lonely men who defended their shyness with a barrage of sarcasm, held simplicity and bareness to be the highest qualities of style, and remained intransigent to the end.* They were happiest with ordinary folk, Léautaud in Fontenay-aux-Roses and Satie in Arcueil. Those who knew them best, while acknowledging their disinterestedness and their prickly independence, realised at the same time that these qualities also made them very difficult characters. Both men were abysmally inept at human relationships. Léautaud found love and companionship in the society of animals. To a lesser extent so did Satie. For animals cannot answer back and they cannot hurt you with wounding words. Their devotion is a flattery, and after the devious ways of men their simple behaviour comes as a refreshment.

An inhabitant of Arcueil remembers Satie's distress when he came across a child trying to catch a lizard which he obviously planned to torment. Posting himself quietly beside a wall, Satie abruptly clapped his hands. The lizard, warned in time, shot off to safety and foiled the child. Satie went on his way, happy with his good deed.

He once gave a lecture introducing a concert of music relating to animals. "Michelet has said, modestly, that animals are our inferior brother," he began, "which is the same thing as saying that man is the superior brother of animals. We do not have the animals' opinion on this matter. What we do know about them is that they are good citizens of Nature; that they have rights and duties; and that they have considerable intelligence. Some are termed: domestic. Why? I don't know."

If, he went on, painters and sculptors have often represented animals, the latter themselves do not seem to know about the plastic arts:

On the other hand, architecture and music have attracted them. The rabbit makes burrows for itself and for the 'fox' [a pun on *terrier* meaning burrow] of the same name; the bird makes a nest, a wonder of art, to live in with its family. We could go on quoting examples for ever.

* In 1938 Léautaud heard a lecture on Satie given by Milhaud. "Simple, sober, Satie's life in full," he wrote, "not a word too much, not a single trick of the voice, no mannerism, an artist talking about another artist, friendship and admiration combined. Then a M. Quénot [?Cuénod] sang some little things by Satie to whimsical poems by Fargue, if I'm not mistaken. Wonderfully sung, without taking away any of the fantasy, the near-clowning, of the real charm of these poems, as singers often happen to do." *Journal littéraire*, vol. XII, Mercure de France, 1962, p. 195.

So much for architecture.

Let's pass on to music. No one can doubt that animals love and practise music. This is obvious, but it seems that their musical system differs from ours. It is another school.

You should hear them whinny, cluck, miaow, bray, croak, bleat, low, gobble, coo, yap, howl, roar, purr, chatter, bark, to get an idea of their art in sound.

The repertory and the way to use it are handed down from father to son through simple imitation. The pupil, highly gifted, doesn't delay in equalling the master.

We do not know their textbooks. Perhaps they have none. The physical aspects of certain species indicate a particular aptitude: the beak, in the case of birds, relates them to the clarinet. By contrast, others have a general conformation that forbids them to launch on an artistic career: fish, for example. These poor beasts don't even think about it.

But nothing prevents us from considering most animals as being suited to exercise an art for which nature has prepared them with so much care. That is why musicians of the human kind have the right to interest themselves in the efforts of their dear colleagues among the animal species.

They have, in fact, always done so with enthusiasm.

He blamed man for not having tried to educate animals, those highly intelligent "fellow citizens". Homing pigeons needed lessons in geography for training in their craft. Fish were denied the opportunities of studying oceanography. And then, his irony growing sharper, he pointed out that oxen, sheep and calves were kept in ignorance of the admirable organisation of modern slaughter-houses and of their own nutritive rôle in the society organised by man. Few were the animals that benefited from human education. Dogs, mules, horses, donkeys, parrots, blackbirds and a handful of others were the only ones to receive the simplest of instruction. In the sphere of music, horses had learned to dance and spiders had nestled beneath pianos throughout a whole concert. But apart from that? As for the nightingale, its musical knowledge was pitifully small. It knew nothing of key, tonality, modes or tempo. Perhaps it had talent?

Animals for Satie were an object of amused fascination. They were observed with tenderness and delight. His piano music was to include portraits of a "dreamy fish", an octopus, dogs, crustaceans of weird appearance, and other creatures whose grotesqueness owed as much to his own fantasy as to nature. He enjoyed the antics of children as much as those of animals. Child-like by nature himself, attached forever to the mood of those early years that had vanished so quickly but had conditioned his mind for the rest of life, he could sympathise instantly with boys and girls. He knew what they liked and what they wanted, what pleased them and how to gain their confidence.

He would walk through the streets of Arcueil, a bowler-hatted Pied Piper with clusters of ragged children about him. They laughed and chattered and did hand-springs on the pavement. From his slender purse he would take a few sous he could ill afford and hand them round. It was his idea to found a "Patronage laïque", a club for young people. This enabled him to organise expeditions and pleasure jaunts. He escorted bands of excited youngsters to the fort at Bicêtre and persuaded the gunners there to explain to a fascinated audience just how the cannon worked. There were all sorts of outings and concerts at reduced prices. At each event he circulated among the young people distributing cash and small gifts without the slightest care that tomorrow he would not have enough to buy his own dinner.

His activities were rewarded. On 4 July 1909, at an official ceremony in Arcueil town hall, the Prefect of the Seine decorated him with the Palmes académiques for "civic services". The cabaret pianist, the tippling Bohemian, had joined the ranks of the earnest school teachers and public-minded civil servants for whom the award is usually reserved. Next month, on the 7th, a "Vin d'honneur" was offered to the new officier d'Académie.

A group of friends hired the Restaurant Donau for the occasion. Guests paid a franc for the privilege and children were let in at half-price. About fifty people joined in the proceedings. One of the town councillors made a formal speech congratulating Satie and recalling the services he had rendered to the Patronage laïque. Then stepped forward Monsieur Poensin, vice-chairman of that institution. He appears in the group photograph of committee-members, all bowler-hatted save one, who, with his peaked cap, might have been the postman or some minor official. Beards are much in evidence, and overcoats well buttoned up to the top. Satie stands at the rear, hands in pockets, eyes lively, bowler tipped a little forward.

Monsieur Poensin attached to Satie's lapel the decorative insignia of the Palmes académiques which had been subscribed for by his friends. A concert followed. Two of Satie's music-hall songs, *Je te veux* and *Tendrement*, were sung to great applause. A comedian entertained the gathering with monologues and funny stories. After which everyone danced until three o'clock in the morning.

Not long after this the composer arranged a concert in Arcueil. He persuaded his old friends Vincent Hyspa and Paulette Darty to come out and sing for him. The Honorary President of the Patronage laïque accompanied them at the piano. His fellow citizens enjoyed it all enormously. Their opinion was summed up by an account which noted that Satie's "musical knowledge is equalled only by his devotion to the work of the Patronage".

He was closely involved in local life. Concerts and work for children's clubs were not his only preoccupation. The Arcueil fire brigade appears on the roll of his interests – an effect of heredity perhaps, for had not his grandfather been captain of the Honfleur brigade? – and he attended a meeting at which corporals vied for promotion to sergeant. Then, suddenly, he gave it all up. His paper-thin sensibilities had been offended. On 15 March 1910, he wrote to the Mayor of Arcueil resigning from the Patronage laïque. He referred darkly to some person or other who, "a stranger to the committee of management, has taken the liberty of distorting, through contemptible rumour-mongering, the facts at issue."

It was sad to leave the children and he missed the fun of their outings together. A few months later, on 4 August, he wrote again to the Mayor. This time he had a more cheerful message to deliver. He informed the Mayor that:

The town council is organising – as in previous years – an excursion for schoolchildren during the holidays. The resources at the town hall's disposal make it necessary to limit the number of children able to take part in this pleasant trip.

With the object of avoiding, as far as possible, this regrettable state of affairs, I have been able to collect among my acquaintances a sum of money which would allow me to help a few children – a dozen, six girls and six boys – to join in a pleasure that's rarely offered them.

I am asking you, Your Worship, if you would kindly agree to my bringing with me the dozen children I have chosen.

I enclose herewith the list of these children's names so that the organisers won't include them among the ones they are to nominate themselves. Given the permission of the parents of the children involved, I will take on, as my entire responsibility, the supervision and conduct of those who are kindly entrusted to me.

This was his last expedition with the boys and girls of Arcueil. Although they still ran up to him in the street and joked and chatted with him, he could no longer afford even the tiny sums and little presents he once had given them. For he was harder up than ever. Poverty, he said, had come to him "like a sad little girl with great green eyes".

XV

New Friends

Other reasons than poverty tended to loosen his ties with Arcueil. Slowly but unmistakably musical circles in Paris were beginning to take notice of him. Ravel, of course, for several years had been spreading word of his music. Another keen young admirer was Roland-Manuel.

Named on his birth certificate as Roland Alexis Manuel Lévy, he was the son of a mining engineer who, despite success in his profession, was more interested in the music which he played enthusiastically on the piano and cello as well as composing. The boy inherited this passion. Brought up on the traditional Romantics – Berlioz, Wagner, Schumann – he outraged his father by discovering and enjoying Borodin. "You're a fool!" was the paternal reaction. Borodin, said M. Lévy, wrote appalling harmonies.

In time Roland-Manuel was to become a well-known name in French music. He composed symphonic poems, one of them enticingly called *Le Harem du Vice-roi*, and several comic operas of which *Isabelle et Pantalon*, with a quaint libretto by Max Jacob, was the most successful. Ballets, music for plays and films, a piano concerto, songs and chamber music, all showed a sensitive musical personality. Then he went through a mystical period, sojourned for long spells at the Abbaye de Solesmes, chose to follow his mother's faith, and became a Catholic. His interest in Gregorian music inspired the *Benedictiones*, a setting of seventeenth-century devotional texts.

Besides composing music he wrote well about it. Three of his books are devoted to Ravel. Others have as their subjects Manuel de Falla and Satie. Though he specialised in fifteenth-century music his scholarship was broad. He edited the Pléiade history of music and sponsored many popular broadcasts on French radio. As a teacher at the Conservatoire he influenced the younger generation with his aesthetic ideas. His wife Suzanne, an artist, designed the scenery for Ravel's *L'Heure espagnole* at the Opéra-Comique.

When Satie made his acquaintance Roland-Manuel was about nineteen years old. He lived with his mother, now a widow, and had begun studying at the Schola Cantorum. The great revelation for him had been *Pelléas et Mélisande*. It wrought such an effect upon him that, after hearing it for the first time, he was obliged to go to bed with a high temperature in a state of shock.

He found by chance that Debussy had orchestrated one of Satie's *Gymnopédies*. If his idol Debussy was interested enough to do this, thought he, then Satie must be a considerable musician. One evening at the Chat Noir he approached Paulette Darty who was singing *Je te veux* there. She invited him to lunch with Satie. Roland-Manuel was astonished: how could this prim, old-maidish creature be an artist?

"Do you know Debussy?" ventured the young man.

"There are only two musicians who count," replied Satie with amused malice: "Ravel and Roussel."

Once Satie had had his little joke he proved to be helpful. "You ought to study composition with Ravel and counterpoint with Roussel," he told him. A little intimidated by Ravel's cold elegance, Roland-Manuel suggested himself as a pupil. He was accepted on condition that no fee be paid.

"You know nothing," Ravel observed, "and you must learn your craft. Though it's not your own craft you learn, but others'! Copy, imitate, write pastiche, and if you've nothing to say it doesn't matter; if you have, then however much you copy, your personality will come through." With deliberate cunning Ravel held up for praise technical examples from music which his pupil disliked. He pointed to Massenet's *Manon*, for instance, and singled out some admirable modulations. "Take these as your starting-point," he advised mischievously.

The method worked. "Ravel did me an enormous favour by killing off my deplorable facility. But," sighed Roland-Manuel, "his teaching of composition was negative on the whole."

At his mother's flat in the rue de Chazelles he had a room which he decorated with sombre materials. The oriental atmosphere was enhanced by the exotic robe he liked to wear and the candle that burned while, curtains drawn, he read with a slight lisp poems by the Sâr Péladan and by Mallarmé. His mother encouraged him to bring home his friends, poets, musicians, writers, and greeted them with benevolent delight when they emerged from her son's mysterious lair to gather in the drawing-room. Once they all joined in a mock ballet, irreverently adapted from Diaghilev's production of *Schéhérazade*, which then was much in the mode, to the accompaniment of the *Trois Morceaux en forme de poire*.

Tall, bearded, clad when out of doors in the broad-brimmed hat affected by artists of Montmartre, the intense young aesthete was at first highly disconcerted by Satie. The contrast between his formal bourgeois presence and his music – cake-walks, cabaret songs, Rosicrucian preludes – bemused him. Just as baffling were Satie's opinions. Debussy? A musician of the past. Ravel was the musician of the present and Roussel of the future.

Only gradually did Roland-Manuel come to appreciate Satie's irony and how it worked. It was cloaked, he realised, in what at first appeared to be conformism. The method was initially to flatter the inaccurate and the ridiculous. It encouraged the commonplace, the hackneyed and the foolish. Then, once confidence was established, Satie unleashed his sarcasm to its deadliest effect. Roland-Manuel remembered him discussing Schumann with an ex-fellow pupil at the Schola Cantorum, now a retired bandmaster. The debate continued gravely and reasonably. "Poor Schumann," concluded Satie, "he just didn't know how to develop. But you, Commander, you do, don't you?"

It became a custom for Satie to meet Roland-Manuel at the Chope latine, a tavern near the Schola Cantorum and the railway station for the Sceaux line to Arcueil. They would drink there, and, over a glass of beer and a salad, the older man held forth to his listener. Roland-Manuel was struck by the subtlety and wisdom that lurked behind the mockery. Then Satie would go to catch his train, vanishing to the suburban home where no one ever accompanied him.

Among the young people who came to Roland-Manuel's home was the actor Pierre Bertin. He was then in his mid-twenties. Since that time he has appeared in many plays and films and made his reputation with a musical speaking voice (he is also a singer) and a typically mobile actor's face. At first he divided his time between medical studies and acting. On matinée days he sped from dissecting-room to stage and back again. Then acting claimed him entirely. His early training as a doctor, he says, gave him valuable insights into psychology. It also had practical uses. Once, while he was playing in Molière's *Le Médecin volant*, a lady in the audience sprained her ankle. He leaped into the auditorium and, wearing the bizarre robes of a seventeenth-century quack, administered treatment on the spot.

Bertin took part in the joke ballet, already mentioned, which Roland-Manuel arranged to Satie's *Trois Morceaux en forme de poire*. This was his first meeting with the composer. Roland-Manuel introduced him to a man he thought looked like an elderly piano teacher who beamed through a beard that quivered to the rhythm of his speech. Intelligent eyes glittered out of the pince-nez clamped on his nose. That day Satie was a little on edge since an extra pianist could not be found. Bertin, after a little prompting, offered himself. He played courageously, blushing at the wrong notes he scattered. Satie remained in good humour. "Well, there were one or two little things . . ." he murmured. The music alone interested him and he did not pay the slightest attention to the action of the ballet. This, Bertin recalls, was characteristic. Once his music had been settled he had no concern for anything else. If, at a concert, some of his own pieces happened to be on the programme, he would loiter outside in the corridor until their turn came. Having heard them he would leave immediately. Perhaps the only exception he made was for anything by Chabrier.

Satie, when Bertin first knew him, was still the simple musician whom Debussy befriended, the humble graduate of the Schola Cantorum. How, wondered Bertin, did he manage to live, and on what? No one knew. Despite the difference in age they became friends. Satie was fond of youth. The gulf created by the years did not trouble him. When Bertin a few years later married the pianist Marcelle Meyer, Satie was a frequent visitor to the house. They lived in the boulevard Montparnasse, a convenient staging point for him whenever he missed his train. Very often he lunched or dined with them. Surprisingly, he showed himself to be something of a gourmet. He would bring delicacies to the feast and give precise instructions on how they were to be prepared. One of his recipes involved the cooking of a cutlet. It ensured that a crust formed to protect the blood inside the meat and bestowed an extra succulence.

Another attraction of the household in the boulevard Montparnasse was Marcelle Meyer herself, a very fine pianist who played Satie's music exactly as he wished to hear it. He, an indifferent pianist, appreciated her complete sympathy with his thought and style. She played everything he wrote. For her he reserved the title of honour, the salutation which he gave only to those women of whom he thoroughly approved: "Dadame."

The third friend Satie made at Roland-Manuel's house was the beautiful Valentine Gross, artist, illustrator, and eventually the wife of Jean Hugo, the poet's great-grandson and a distinguished artist. Her ballet drawings had gained attention for their brilliance. She was young and full of talent. Soon she was a notable figure in Parisian artistic and social life. At one point it was thought that she might marry Jean Cocteau. Or so Madame Cocteau urged, impressed by her looks and her intelligence. But even in Cocteau's world of gilded paradox, such an event was, and turned out to be, wholly improbable.

She was amused by Satie's drollery and, at the same time, by his more serious aspect which he camouflaged with jokes. From the start they felt drawn to each other. Their affection survived all his tantrums and all the queer outbursts of temper to which he became increasingly subject as he grew older. It lasted until his death. As soon as he had an idea for a new piece of music he would make an appointment with her so as to be sure that his "chère grande fille" would be at home when he called, ready to hear him play and sing his initial ideas:

And in that way [she wrote] I gradually became his child, his friend, his sister.

He put his trust in me very simply, as much by letter as by conversation. He told me about his joys, which were, alas, very rare, and about the cruel disappointments and worries that were far too numerous. Poor dear Satie! As best I could I soothed the anger and the resentments which were, most of the time, quite justified. Sometimes I had to resort to the most fantastic guile to rescue what he'd destroyed, and then I'd receive a little letter from him, in the usual fine calligraphy, like this one, for example, written on music paper: "It's not nice when you gently say to me: Satie, you mustn't get angry with them."

Long before he discovered Plato's *Socrates* I'd been very moved by our dialogues together. I couldn't help but find them "Socratic". I played a very modest part in them, but I could listen. I'd just finished a big book, since lost, on Greek dance, intended as a successor to the one I'd published on Egyptian dance, and I was well acquainted with the rhythm and substance of the classic conversations. Often there came into my mind then those words of Socrates which were, for me, a difficult line of conduct to follow: *When people make long speeches to me, I lose sight of the subject under discussion . . . Cut down your answers and make them shorter if you want me to follow you.*

From Roland-Manuel's home, as from the centre of a spider's web, the filaments radiated to shape a network of acquaintance. Satie moved inevitably along them. He met new faces and new groupings. He enjoyed a reputation in a world that was small but not without influence. Almost apologetically he would sidle into a room, his hand held in front of his mouth. At first his speech was hesitant. Suddenly it would become hurried. Always it would be masked by the hand spread out like a fan. Those to whom he spoke were addressed with polite ceremony as "Monsieur" and "Madame". He spoke confidentially, as if passing on a secret. And when contact had been established, when it was clear that the atmosphere was sympathetic, he would burble softly: "Bonjou, Bonjou, ma bonne dame, alors . . . alors . . . ma bonne dadame."

XVI

"An Inspired Forerunner"

The occasion that brought Satie into prominence was a concert organised by the Société Indépendante de Musique. This body competed to some extent with the much older Société Nationale de Musique which had been founded in 1871 after the Franco-Prussian War. The Société Nationale aimed at helping French composers to find an audience for their work. Up to that time concert programmes were dominated by the classic names of Beethoven, Mozart, Haydn and Mendelssohn. Conductors were reluctant to play modern music which might frighten off their staid subscribers. Under the proud device *Ars Gallica*, the Société Nationale launched its own concerts and, over a long period, eventually succeeded in persuading French audiences to listen to music written by their compatriots. New works by Franck, Lalo, Chabrier, Fauré, Debussy, Ravel and Dukas were heard for the first time and given an opportunity to make their mark.

One of the most active founders of the Société Nationale had been Saint-Saëns, in his time an innovator and the sponsor of much new music both French and foreign. By the early nine-teen-hundreds the Société had begun to lose some of its impetus. Saint-Saëns was displaced by Vincent d'Indy, who in turn found that his other heavy commitments, notably the Schola Cantorum, were taking up his energies. In 1910 history repeated itself. A group of young musicians established the Société Indépendante de Musique.

The president of the new organisation was Gabriel Fauré. He had been Saint-Saëns' favourite pupil and was treated by the older man as a son. Saint-Saëns' reaction to his protégé's venture was typical of the older generation. "I very much hope," he snapped, "that you'll give up that gang of hooligans!" The difference of opinion did not last long and their affectionate relationship was soon restored.

The rival societies went their own ways and continued to do valuable work. The SIM, while presenting new French music as the Société Nationale had done, broke with tradition by introducing a greater number of foreign compositions. The "hooligans", in Saint-Saëns' phrase, who made up its committee included Ravel, Florent Schmitt and André Caplet.

It was Ravel who, in the second year of the SIM's existence, gave Satie his first chance of an important hearing. On 16 January 1911, he himself played at an SIM concert the second of the *Sarabandes*, the prelude to *Le Fils des Etoiles* and the third *Gymnopédie*.

What must have been Satie's feelings, after years of obscurity and indifference to his music, when he read the following in the programme note?

Erik Satie occupies a very remarkable place in the history of contemporary art. Although isolated from the mainstream of the age, he has already written several short pieces which show him to be an inspired forerunner. These works, unfortunately few in number, are surprising in the way they anticipate the modern idiom and for the almost prophetic character of certain harmonic discoveries ... M. Claude Debussy paid a striking tribute to this subtle explorer by orchestrating two of the *Gymnopédies* which were given at a Société Nationale concert. By playing today the second *Sarabande*, which carries the astonishing date of 1887, M. Maurice Ravel shows the respect which is felt by the most "advanced" composers for a creator who, a quarter of a century ago, was already speaking the musical "jargon" of tomorrow.

The concert was successful. Influential critics spoke well of Satie's music and general comment was favourable. A little triumph, his first, had come the way of the middle-aged composer. But, as always in life, there were flaws. Among them was Debussy's attitude towards his old friend's modest success. He was not on good terms with Ravel at the moment, and it vexed him perhaps that Satie should have emerged into the limelight under different auspices. "Somebody who's not satisfied," remarked Satie, "is the worthy Claude. It's all his own fault. If he'd done earlier what Ravel has, his position wouldn't be the same." A few months later Debussy conducted the two *Gymnopédies* he had orchestrated and confessed himself surprised at the favour they won. "Why won't he leave me just a tiny little place in his shadow," complained Satie. "I don't want to hog the sun." From now on their relationship began to deteriorate.

After the first excitement, too, Satie began to wonder if the motives of the SIM faction were not unmixed. He expressed his doubt in a letter to Conrad:

> In 1905 I set to work with d'Indy. I was tired of seeing myself reproached for an ignorance of which I was only too well aware, because competent judges had pointed it out in my work.
>
> After three years of solid hard work I obtained at the Schola Cantorum my diploma in counterpoint signed by the hand of my excellent master, who is certainly the best and most learned man in the world. So there I was, in 1908, holding a degree conferring on me the title of contrapuntalist. Proud of my knowledge, I started to compose. My first work of this kind was a four-handed choral and fugue [*Aperçus désagréables*]. I've been slanged often enough during my wretched existence, but never had I been treated with such contempt. What had I been up to with d'Indy? I'd written so much before that was full of charm. But now? How pompous! How boring!
>
> Whereupon the "angry young men" started a campaign against d'Indy and began playing the *Sarabandes*, *Le Fils des Etoiles*, etc., music that once was considered the result of my vast ignorance – quite wrongly, though, according to the youngsters.

That's life, old chap.
It's beyond all understanding.

Another concert was given in June 1912. Roland-Manuel, following in Debussy's footsteps, had orchestrated one of Satie's works. This was the *Prélude de la Porte héroïque du ciel* which the orchestrator conducted himself. The Rosicrucian music seemed to fascinate the young "hooligans" of the SIM. A year later Ravel was to orchestrate the prelude to Act I of *Le Fils des Etoiles,* and Roland-Manuel other portions of the suite.

The concert sustained and encouraged the interest in Satie which had been stimulated by Ravel's initiative the previous year. Satie did not attend. He was so poor, he explained, that he had no decent clothes to wear. Reports of the event delighted him. The enthusiasm of his supporters won for them the name of "Satistes", much as an earlier generation had become known as "Wagnerians".

Just about that time Paul Fort had been elected "Prince of Poets" in succession to the now forgotten Léon Dierx. This was a title conferred in Bohemian circles as a reaction against the official honours awarded by academies and such. Paul Fort, who died at the age of eighty-eight in 1960, was a traditionally Romantic figure. He wore a large Rembrandtesque hat and long black hair. His work took its inspiration from folk-lore and opposed a lyrical simplicity to the subtle obscurities of Symbolism. As the magazine to which he contributed paid only for prose and not for poetry, he ran the lines of his verse together so that it looked like the former. In this way he both received a fee and established a famous mannerism.

Satie probably knew Fort and his admirers. He certainly was aware of Fort's election. The young men of the SIM now put Satie forward as "Prince of Musicians". The composer took the idea seriously. On 3 July, a month after the concert, he wrote to Roland-Manuel complaining about various music critics who had not responded. "Music has need of a Prince," he declared. "She shall have one . . ."

However great the need it failed to be met and the project aborted. If, though, he was not to be Prince of Musicians, another opportunity for him to catch the public eye offered itself through the medium of the review published by the SIM. On 15 April 1912, his first contribution appeared under the humorous title of "Mémoires d'un amnésique". The sufferer from amnesia begins his memories with the statement: "Everyone will tell you that I am not a musician." He then goes on to state, in a vein of the purest Alphonse Allais, that he is instead a "phonometrogapher", one who examines, classifies, weighs, cleans and indexes musical sounds. The fantasy concealed his feelings of hurt – "Everyone will tell you that I am not a musician" – and he met his detractors with a jest.

Another instalment of his "mémoires" appeared in the issue dated 15 February 1913. Under the title of "A Musician's Day", he wrote:

The artist should regulate his life.

Here is the precise timetable of my daily acts:

My awakening: at 7.18; inspiration from 10.23 to 11.47. I dine at 12.11 and leave the table at 12.14.

A wholesome ride on my horse around my estate: from 13.19 to 14.53. More inspiration from 15.12 to 16.07.

Various activities (fencing, reflection, immobility, visits, contemplation, dexterity, swimming, etc. . . .) from 16.21 to 18.47.

Dinner is served at 19.16 and ends at 19.20. Then come symphonic readings aloud from 20.09 to 21.59.

I go to bed regularly at 22.37. Once a week I awake with a start at 3.19 (on Tuesdays).

I only eat white food: eggs, sugar, grated bones; the fat of dead animals; veal, salt, coconuts, chicken cooked in water; fruit mould, rice, turnips; camphorated black pudding, paste, cheese (white), cotton salad and certain kinds of fish (without skins).

I have my wine boiled and drink it cold with fuchsia juice. I've a good appetite; but I never speak while eating for fear of strangling.

I breathe carefully (not much at a time). I very rarely dance. When walking I hold my sides and stare behind me.

My appearance is very serious, and if I laugh I do so without deliberate intent. I always apologise graciously for this.

I only sleep with one eye shut; my night's rest is very hard. My bed is round and pierced with a hole to let the head through.

Every hour a servant takes my temperature and gives me another one.

For a long time I have subscribed to a fashion magazine. I wear a white bonnet, white stockings and white waistcoat.

My doctor has always told me to smoke. He adds to his advice: "Smoke, my friend: but for that, somebody else would smoke in your place."

Again, the humour cloaks resentment. While the jokes about his temperature and his smoking are worthy of Allais himself, the amusing timetable of his activities can be seen as a gibe at the conventional wisdom of his schoolmasters and the teachers he studied under at the Conservatoire. Had they not continually impressed upon their idle and rebellious pupil the virtues of working systematically, of following a logical method, of dividing up the time so that every minute was profitably employed in useful tasks? At last he was able to answer them back

PART FIVE

Preludes and Descriptions

XVII

Words and Music

The discovery of a public, however small, and the support of his young friends at the SIM seem to have reawakened Satie's urge to compose. From 1913 onwards he turned out a stream of piano pieces, many of them written, it appears, at speed.

Up to then he had composed little of account since entering the Schola Cantorum. In the September of 1908, a few months after graduating with his diploma, he started work on the *Aperçus désagréables* for piano duet. He tinkered with them, on and off, until October 1912. They comprise a pastorale, choral and fugue. That they gave him much trouble is shown by the amount of time he spent on them over the years. They may also have inspired Roussel's fear that his submission to academic disciplines might harm his originality – an attitude less kindly expressed by those against whom Satie protested in his letter to Conrad. In any case, it is difficult to avoid the general opinion, both then and now, that the *Aperçus désagréables* are a laboured exercise.

By 1911, still under the spell of his academic training, he had written *En habit de cheval*, again for piano duet. This, consisting of two chorals and two fugues, is more successful. When Satie played some of it over to Roussel the latter was amused and even approved of the novel ideas in what the composer called the "Paper Fugue" to distinguish it from its mate the "Fugue litanique". There is a hint that the title, far from picturing Satie in riding habit, implies a situation where he is harnessed unwillingly to the rules and kicking against them, as against the shafts. He later orchestrated the suite for chamber ensemble, limiting himself to a pair of trumpets in the brass. Three trumpets, he quoted d'Indy as saying, meant the end of the world.

In August 1912 the *Véritables préludes flasques* (*pour un chien*) proved that he had now been able to evolve his own distinctive form of expression. These doggy preludes, whimsically misnamed "flabby", are in fact clean-lined and wiry. The contrapuntal manner is rigorous and the texture lucid. Only in the third of these piano pieces, "On joue", with its fleeting reference to the tempo of the cake-walk, is there any suggestion of skittish dogs at play. The sole concession to verbal humour is found in the "Latin" words added at various points: Nocturnus, Caeremoniosus, Paedagogus, Illusorius, and so on.

Throughout the summer of 1913 he was busy with many more piano pieces. It seems from internal evidence that he wrote each item separately, none much longer than a minute or so, before deciding how to group them according to his favourite number of three. The *Descriptions automatiques*, composed towards the end of April, open with "Sur un vaisseau" which, in its stylised representation of a ship pitching and tossing, adopts an "automatic" rhythm. But we know that the ship is a toy one, that the waves it crosses are made of painted paper, and that the jerky tempo is created by the turning of a handle. Against this rocking of the boat a popular refrain cuts in, "Maman les p'tits bateaux . . . ont-ils des jambes?" which he would have remembered from his seaside childhood in Honfleur. "Sur une lanterne", dedicated to Ravel's mother, could well picture a ship's lantern swaying to the rhythm of the sea. It incorporates in the left hand a melody that echoes the Gregorian mode. The third item, "Sur un casque", offers a military parade. Drums roll, trumpets bray, the *Carmagnole* flitters in the background, helmets flash, troops march past, and the Colonel, "ce bel homme", leads them bravely. It would be interesting to know the reaction of Paulette Darty, the music-hall queen to whom this item is inscribed.

With the *Embryons desséchés*, which he wrote in a few days at the end of June and the beginning of July, Satie indulged to the full his taste for pairing elaborate commentaries with the music. The "dried embryos" are those of crustaceans whose acquaintance he made in the pages of textbooks on sea life. What he found there stimulated his surrealistic imagination. The "Holothurie", he explains correctly, is popularly known as the "sea cucumber". It climbs, he says, on stones and rocks, purrs like a cat, spins a sort of damp silk, and avoids the light. (What he does not add, except in the reference to damp silk, and what, one imagines, would have greatly appealed to him, is that the holothuria expels clumps of thread when attacked. These threads entangle and confuse its enemies. In times of grave crisis it goes even further and throws out its innards completely, which it then replaces by growing a new set afterwards.) However, Satie tells us enough about the holothuria to establish its claim to uniqueness. Having observed it in the bay of Saint-Malo, he has an excuse for weaving the tune of "Mon rocher de Saint Malo" into his music. The holothuria purrs as expected. At one point the executant is instructed to play "Like a nightingale with toothache". The crustacean goes out in a blaze of glory amid a climax that parodies those rhetorical but protracted endings favoured by Romantic composers: chords repeated aloft and below which continue for so long that the uninitiated are often tricked into applause before the fun is over.

Next comes the "Edriophthalma". Satie describes it as being prone to melancholy, for it rejects the world and chooses to inhabit holes pierced in cliffs. The music is frankly parodistic. The crustacean's sadness is conveyed by a handful of bars from Chopin's Funeral March which are labelled in the score: "Quotation from Schubert's famous Mazurka." ("The father of a family speaks up . . .") The third item hymns the "Podophthalma". From Satie's description this is a crustacean familiar to marine biologists, however fanciful the name he gives it. There are indeed creatures living in the darkest fathoms of the water which have developed eyes at the top of long stalks that move ceaselessly around in quest of the slightest phosphorescent gleam. Satie is right, too, in giving his podophthalma carnivorous habits. It sets off for the hunt to a scurrying figure which incorporates a horn call and a tune from the operetta, *La Mascotte*, which cautions:

"Ah! n'courez pas comme ça." As with the holothuria, there is a grandiose climax which offers, by way of bonus, an "obligatory" cadenza. ("By the composer", adds a note, making a sly tilt at those in the habit of remedying, for example, Mozart's deficiencies by supplying his piano concertos with cadenzas both out of character and out of style.)

At various times in June, July and August he wrote the *Croquis et agaceries d'un gros bonhomme en bois*. They are straightforward parodies. The "Tyrolienne turque", mincing and precise, takes off Mozart's Turkish March. The "Danse maigre" is something of an intruder, having been written out of chronological sequence and added, presumably, to make up the number of pieces to three. Finally, "Españaña" mocks French composers' liking for exoticism, particularly in the example of Chabrier's *España* from which direct quotations are given. The labels tell the story: Puerta Maillot, Plaza Clichy, Rue de Madrid.

Soon after these, between late August and early September, Satie wrote the *Chapitres tournés en tous sens*. The group opens with "Celle qui parle trop", a brilliant and amusing portrayal of a loquacious wife who talks her husband to death. She wants a hat in solid mahogany, she envies Madame So-and-so her bone umbrella, she reports that Madame Such-and-such has married a man who's dry as a cuckoo ... The music patters on remorselessly with the aid of "Ne parle pas, Rose, je t'en supplie", a favourite opera tune of many years ago, until the husband gives up and dies of exhaustion.

"Le porteur de grosse pierres" relies for its humorous effect on the title and on the commentary. The musical quotation this time is from an operetta by Rip, "C'est un rien, un souffle, un rien" ("It's a trifle, light as air, the merest trifle"). The point would be missed if the "programme" were not known. The carrier sweats and strains, reeling beneath the enormous weight of stone a hundred times larger than himself. Children marvel at his strength. Pauses on notes at unexpected places illustrate his unequal grapplings. The stone, at last, falls to the ground. But it was pumice stone! The "Regrets des enfermés (Jonas et Latude)" is little more than an excuse for Satie to tantalise his audience with obscure erudition. The sixteenth-century German Protestant Jonas and the eighteenth-century Frenchman Latude were both imprisoned in their day for offences against authority. "Several centuries separate them," says a note, "all they can think of is getting out." The musical interest is slight and depends on a treatment of the folk song "Nous n'irons plus au bois", which, under the circumstances, adds a dash of irony.

A few days later Satie was busy with *Vieux séquins et vieilles cuirasses*. "Chez le marchand d'or" depicts a thirteenth-century miser fondling his coins, kissing them, talking lovingly to them, and then jumping into the coffer and rolling in them. A faint suggestion of Mephistopheles' aria about the golden calf (Gounod's version) is heard here. The "Danse cuirassée (Période grecque)" is less complicated, being an unpretentious little measure. The "nightmare" of the "Défaite des cimbres" makes extended use of "Malbrouck s'en va-t-en guerre".

In October he wrote the three sets of pieces for children which he called *Menus propos enfantins, Enfantillages pittoresques* and *Peccadilles importunes*. The lover of Hans Andersen, the Pied Piper of Arcueil, was a natural composer for the young. These five finger exercises include a war song for the King of the Haricot Beans, a lullaby for the Princess of the Tulips, and a Chocolate and Almonds Waltz. "Maman, there's a bone in my chocolate." "No, mon petit, it's an almond." In the "Marche du grand escalier" the composer seems to be remembering his Uncle Adrien, the "Sea Bird" who used his yacht but rarely, his handsome carriage never, for fear of damage. "The stairway is big, very big. It has more than a thousand steps, all in ivory. It is very beautiful. No one dare use it so as not to spoil it. The King himself has never set foot on it. To get out of this room he jumps through the window. He often says :'I love these stairs so much I'm going to have them stuffed.' Isn't the King right?" The "Peccadilles" warn little people to avoid such undesirable emotions as envy. They must get used to seeing bread and butter without feeling the need to steal it. Taking a friend's bread and butter could make your head swell up. Why, says the composer, I had a dog once that smoked my cigars in secret. His punishment was a stomach illness. Though of no great value musically, these pieces for small fingers demonstrate Satie's bond with children and his ability to see things from their point of view without self-consciousness. While Schumann re-creates childhood by looking back through the eyes of a nostalgic adult, Satie starts in the opposite direction from the original source.

Next month came *Les Pantins dansent*, an agreeable little number which he wrote for a "poème dansé". After this he seems to have composed no more for the piano until the spring of 1914, when he produced the *Sports et divertissements* and the several groups that conclude the series which began with the *Véritables préludes flasques (pour un chien)*.

His passion for dressing up the music with words attains a riotous flowering with these last piano pieces. Yet a footnote to the *Heures séculaires et instantanées*, which date from June and July, reads like an echo of the Rosicrucian declarations: "To whom it may concern. I forbid the text to be read aloud while the music is being played. Any failure to observe this will incur my just indignation with the presumptuous sinner." The scenario of the "Obstacles venimeux" presents a Negro alone in a vast landscape. The shadow of age-old trees shows that it is seventeen minutes past nine in the morning. The toads call to each other by their surnames. The Negro holds his cerebellum in his hand the better to think. From afar he looks like a distinguished physiologist. Of the "venomous obstacles" which give the piece its title there is no sign – unless they are the snakes and the old mango tree later brought into the picture. The music, on its own, is a perfectly acceptable exercise based on a typical nonchalant theme, plain and angular.

Satie's dislike of the sun, to which he preferred rain and stormy weather, was notorious. "What a bore the sun is," he would say, "what a twerp! It looks like a clumsy great lout with its head as red as a cockerel. It's a disgrace!" In the second of the *Heures* he presents "Crépuscule matinal (de midi)", thus putting the sun in its place with morning twilight at midday. "The sun arose early and in a good temper," he writes. "The heat will be above average because the weather is prehistoric and likely to be stormy. The sun is high up in the heavens; he looks a good sort. But let's not trust him. He may be going to burn the harvest or loose off a heavy stroke – sunstroke. Behind the shed an ox is eating itself sick." This time the music vaguely follows the programme: a fanfare as the sun wakes up, chromatic shimmerings for the heat, abrupt little snatches to figure sunstroke.

In the final piece, "Affolements granitiques", a clock in a deserted village strikes thirteen (you hear it thudding in the bass), a rainstorm surges from clouds of dust, the trees tug at each other's branches, and great chunks of granite jostle among themselves in a panic.

Even more baroque was the verbal scaffolding erected round the *Trois Valses distinguées du précieux dégoûté* which were written in the same month of July. Each waltz presents an aspect of the world-weary and precious dandy: his waist, his spectacles and his legs. "Sa taille" is prefaced with a quotation from La Bruyère reproving those who sacrifice truth for the sake of a witticism. The commentary shows the *précieux* looking at himself, humming a fifteenth-century tune, and paying his person a discreet compliment. Isn't he the most handsome of all, has he not a tender heart? He takes himself by the waist. It's a delight for him. "What will the pretty marquise have to say? She will fight but will be defeated."

The second waltz, "Son binocle", is headed with a remark from Cicero which points out that the ban on young men appearing naked at public baths was an incentive to modesty. The narrative above the music this time speaks of our hero cleaning daily his silver spectacles and their lenses of smoked gold. A beautiful lady gave them to him. But, alas, the *précieux* is overwhelmed with a great sadness; he has lost his spectacle case.

Finally "Ses jambes", introduced by lines from Cato on the first duties of a landowner when arriving at his estate, imagine the *précieux* admiring his legs. "He is very proud of them," runs the slapstick note. "They only dance the best dances. They are fine slim legs. At night they are dressed in black. He wants to carry them under his arm. They slip about in melancholy fashion. Now they're indignant and very angry. (Don't cough.) Often he embraces them and puts them round his neck. How good he is to them! He refuses most emphatically to buy gaiters. 'A prison!' he calls them." "Ses jambes" is dedicated to the poet and critic René Chalupt. He believed that the reference to dancing may have been a humorous side-glance at his liking for the tango and the "hesitation waltz" that were fashionable then.

Like all the piano music Satie wrote at this period, the *Trois Valses distinguées du précieux dégoûté* are innocent of bar-lines. Yet the rhythm falls into place so naturally that their absence goes unnoticed. Text and music are entirely independent. The waltzes can be enjoyed for themselves alone. The second, "Son binocle", is in effect another "gymnopédie", calm, lucid and poised.

Perhaps the regular waltz tempo imposed a discipline that concentrated Satie's thought. In any case, the *Trois Valses* contain examples of his most elegant writing for the piano.

The ultimate in his series of trinitarian piano groups was the *Avant-dernières pensées* of August and October 1915. These "last-but-one thoughts" follow the usual pattern of incongruous text plus music. The stream is soaked to the skin, the trees look like badly made combs. The "Idylle" is a contemplative nocturne with a dedication to Debussy which shows that their friendship still existed, in however fragile a condition, at this date. The "Aubade" returns to the idiom of the *Descriptions automatiques*. The busy nature of the concluding number, humorously mis-called "Méditation", carries a reminder of Chabrier, though the dedicatee is Satie's old teacher Roussel.

The essence of his writing for piano, however, is to be found in the *Sports et divertissements*. The story of how they originated is both odd and typical. There is a parallel with Dickens, who was commissioned to write the accompanying text for a series of sporting illustrations, and who went on to produce, almost by accident, *The Pickwick Papers*, having soon outpaced the original modest conception of the work. Likewise, the music publishers Lucien Vogel sought a composer to illustrate with music an album picturing various sports and entertainments. They put the idea to Stravinsky. The fee he asked was too large. Then Roland-Manuel intervened and suggested his friend Satie for the commission. A different problem now arose. Although the fee offered was lower than Stravinsky's, the unpredictable Satie thought it too high. Indeed, he felt he had been insulted. The notion of earning big money from his art quite shocked him, and Roland-Manuel, who had thought to do him a good turn, was assailed with angry reproaches. In the end Satie was pacified and a suitably low fee calmed his outraged conscience.

As in the case of *The Pickwick Papers*, the *Sports et divertissements* outlived the drawings which they had been intended to complement. Charles Martin's pictures survive, with their curiously dated air, as a pendant to the music. Satie's manuscript, beautifully drawn and lettered in his exquisite hand, was reproduced as it stood. Ironically enough, the fact that Lucien Vogel published it in a *de luxe* edition, highly priced and limited to a small number of subscribers, meant that Satie's most considerable achievement for the piano reached for the time being an audience even more restricted than the one he usually enjoyed. The first of the twenty pieces that make up *Sports et divertissements*, "La Pêche", was written on 14 March 1914. The others followed at various intervals throughout the rest of March, April and May. None of them last more than a minute or so. The thought is concentrated and precise. As in the piano pieces which lead up to these compositions there are no bar-lines. Verbal embroidery is present, of course, but it is not so obtrusive as in earlier writing, and the humour is more controlled. Parodistic references are few and include a brief snatch of "Frère Jacques, frère Jacques, dormez-vous". An unintentional one emerges, nonetheless, in "Le Golf", where a strange prophecy of "Tea for two" strikes the surprised ear.

In his preface the composer writes: "I advise the reader to leaf through this book with a friendly and benevolent hand, for it is a work of fantasy. No more should be read into it. For the Stunted and the Stupid I have written a serious and respectable Choral. It is a sort of bitter preamble, a kind of austere and unfrivolous introduction. I have put into it all I know about Boredom. I dedicate this choral to those who do not like me. I withdraw."

The "unappetising" Choral, as he baptised it, "surly and peevish", is a taut piece of musical argument such as he had learned to write at the Schola Cantorum. It is followed by "La Balançoire", in which the gentle motion of the swing is represented by the simplest of means in the left hand while the right spells out a succession of single notes which, perhaps because of its very bareness, holds the attention completely.

"La Chasse", inevitably, utilises a hunting call in the manner of the "Podophthalma" from the *Embryons desséchés*. It is embellished with a nonsense text: "Can you hear the rabbit singing? What a voice! The nightingale's in its burrow. The owl suckles its young. The wild boar's about to get married. And I? I'm shooting down nuts with my gun." In "La Comédie italienne" Scaramouche vaunts the beauties of the soldier's estate with a particularly elaborate flourish which somehow captures to the life the gestures of this flamboyant character.

"Le Réveil de la Mariée" is more surrealistic: guitars are made of old hats and a dog dances with its betrothed. A military reveille is heard and the piece ends with an echo from *Jack in the Box*. "Colin-Maillard" presents, in a game of blind man's buff, a complete little love story. "La Pêche", on the other hand, is a quick impression of a river scene. The water murmurs gently, a fish swims into view, another follows, two more arrive, they chance to spot the angler, they go away . . . and so does he.

In "Le Yachting" the sea has wound down. "I only hope it won't break on a rock. Nobody can wind it up again. 'I don't want to stay here,' says the pretty passenger. 'It's not an amusing sort of place. I'd prefer something else. Go and get me a car.'" The theme is continued in "Le Bain de mer", with its superb picture of giant waves boiling up. "The sea is wide, Madam. In any case, it's very deep. Don't sit on the bottom. It's very damp. Here are some good old waves. They're full of water. You're quite wet! 'Yes, Sir.'"

Confetti drifts slowly down in "Le Carnaval", and in "Le Golf" a surprised colonel and his caddy see a club shatter into pieces. The reference to "astonished" clouds and "trembling" holes suggests the style of a Bateman cartoon. A latter-day member of the *Embryons desséchés*, "La Pieuvre", an octopus which swallows a crab the wrong way, is followed by a vivid miniature of the races, "Les Courses", ending with a distorted quotation from *La Marseillaise*. Another example, like "La Balançoire", of Satie's genius for using the most economical of methods to achieve a striking effect, is "Les Quatre Coins". The wary manoeuvring of cat and mouse is hinted at with a tangible feeling of suspense and bated breath – yet the technique is the essence of simplicity.

"Le Pique-Nique" sketches in polka rhythm a suburban day trip complete with the sort of banal and inconsequent remarks that James Joyce liked to record in his notebooks for later use. Two more dances, a valse-musette ("Le Water-Chute") and a "Tango perpétuel" carry on the tale. The latter, with its self-plagiarism of "Sur un vaisseau" in *Descriptions automatiques*, was probably known to Lord Berners, whose "Strauss, Strauss et Strauss" embodies a like satirical idea. The "Tango perpétuel", incidentally, emphasises its point by being the only one of the *Sports et divertissements* to have a repeat. "Modéré et très ennuyé" reads the direction, with an obvious reference to the blasé expression and languid movements it was fashionable to adopt when treading this measure which had just become a craze in tea-

1 Satie's Norman father, Alfred

2 Satie's Scottish mother, *née* Miss Jane Leslie Anton

3   Satie as a child

4   The composer as a young man of twenty

5   Portrait of Satie in his mid-twenties by his mistress Suzanne Valadon

6   "The Velvet Gentleman" of Arcueil in his mid-thirties

7   Satie in 1910 at the age of   8   Satie in 1918
        forty-four

9   Posing with Debussy

10 An example of Satie's calligraphy: "The Community of Poor Knights of the Holy City . . ."

11 A letter from Satie to Valentine Hugo

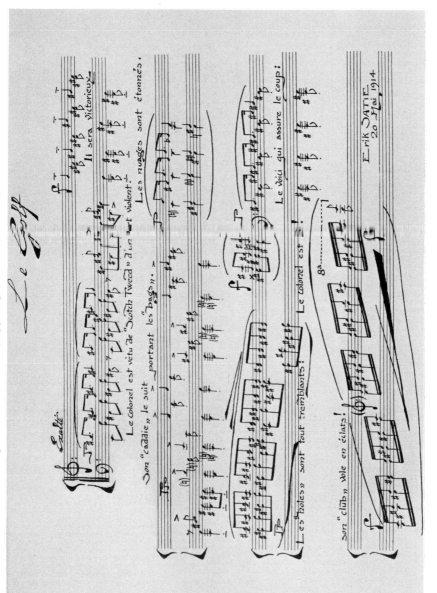

12 Manuscript of "Le Golf" from *Sports et divertissements* (1914)

13 Léon-Paul Fargue, poet and friend

14 22 rue Cauchy, Arcueil – Satie's room was on the second floor

15   Satie pen and ink sketch

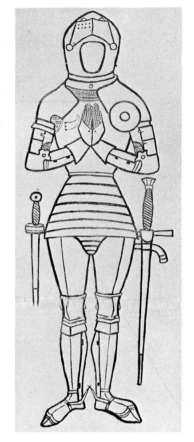

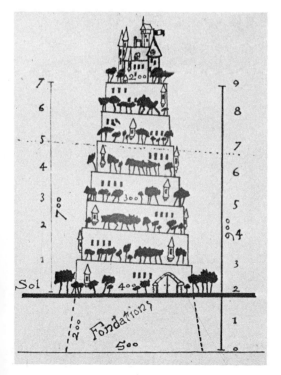

16   Mediaeval fancy by
Satie (drawn about 1875)

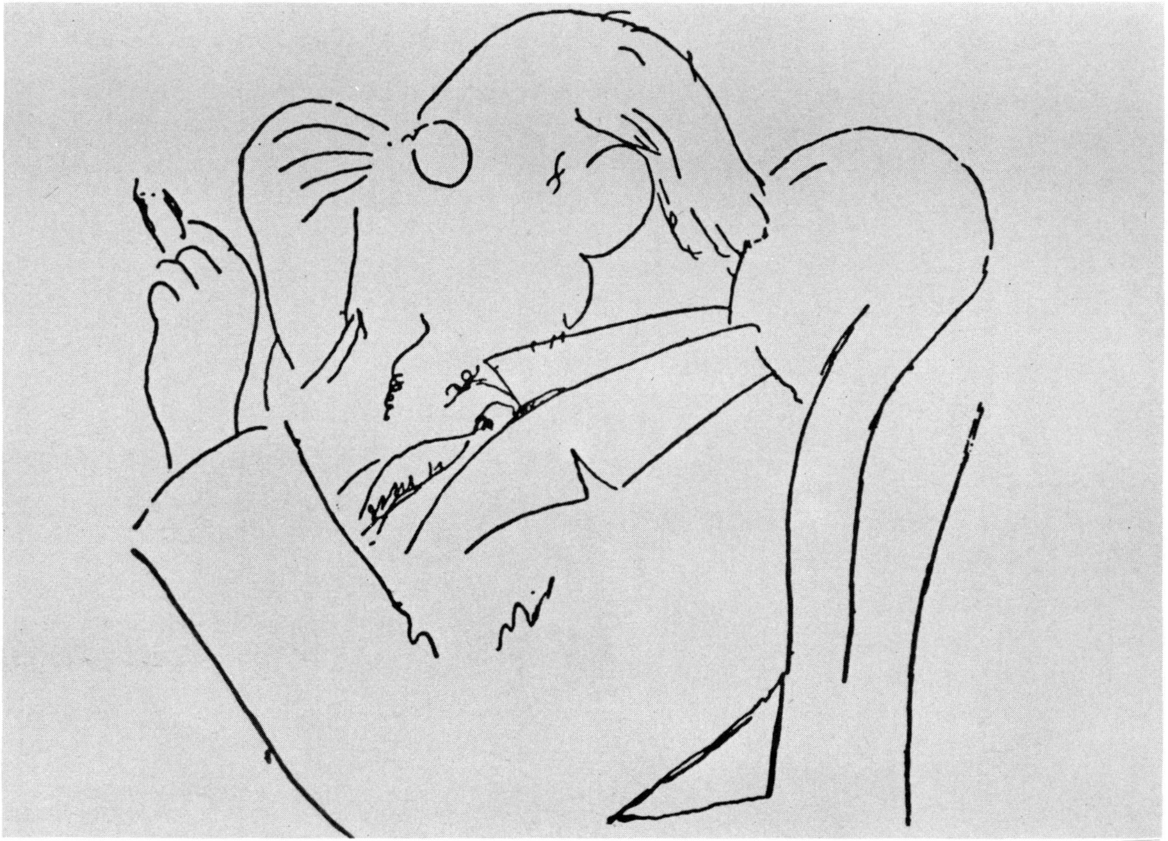

17 Cocteau's view of Satie

rooms and dancehalls. "The tango is the Devil's dance," remarks a note. "It's his favourite. He dances it in order to cool down. His wife, his daughters and his servants also cool down this way."

"How cold!" says the remark attached to the few chilly dissonances that introduce "Le Traîneau". The ladies are wrapped up to the nose in furs. You can hear them shivering in the music, as well as the horses. "The countryside is so cold it doesn't know where to put itself." The sledge departs.

After the manner of "Le Pique-Nique", "Le Flirt" (sport or entertainment?) records odd scraps of hackneyed conversation. It is suddenly outshone by the dazzling "Feu d'artifice", a flash of fireworks that explode into a golden bouquet. The left hand conjures up darkness from the bass to contrast with the mercurial brilliance traced by the right. "Le Tennis", the final piece in the suite, imitates the click of ball on racket and ends with the cry "Game!"

Sports et divertissements represent the culmination of Satie's work for piano. All the characteristics which had shown themselves, though raggedly, in the earlier piano groups are here refined and crystallised. He transcribes with concision what he has observed so acutely. There is no need to study the verbiage around the music to appreciate, for example, the wry hesitations of "Les Quatre Coins". Brevity is all. The evidence of the notebooks shows that Satie worked very hard at his initial ideas, paring them down to the bone, simplifying always, reducing the material to as small a compass as possible, and cutting out inessentials to achieve the lithe bare style that was his ideal. Each bar of *Sports et divertissements* resulted from this continuous process of stripping down and polishing. Having set himself very strict limits, he succeeds completely within the area he has chosen. Like Jules Renard in the *Histoires naturelles*, he makes an asset out of smallness and capitalises on the virtues of brevity. The *Sports et divertissements* remain unique.

In the same year as the *Sports et divertissements* he also wrote two quite different works. January saw the composition of *Choses vues à droite et à gauche (sans lunettes)* for violin and piano, a combination otherwise strange to him. The things he saw to right and left (without glasses) comprised a "Choral hypocrite", a "Fugue à tâtons" and a "Fantaisie musculaire". A note observes: "My Chorals are as good as Bach's, except that there are fewer of them and they're less pretentious." The satire here is directed at the airs and graces of the violin virtuoso with his showy cadenzas and swashbuckling technical feats. This is emphasised in the aptly named "Muscular Fantasy", where the soloist hurdles over various acrobatic passages. Yet the theme of the "Fumbling Fugue", the simplest of tunes, is very charming and very attractive in its naïveté. At its first performance there were derisive whistles ... but applause from sympathisers in the audience urged the performers to encore the cadenzas, so that in the end the satire on complaisant virtuosos was emphasised even more neatly than the instigator had planned. Accompanying at this recital was the pianist Hélène Jourdan-Morhange. Satie was so delighted with her performance that he wrote her one of his finely indited letters promising the dedication of a piece to be called *L'Embarquement pour Cythère*. But illness prevented this, and she was never, she regretted, to embark for Cythera with her bowler-hatted admirer.

This year also he ventured into the field of songwriting. The *Trois poèmes d'Amour* are settings of his own words. "I am but a grain of sand," pleads the first, "ever hale and lovable." The second, "I am bold by birth through sheer good breeding", is governed by the need to find rhymes for *naissance* – so his incongruous lines end in *bienséance, confiance, vaillance, arrogance,* and *Hortense,* the only girl's name admissible in this rhyme-scheme. The last song, "Ta parure est secrète", addressed to the "douce luronette", or strapping little lass, again produces nonsense verse in response to a tyrannical rhyming pattern. The most notable feature of these songs is that they are heavily Gregorian in atmosphere and that the first actually reproduces with little alteration the "Victimae paschali laudes" sung at Easter service. They show that even at this late period Satie had still not forgotten the earliest of his musical enthusiasms.

XVIII

Five Grimaces

Roland-Manuel's home continued to be a hospitable centre for the musician of *Sports et divertissements*. It was here, at some time during the winter of 1913 to 1914, that *Le Piège de Méduse – comédie en un acte de M. Erik Satie (avec musique du même Monsieur)* was first performed with a cast made up of friends. The author himself played the leading part, that of Baron Méduse, with a seriousness that gave edge to the comedy. The rôle of his daughter Frisette was taken by Suzanne Roux, soon to become Madame Roland-Manuel.

The title owes everything to Satie's memories of his classical education and little to the plot. Medusa, the only one of the three Gorgons to be mortal, incurred the wrath of Athena, who changed her lovely hair into serpents, after which the luckless girl was destroyed by Perseus. Her snaky coiffure turned into stone those who looked at it, and this is the tenuous connection that links her with Satie's play. For Baron Medusa's daughter is pursued by a suitor Astolphe. The Baron sets a trap for Astolphe when he asks him about dancing with his eyes. The suitor avoids the *piège* by replying correctly, so the Baron gives him permission to marry Frisette.

Other elements in this farrago, which springs from Allais and proceeds by way of Jarry to anticipate Ionesco, include the Baron's manservant Polycarpe, who treats his master to a perpetual stream of irreverent insult, and a stuffed monkey called Jonas. From time to time the action is interrupted while Jonas performs a little dance. There are seven of these interludes, each of them an attractive enough pleasantry. The first, a quadrille, invokes a grotesque fairground atmosphere. "Be decent, please," runs a note, "a monkey is watching you." The second, a waltz, is very similar to the third of the *Trois Valses distinguées du précieux dégoûté*. The remaining numbers mingle the rhythms of *Jack in the Box* with music-hall ragtime. A final "Quadrille" verges shamelessly on "Yankee Doodle". At the first performance sheets of paper were slipped between the strings of the piano for added musical effect.

But the amiable idiocies of *Le Piège de Méduse* went no further for the time being than the walls of Roland-Manuel's drawing-room. Within months came the declaration of war. The clamour of excited patriots and the fervour of anti-German orators drowned out all other things. There were demands that German music should be banned. Sophisticated arguments raged about the hypothetical case of the brave musician who fought at the front and lost an arm. Suppose he were a Wagnerian. He would no longer be able to play his favourite music. Would it therefore be just to prevent him from listening to Wagner played by others?

Satie was in despair. "Certainly the Germans are an unpleasant lot and continue that way," he wrote. "So why should we drive them to the wall? What a century we live in! This business is nothing more than a version of the end of the world, but sillier than the real one. Let us be meek, even towards our enemies, let us not forget to turn the other cheek, always the other cheek. By doing this we shall be the stronger morally."

He belonged to the minority. Jingoism triumphed everywhere. Men who in time of peace were sober and logical of judgement now vied with each other in the extravagance of their emotions. Never had Joan of Arc and the provinces of Alsace and Lorraine inspired so much passionate absurdity. Ultra-nationalists went so far as to claim as their own the great men of other countries. Satie commented ironically: "The Germans rob France of everything – you know only too well that Wagner was French ... He was

Franco-German, in fact." Other excesses urged him to remark: "And Goethe? Goethe was a Frenchman who ... wrote in German – that's all ... But he was certainly French, the dear man ... Besides everybody knows it."

One of the most belligerent patriots was Saint-Saëns. Now a venerable figure on the musical scene, he plunged vigorously into the debate. He called strenuously for the complete suppression of all German music. Although he had been an early champion of Wagner, he had gradually come to realise the political implications of the composer's philosophy and sought to warn his native land, which for the second time in his life was being invaded by German troops, against these dangerous ideas. Hot and angry was the polemic, violent and harsh were the insults. There were accusations of treason, pederasty and eunuchry. His opponents claimed that Saint-Saëns was the illegitimate son of a Catholic priest, and, worse still in a country where echoes of the Dreyfus case had not yet died down, that he was a Jew.

Satie observed coolly: "No – M. Saint-Saëns isn't a German ... He's just a bit thick in the head ... He gets hold of the wrong end of the stick, that's all ... But he means well, to be sure ... At his age you can say what you like ... What does it matter?" As for himself: "Am I French? Of course ... Why do you expect a man of my age not to be French? ... You surprise me."

All these arguments, however, had little to do with the hard facts of Satie's life at the time. He was poor, poorer than he had ever been, and it was becoming even more difficult simply to exist. In his need he appealed to Paul Dukas, an acquaintance whose official connections might be of help.

Although they were not intimate friends the two men were sympathetic to each other. Like Satie, Dukas had rigorous standards. A great deal of the music he wrote will never be heard, for he judged his own efforts with severity and destroyed most of them ruthlessly. There remain, for piano, the massive sonata and the thoroughgoing Rameau variations. His luscious and very beautiful opera, *Ariane et Barbe-Bleue*, had an enchanting libretto by Maurice Maeterlinck. When produced at the Opéra-Comique in 1907 with Georgette Leblanc, the poet's mistress, in the leading rôle, it laid the foundation of one of the few successes this stern self-critic allowed himself. Then came the eastern splendour of his ballet *La Péri*, a manuscript which friends begged him not to put on the fire as he had intended. He allowed it with reluctance to be performed. Between 1912 and his death in 1935 he published little. The sensational triumph of his early *L'Apprenti-sorcier* labelled him unjustly as the composer of a single work. In his ardent Wagnerian youth he had copied out the full score of *Parsifal* as an act of piety. He developed into a composer with a rich vision of music as architecture and with a marvellous grasp of orchestration. At the Conservatoire he was a kindly teacher of Messiaen and others. He wrote music criticism for several newspapers and had many valuable things to say. His editions of Rameau and Scarlatti were models of careful scholarship. A cigarette dripped constantly from his mouth and stained his moustache with varying shades of yellow. His collection of pornographic pictures, notable for its bold variety of subject and brilliance of colour, was the delight of close friends.

When Satie asked him to intervene with the authorities on his behalf, Dukas good-naturedly agreed. As one who enjoyed the affectionate admiration of such widely differing personalities as Debussy and Saint-Saëns (to whom his piano sonata is dedicated), as Fauré and d'Indy, he was catholic enough in his taste for men and music to include Satie among them. He used what influence he had with the Ministry of Fine Arts. More, he advised Satie to apply as well to the pianist Alfred Cortot who was doing warwork as an attaché there.

The care Dukas took over the matter is shown by a letter he addressed to Satie on 21 August 1915:

At any moment now, I'm expecting a reply from the Sous-Secrétariat des Beaux-Arts to which I sent an immediate appeal on your behalf. I hope this appeal will be followed by the quick and satisfactory result I spoke to you about in my last letter.

But to hasten things up, why don't you yourself approach the *Fraternelle des Artistes* by way of Cortot, who is very deeply involved in it? He'll give you the nicest possible reception, I'm sure, and it's quite unnecessary for you to be recommended by me, as you may, if you think fit . . .

That would give you two strings to your bow. The beginning of a lyre! . . .

I'd be delighted to see something of you. But an awful event is happening in my life this fortnight: I'm moving house! I'm leaving the rue de l'Assomption for the rue Singer, and I'll write to you from there as soon as I'm more or less settled in.

Between now and then I'm confident we'll have achieved a result that will give some justification for the thanks you have been much too kind in sending me in advance.

War . . . is war, as they say in *Carmen*. I don't know whether I myself understand anything of it. But I do think our planet will be a beastly place for the next twenty years after this dress rehearsal for the Last Judgement.

It is very probable that Dukas succeeded in his benevolent purpose. Six weeks or so after he wrote the letter quoted above he found himself the startled dedicatee of "Aubade", which Satie wrote on 3 October as the second of the *Avant-dernières pensées*. The layout of the piece is the same as that of "Sur une lanterne" in the *Descriptions automatiques*. Abrupt chords in the right hand imitate a guitar while the melody is played in the bass. "Listen to the voice of your beloved," pleads the commentary. "He's picking out a rigadoon. How he loves you! He's a poet. Do you hear him? Is he mocking you, perhaps? No: he adores you, gentle Beauty." This mockery of the conventional *aubade* – which reminds us that the word has the secondary meaning of din or noisy cat-calling at dawn – is emphasised by a pun about the elderly poet who is serenading his loved one and catches a cold from the morning chill: "Il repince un rigaudon et un rhume."

Another good friend in need proved to be Valentine Hugo. Through her journalistic connections she was able to arrange for the publication in a magazine called *La Gazette du bon ton* of three songs. This occurred in the winter of 1914–1915, and the commission brought Satie fabulous wealth: three thousand francs, a sum he had never dreamed of before, let alone handled. The songs were probably the *Trois poèmes d'Amour*, since he did not compose the *Trois Mélodies* until the following year.

Urged by the direst poverty, he did not scruple to accept the money. (It is true that, once promised a loan, he replied: "Monsieur, what you have said did not fall on a deaf ear.") His gratitude towards Valentine was intense. When, in October 1915, she asked if he would like to meet Jean Cocteau, he gladly fell in with her request.

Cocteau was then already a dazzling Parisian celebrity, adored by some for his mercurial wit and detested by others as a self-advertising charlatan. Before he was twenty years old he had founded, with the precious Maurice Rostand, the playwright's son, an exotic magazine called *Schéhérazade*. It published, on fine paper in beautifully designed issues, drawings by Marie Laurencin and Dunoyer de Segonzac, music by Reynaldo Hahn and Massenet, and poetry by the distinguished elder Rostand and Cocteau himself.

Cocteau knew everyone. His appetite for the famous was insatiable. His acquaintance ranged from Proust to Gide, from Péguy to Mauriac. Among his most glittering conquests was Serge Diaghilev, at whose court he officiated as a privileged entertainer. His charm and his conversation were irresistible. Diaghilev, though shrewdly aware of the self-interest that inspired Cocteau's flattering attention, like many others gave way to the spell. But Cocteau's non-stop public display of fireworks exacted a price. It meant eternal vigilance lest, wherever two or three were gathered together, the mask should be seen to slip. It called for continuous rehearsal of his epigrams and unremitting calculation of the effect on his audience. It obliged him, when visiting the home of a friend or admirer, to prepare and polish his repertoire even while going up in the lift and walking along the corridor.

The reason for Cocteau's wish to meet Satie was a new project that engaged him at the time. For emotional and artistic reasons he was currently obsessed by the circus, an element that recurs in his writings and theatrical ventures. The idea was to produce a modern version of *A Midsummer Night's Dream* at the Cirque Médrano, that famous entertainment in Paris where Cocteau, enthralled by the techniques of the performers and the glamour of the ring, was an eager observer. He wanted to cast the Fratellini brothers, the well-known clowns, whom he later used in his ballet *Le Boeuf sur le toit*, as Bottom, Flute and Starveling. There would be sets and costumes designed by the Cubist Albert Gleizes, and music by some contemporary composer. Whereupon the ever-reliable Saint-Saëns offered himself as a target again by protesting that it was impossible to contemplate such a production without using Mendelssohn's famous music.

The composer Edgar Varèse was already involved as musical director. Having studied the science and mathematics which no doubt played their part in his later researches into electronic music, he had given them up and studied music under d'Indy and Roussel. Soon after his association with the *Midsummer Night's Dream* plan he left for New York, settling there in 1916 and becoming eventually a naturalised citizen. "Ce brave garçon", as Satie called him, was to give the first American performance of the *Gymnopédies*.

The future composer of the *Poème électronique*, of *Ionisation* and of *Density 21·5* found in Satie a character to like and a musician to admire, especially the musician of the *Gymnopédies* and the *Messe des pauvres*. Having learned that Satie's visits to friends would usually last until the bottle of cognac was emptied, Varèse took care that meetings with him were suitably lubricated. The thought was appreciated. Long after Varèse had established himself in America Satie was writing to him with news of Paris and sending copies of his music. To Madame Varèse Satie confided his ambition of turning *Alice in Wonderland* into a ballet. Would she put together a scenario? He was, he said, the only Frenchman to understand English humour, and the only one whose music "understood Alice".

Varèse had been distantly associated with Max Reinhardt's Berlin production of *A Midsummer Night's Dream*, and it may be that news of a revival had stimulated him and his friends to create a subtler, more Gallic version. At first they intended to use the *Gymnopédies* and various pieces by Florent Schmitt, Ravel and Stravinsky. In the end Satie wrote his *Cinq Grimaces pour le songe d'une nuit d'été* which are all that remain of this unrealised project. For the original enthusiasm which inspired Cocteau somehow fell away. The practical difficulties of mounting such an operation were not small, and the problems of wartime magnified them. But even the people most directly concerned were vague about reasons for the demise of the venture.

Before he went to America Varèse is reported to have given Satie aid in orchestrating the *Cinq Grimaces*. The five pieces that make up the suite are written for a "circus" ensemble. The *Préambule* opens in the manner of *Jack in the Box*, easy and nonchalant with gauche ambling phrases. Even more typical is *Coquecigrue*, a title referring to the chimera, or fire-breathing monster with lion's head, goat's body and snake's tail. *Chasse* is a straightforward hunting piece including the motif Satie had already used in his piano works. The *Fanfaronnade* suggests the bounce and swagger of Bully Bottom, and there is a concluding *Pour sortir* which incorporated a trumpet call after the style of similar items in *Geneviève de Brabant*.

How much of this was Cocteau and how much Satie? No written plan exists. The importance of the *Midsummer Night's Dream* project, however, lies in the introduction to Picasso which Varèse arranged for Cocteau. "Picasso was *the* great meeting for me," said Cocteau afterwards. From it was to spring, two years later, the ballet *Parade* with designs by Picasso and music by Satie.

XIX

The Poet of Paris

In the April and May of 1916 Satie wrote his *Trois Mélodies*. They
are settings of poems by various friends. The words of "Daphénéo", for example, are credited to a "M. God", otherwise thought
to be Cyprien Godebski, who with his wife Ida entertained in
their famous salon writers like Gide, Valéry, and Cocteau, and
composers such as Roussel, de Falla and Stravinsky. Ravel's
Ma mère l'oye was written for their children Mimi and Jean, for he
was close enough to be almost a member of the household.

Although "Daphénéo" is generally assumed to have been
written by "Cipa" Godebski, as he was known to his friends, it
seems that the true author was his daughter Mimi. "M. God"
therefore becomes Maria, or Mimi, Godebska. Later to die pre-
maturely in a car accident, she was only sixteen at the time of
"Daphénéo". The poem has that atmosphere of childhood innocence characteristic both of Satie and of the young friend with
whom he was able to establish so quickly a bond of conspiratorial
sympathy. What, asks Chrysaline, is the tree that produces fruit
in the shape of weeping birds? Daphénéo replies that it is a bird-
tree *(oisetier)*. "Ah!" breathes Chrysaline with astonishment, I
thought, she continues, that *noisetiers* (nut-trees) gave nuts. You

are right, says Daphénéo, nut-trees give nuts . . . and bird-trees produce weeping birds. "Ah!" responds Chrysaline again. This delightful non-sequitur is couched in musical terms utterly straight-faced except that at one moment a turn of phrase from *Madame Butterfly* ("One fine day") insinuates itself.

The words of "Le Chapelier", after *Alice in Wonderland*, were supplied by René Chalupt, the critic and poet. The Mad Hatter is surprised to note that his watch is three days slow, even though he takes care always to grease it with nothing but the best butter. The reason, of course, is that he has dropped breadcrumbs into the works, and however often he dips the watch in his tea it will never catch up on lost time. There was no need for Satie to include the direction "Allegretto (genre Gounod)". The tune is stolen complete from the "Chanson de Magali" in *Mireille*.

The last of the songs to be composed, though the first in order of published appearance, was "La Statue de bronze" by Léon-Paul Fargue. Here a garden ornament, cast in the shape of a frog, its mouth eternally open, expresses its boredom at being the statue always about to say "The Word" but never actually pronouncing it. The frog would much rather be with its fellows, blowing bubbles of music out of the soapy moonlight. Yet all it gets is small change thrown into its mouth by frivolous passers-by. And at night disrespectful insects sleep in that ever-open orifice.

This is the most original and successful of the *Trois Mélodies*. A lugubrious accompaniment hints at the ornament's weary complaint, while the vocal line with its grotesque little skips underlines the pathetic absurdity of the verse. In setting the poem the composer had cut out three words. It took the poet a certain time to forgive him. When Fargue had recovered from this betrayal their friendship, which had probably begun in the Godebskis' drawing-room, went on as amiably as before.

Fargue was already a Parisian legend. Born in les Halles among the reek of fruit and vegetables of that now vanished market, he spent there a secret and melancholy childhood. His father ran a ceramics workshop. His mother, who was devoted to her son, looked after and tended him until her death at the age of ninety-three. But over what should have been a happy little family there hovered a strange cloud. The father's mother had disapproved of his choice of a humble bride and forbidden him to marry. Only at her death did they venture at last to regularise the situation. Fargue was then nearly thirty years old. His early years had been shadowed by the uneasy secret. He felt that he and his parents were outcasts. This feeling of rejection would help to account for his bohemianism as an adult, his inability to conform with social customs, and at the same time his excessive delight in honours, however insignificant. Long before he was entitled to wear the Légion d'honneur he displayed a convincing forgery in his buttonhole. He signed himself "Léon-Paul Fargue, de l'Académie Mallarmé" with a proud flourish.

Despite a brilliant career at school he did not want to take his studies further. He preferred writing, drawing, playing the piano. At the age of fourteen he had painted his first picture and could play Saint-Saëns' *Danse macabre* with something more than amateur skill. He went to the famous Tuesday evening gatherings where Mallarmé was host. Poetry, he decided, had chosen his fate for him. He wrote a lot, often taking crumpled scraps from his pocket to read to friends. But he could not bring himself to publish it. This was due to his state of chronic uncertainty. It is told that he was once three hours late for an appointment. The reason, he explained earnestly, was that his mother had put out two pairs of shoes for him that morning and he had been unable to make up his mind which to wear. It was the same with his poetry. Constantly revising and crossing out, he could never bear to let his manuscript go. He had the Balzacian habit of re-writing on the proofs. The printer of his *Nocturnes* gave up in disgust after six months of continual revision. If ever a magazine sent him proofs, it was rare for them to be seen again. The manuscript of *Tancrède*, which acts as a strange hyphen between Symbolism and Surrealism, a beguiling mixture of prose poem and free verse, had to be snatched away from him and seen through the press by friends.

Music and art he loved as much as poetry, and music perhaps more than art. Certain things, he said, he could only express through music. Ravel was a close friend and dedicated to him *Noctuelles*. Fargue would have liked composers to set his poems, and was delighted when Satie emerged as the first to do this, even at the cost of those cherished three words. Ravel later followed Satie's example, and so did Florent Schmitt and Georges Auric.

When his father died the ceramics business withered. Fargue

lived quietly with his mother in a small flat overlooking the Canal Saint-Martin. Journalism was his main source of income and he held forth on any subject editors proposed to him. The best of his many articles were those he wrote about his beloved city and which he later collected into Le Piéton de Paris: impressions of Montmartre cafés, twilight meditations in the rue de Lappe, sketches of street life, digressions on the charm of the quays by the Seine, sharp little cameos of the stars of the Comédie-Française, essays on the waxwork mysteries in the Musée Grévin. To be a Marseillais, he wrote, you have to be born in Marseille. But you need not have first seen the light of day in Paris to be a Parisian. Because a Parisian is, above all, a Frenchman. A rich foreigner is a foreigner. A rich Parisian is a Parisian . . . and so is a poor one.

The poetry he reluctantly published gradually made him known. Proust spoke of his "admirable talent" and Rilke described him as "one of our greatest poets". He became the darling of rich society hostesses who loved to treat the old bachelor as a wayward little boy and to spoil him with the gourmet dinners and fine wines he loved. He slept during the day and lived during the night. By the end of the afternoon he would decide to get up. Dressing was an intricate ritual involving many compulsive neuroses – the tie to be tied in a certain way, garments to be handled according to an involved ceremony – and only at twilight was he ready to step outside and find a taxi. Taxis were a part of his life. In them he drove from bar to bar, from café to café. They waited outside, the minutes dissolving remorselessly into cash, as he held court with his friends over the zinc-lined counter. Usually the same taxi would stay with him until dawn, when he finally had to make the awful decision: should he go home? Afraid of insomnia, of wakeful terror in a lonely bed, he put off deciding until he was purple with fatigue. At last he paid off his taxi which had been, for twelve hours, a mobile home, a comforting womb, a shelter against the harsh world outside. It was, to him, what the shell is to the snail.

His face, a Chinese mask with a crumpled Gauloise for ever attached to it, was known in all the bars of Montmartre and the Champs-Élysées as well as at the dinner tables of princesses. He enjoyed the company of chauffeurs and plumbers as much as that of aristocrats. Sometimes a rich friend persuaded him to accept a free cruise on a luxury yacht. No sooner had it left harbour than he was pining for the dusty streets of Paris and the smell of dark, crowded *bistrots*.

In 1943, while chatting with Picasso at a restaurant in Saint Germain des Prés, he collapsed of a stroke. So many cigarettes, so much rough red wine and Pernod, so many white nights, had caught up with him. Now he no longer went out by taxi. An occasional trip in an ambulance took the place of those nocturnal meanderings. Though paralysed, he was spared the use of his right hand. He sat up in bed scribbling. His mother had died and he married the artist Chériane who became his nurse. He liked to entertain his friends as they crowded noisily around his bed to hear his talk, lively, malicious, on occasion hugely obscene.

He resembled, when he gave audience to those who called, a monarch of the old régime. Visitors gathered in the dining-room. At a given moment Chériane swung open the double doors and allowed the chattering group into Fargue's presence. His shoulders were draped with an old shawl. Scattered over the sky-blue coverlet lay books, open newspapers, unfinished articles. In his early days he had looked, said his fellow poet Valéry, like the young Nero. Now, said another friend, he had the air of Napoleon on Saint Helena. His old acquaintance Colette arrived one evening for dinner. Her health was only just a little bit better than his, for she had arthritis of the hip. Since the lift did not go all the way up, she travelled in the goods hoist.

His room filled with smoke and grew over-heated. One Sunday in 1947, after his friends had gone, a window was opened to let in fresh air. It also let in a draught. He caught bronchitis. Three days later, surrounded by his pills and medicines and tablets, he died.

"My whole existence," he once wrote, "has been a commingling of secret sorrow and an apparent joy in living." It was this, perhaps, which enabled him to look at the things of everyday life – a table, a chair, a railway engine, so comforting in their ordinariness – and to turn them into monsters of fable. As the poet of Paris he brought a haunting urban flavour to his childhood memories and chronicles of daydreams. Though he was not a great poet, he was an ingenious and entertaining one. And he was thoroughgoing in the way of life he had chosen. "I call bourgeois anyone who renounces himself, the struggles of life, and love, for safety's sake," he remarked, "I call bourgeois anyone who puts anything above feeling."

An observer who knew both Fargue and Satie was struck by their similarity. This was the music critic and writer M.-D. Calvocoressi, who, born in Marseille of a Greek father, made a name for himself as a champion of modern French music. He worked with Diaghilev, was an intimate of Debussy and Ravel and Fauré, and also had personal links with the Russians Glazunov, Balakirev and Rimsky-Korsakov. Then he settled in England and built himself another career, writing English with the same fluency and distinction as he had shown in writing French.

Satie, like Fargue, appeared to be highly amused with himself. This, thought Calvocoressi, was entirely natural and had nothing of a pose about it. The two men were quiet and unemphatic in manner. They had a common liking for dry humour, for the deflating remark, for the surrealist joke. Their contempt for money and bourgeois values was expressed with irony and understatement. They were completely unworldly. One visualises them at a café table sitting late into the night and early into morning, imbibing at a steady but dignified rate and creating extravagant fancies. When Satie rose to walk back to Arcueil and Fargue, unwillingly, looked around for his taxi, it is little to be doubted that their step was as firm and sober as that of any teetotal bourgeois.

In 1923, seven years after "La Statue de bronze", Satie put to music five more poems by Fargue. These were taken from *Ludions*, selections from which appeared desultorily in magazines over the years until they were finally collected as a book in 1933. Fargue's notorious reluctance to publish is shown by the fact that some of these poems dated from the time when he was only twelve years old. It had taken him nearly half a century before he could bear to see them in print. The title, "bottle imps", indicates the nature of the verse. The thought is witty and bizarre, the language unexpected and starred with puns. Illogicality is the source of much of the inspiration, and the drollery is unstinted. The inventive word-play makes translation difficult – as, for example, with "Merdrigal", which is sub-titled "En dédicrasse".

It is natural that Satie should be attracted to Fargue's verse and his personality. The first poem of the group, which Satie also called *Ludions*, was the "Air du rat". This is a nonsense piece ("Un jo, un joli goulifon") set to a galumphing tune which, by careful placing of accents, stresses the incongruity of the words. The second item, "Spleen", is by no means comic. It pictures a crumbling old city square under the rain, drenched and desolate in an atmosphere of morose despair. The concluding phrase, "What is our life?" has a liturgical cadence which exquisitely conveys the mood of hopelessness and sums up the essence of a favourite Baudelaire word.

"La Grenouille américaine" is related to the frog of "La Statue de bronze". He stares at the poet over the top of his glasses, according to the singer, who has to adopt an American accent. But in fact he is a bubble – perhaps in the coffee pot. The accompaniment derives frankly from the music hall. More reflective is the "Air du Poète", an involved conceit which depends for its humour on a trick with the word "Papouasie" (Papua). For your own sake, remarks the poet, I hope you won't be a "Papouète" – a play on "cacahouète", meaning a peanut. This Carrollian squib is set to an appropriately grave melody. The last song is the "Chanson du chat", a grown-up nursery rhyme with many a "Tirelan" and "Tirelo", which gallops along at a hearty pace. For each of these songs the composer found a style and a tone which perfectly marries with Fargue's content – burlesque, ironic, melancholy, eupeptic or droll.

PART SIX

Scandals

XX

Parade

Besides marking the start of Satie's long association with Fargue and his link with the Godebski salon, the *Trois Mélodies* of 1916 also illuminate other areas of friendship. "Le Chapelier" is dedicated to Stravinsky. The composer of *Le Sacre du printemps* was, for Satie, "one of the most outstanding geniuses music has ever known". Satie regarded him as a leader whose strength had won rights for other composers which could never be lost. Stravinsky, he added, was a magician, whatever the critics might say about him.

They had met in 1913. It was Debussy who brought them together. In that same year Stravinsky took a photograph of Debussy and Satie.

"He was certainly the oddest person I have ever known," Stravinsky later told Robert Craft, "but the most rare and consistently witty person, too. I had a great liking for him and he appreciated my friendliness, I think, and liked me in return. With his pince-nez, umbrella and galoshes he looked a perfect schoolmaster, but he looked just as much like one without these accoutrements. He spoke very softly, hardly opening his mouth, but he delivered each word in an inimitable, precise way. His handwriting recalls his speech to me: it is exact, drawn. His manuscripts were like him also, which is to say as the French say: '*fin*'."

Satie played to him many of his own compositions. Privately Stravinsky thought them hampered by the verbal trappings with which they were adorned. He believed that whereas, for example, Paul Klee's "literary" titles did not limit his paintings, Satie's restricted his music. He also found the pieces less amusing a second time. Despite these reservations, he paid a charming tribute to Satie with one of the *Trois pièces faciles* for piano duet which he composed while staying with Diaghilev in Rome during the winter of 1915. The "Polka" was dedicated to his host – whom, Stravinsky told him, he had envisaged as a ringmaster in a circus, complete with top hat and dress coat, cracking his whip at an equestrienne. It took Diaghilev some little time to appreciate the joke. The "Marche" was intended for the Italian composer Alfredo Casella, and Satie's name was linked with the "Valse". Although, as the name implies, these are "easy" pieces with a simple bass, the musicianship behind them is delightful proof that a great composer cannot help showing his quality, however restricted the medium.

The *Trois Mélodies* were given their first performance in May 1916, at a concert in a house belonging to the sister of the dress designer Paul Poiret. Madame Bongard too was in the dress business and directed her affairs from this handsome old building in the fashionable rue de Penthièvre. Satie's music therefore had its première in a glossy setting to which its composer was little accustomed. The audience, made up of wealthy persons who patronised expensive dress-makers, equalled the grandeur of the surroundings. The reactions on this point of the socialist philosopher of Arcueil have not been handed down to us. So far, however, as the propagation of his music was concerned, he showed complete approval.

René Chalupt, who had written the words of "Le Chapelier", was asked to introduce the composer and his work at the beginning of the concert. To a polite but rather baffled gathering he tried to explain the nature of Satie's music, the new ideas he had brought, and to what extent he had been a precursor. But, Chalupt continued, "probably too indifferent to apply them himself, he has left it to others to draw out the consequences of his discoveries." Since it was wartime and German dirigibles had flown threateningly over Paris, he concluded that Satie's "sharp little arrows punctured with their merciless pinpricks the romantic and sentimental Zeppelin."

Satie, much gratified, sent him next day a message. "You were terrific," it read. "Yes, I'm telling you. And so I want to thank you. You can just see how simple it all is . . . you're a good friend".

Sandwiched between items for piano, and the *Choses vues à droite et à gauche (sans lunettes)*, the *Trois Mélodies* were given by Jane Bathori. She was a passionate defender of contemporary music who introduced many new songs by Debussy, Ravel and others. After making her début at Nantes in 1900 she sang at La Scala in Milan, at the Théâtre de la Monnaie in Brussels, and became internationally known. She condensed her practical experience into valuable writings on the art of song and particularly on the interpretation of Debussy's vocal music. "Dear Jane Bathori, what *hasn't* she done for modern music!" Poulenc was later to say, expressing what he and many other composers felt.

Her husband was Emile Engels, to whom "Daphénéo" is inscribed. She herself was the dedicatee of "La Statue de bronze". Though there is confusion here. The concert took place on 16 May, yet the song is dated the 26th. Perhaps this was the day when Satie resolved to associate her with it, or the day when he wrote out a fair copy for the printer. What cannot be doubted is the gratitude he felt towards her and all the other friends who had made the concert possible and helped to further the cause of his music.

The pianist on this occasion was Ricardo Viñes, another who, like Jane Bathori, avoided the easy triumphs his spectacular technique could have won in the established classics by going out of his way to discover all that was new and interesting. Viñes was a Spaniard of Catalan origins who had studied in Barcelona and at the Paris Conservatoire. He was a remarkable pianist with an exuberant appetite for modern music. His moustache attained to heroic size. He always wore a dashing brown sombrero. His disciple, the young Poulenc, remembered that whenever a pupil's foot made a pedalling error, Viñes' button boots would flash out to deliver an exasperated kick on the shins. Like Jane Bathori, he was a pioneer. Debussy, Falla, Albeniz and now Satie were to be in his debt. He had been a fellow student with Ravel. A mutual taste for Baudelaire strengthened their lifetime's friendship. Viñes was the first to play in public nearly all of Ravel's piano works, each bar having earlier been rehearsed with the composer. (A great affection did not prevent the pianist from being reminded, by Ravel's short stature, of a jockey.) They had a taste for sophisticated jokes. Chopin, they agreed, never sounded more beautiful or poetic than when played on one of those ancient, out-of-tune pianos to be found in old country houses. When they went on journeys together they would look out for the most decrepit and worm-eaten instruments they could find in order to give themselves this pleasure.

To Viñes, whom he called his "dear old accomplice", Satie wrote: "I shall never be able to thank you enough. What a terrible bore my old music is! What a load of crap [*connerie*], if I dare say so . . ."

At the end of the year he had fresh cause for gratitude to Viñes. The programme which had been given at Madame Bongard's house "for the benefit of artists suffering from the war" was repeated in a studio at No. 6 rue Huyghens. During the war this cramped little building in a narrow street off the boulevard Montparnasse was used for art exhibitions, readings of poetry and concerts. Here were shown Cubist paintings and here new music was performed. The Satie recital was called an "Instant musical", and Viñes again played the items he had given at Madame Bongard's. In the *Trois Morceaux en forme de poire* he was joined as fellow duettist by the composer. Jane Bathori once more sang the pieces she had earlier introduced.

Cocteau was a prominent figure in the activities at 6 rue Huyghens. He brought Diaghilev with him to Satie's "Instant musical". The impresario was perhaps curious to hear more of the composer whom he had commissioned to write music for a new ballet inspired by Cocteau. For earlier that year Cocteau and Satie had started work on *Parade*. Stimulated by memories of *Petrouchka*, Cocteau had once visualised a ballet to take place at a fair. The action consisted of a *parade*, or the knockabout turn put on by acrobats outside the fairground booth to tempt an audience inside. The hope was that Stravinsky would write the music. But the composer of *Petrouchka* remained wary. There were biblical undertones to *David*, as the ballet was first titled, which did not appeal to him. And then Cocteau was tiresomely persistent, even tactless in his enthusiasm. Besides which Diaghilev resented Cocteau's initiative.

So *David* was never to be composed by Stravinsky. For a year or more the idea slept among Cocteau's papers. Then, on meeting Satie, he dusted it off and presented it anew. Now the ballet was to be called simply *Parade*, the biblical David vanished from the scene, and an acrobat would dance a few music-hall numbers. Though baffled, Satie expressed an interest, his only stipulation being that he should write new music rather than use existing pieces. By the spring of 1916, Cocteau had provided him with a scenario involving a Chinese conjurer, an American girl and an acrobat.

In June Satie had to reassure his impatient collaborator that all was going well. Cocteau's impulsiveness and his tendency to hustle people did not please the independent Satie. He warned him that the music would not be ready until October.

At this point the formidable Misia Sert intrudes on the narrative. She was the half-sister of Cipa Godebski, and, like him, much interested in the arts, particularly in music. On the three occasions when she married she chose a husband who was either very rich or very clever or both. Her first choice fell on Thadée Natanson, an important journalist and co-founder of the *Revue blanche*, whom she espoused at the age of fifteen. Her second husband, whose fifth wife she became, happened to be the extremely wealthy Alfred Edwards. He was fat and unattractive but had great power, an attribute which is as potent an aphrodisiac as any other. His newspaper, *Le Matin*, was the most successful of its kind. On his luxury yacht he and his new wife took their friends, among them Ravel, for easeful cruises. After a palatial existence with Edwards Misia took as her third and final husband the Spanish artist José-Maria Sert, who specialised in grandiose mural decorations covering untold square yards of elaborate, stylised perspective.

At the time Satie knew her she was still Madame Edwards. Her salon, where Ravel figured as her most prestigious exhibit, shone with the brilliance of famous names. She was ruthless in her machinations and imperious in her friendships. For twenty years she was the intimate of Diaghilev. It is a measure of her influence with him that he, who normally detested women, should have made her his confidante, the person with whom he discussed his most secret plans and ambitions. They had violent quarrels and bitter disputes. They insulted each other with Slavonic fury. (Like her half-brother, she had Polish blood.) But always they were reconciled, the storms evaporated as swiftly as they arose, and soon the two conspirators were immersed as deeply as ever in the adorable, the fascinating business of plot and intrigue. She was, without a doubt, the hidden eminence of the Ballets Russes and one whose approval was necessary if favours were to be obtained.

With, for him, unusual diplomatic flair, Satie invited Misia to patronise a concert of his music. Then he told her that he would dedicate *Parade* to her and hinted that she had been the inspiration of it. When, though, she learned that Cocteau had written the scenario, her annoyance was sharp. She made known her displeasure in acrid terms. Cocteau rushed to soothe her with flattering words. He failed. Misia was outraged at what seemed to be his attempt to seduce from Diaghilev and herself their protégé Erik Satie. Perhaps, she threatened darkly, the ballet would in the end be produced with music he had already written. She even spoke disobligingly of Satie himself. When the touchy musician got wind of this, as inevitably he did, he christened her "Tante Trufaldin" in a disrespectful reference to the treacherous valet in Italian comedy. Cocteau, meanwhile, trembled for the outcome of his cherished plan.

The crisis eventually blew over. Calmed by Satie's assurance that he would dedicate *Parade* to her – her name appears, in fact, on the four-handed piano version – Misia subsided without further objection. In August a new excitement broke: Picasso agreed to design the ballet. Cocteau's delight was at first wholehearted. For some time he had been courting Picasso, and now that the artist had joined him his triumph was complete. Picasso already knew Satie, and it may have been this which determined him. In any case, Picasso and Satie quickly understood each other so far as *Parade* was concerned and were even able to veto some of Cocteau's ideas. One of these was to have an amplified voice declaiming spoken phrases after each number. Denied this inspiration, Cocteau later used it for his ballet *Les Mariés de la Tour Eiffel*. Other effects which he planned were likewise rejected. In all these arguments, it seems, Picasso agreed with Satie and urged him to stand up to Cocteau.

At times Cocteau felt badly treated and complained he was not being given full credit for his enterprise. Satie, in turn, was embarrassed to find himself always on Picasso's side and preferring the latter's ideas to Cocteau's. Somehow they composed their differences as they went along, and by the end of 1916 the score was in its essentials complete. On 12 December Satie told Valentine Hugo that he had written the "Petit prélude du rideau rouge", the second item in the sequence which, typically, he composed last. A fortnight later he asked her to get together some friends so that they could hear it played on the piano. In the New Year, from 3 January onwards, they met on several occasions at Ricardo Viñes' home for more hearings of the new work.

Now that the labour of *Parade* was over he found time for other things. He gave a lecture on "Animals in music" and put forward the ideas which have been mentioned earlier. There was also the pleasant business of signing contracts for *Parade*. Satie received not only an amount of money which was, for him, large, but also three thousand francs which Cocteau very generously made over out of his own advance on future royalties. "Satie is buying an umbrella a day," Cocteau joked to Valentine Hugo.

Early in 1917 Diaghilev invited scenarist, composer and designer to Rome for rehearsals. He envisaged Massine as the Chinese conjurer and wanted him to devise the choreography. Cocteau and Picasso sped off enthusiastically. Satie stayed behind. "Do you know Rome, Monsieur Satie?" he was asked. "By name – only by name," he replied.

In Rome, not without the usual disputes and quarrels, *Parade* gradually came to life. The company returned to Paris at the beginning of May and the first performance was arranged for the 18th at the Théâtre du Châtelet. Much has been written about this famous première and there is little need to enlarge on the notorious details of an event which marks an important date in musical history. Tickets had been bought by a well-meaning audience whose money was destined for such deserving charities as those of wounded or sick soldiers, Polish prisoners and other unfortunate cases. Although a sprinkling of young artists and musicians was present, the majority of spectators belonged to more conventional areas of society. They were better accustomed to the other items on the programme, which included *Les Sylphides*, a ballet with music by Rimsky-Korsakov, and even *Petrouchka*, than to the unusual entertainment that took place before their disbelieving eyes.

Wholly unprepared for Satie's novel music and Picasso's cubist designs, they showed their indignation with noisy vigour. Cocteau reported vividly that there were insulting cries of "Boches!" and demands that the perpetrators be sent to the Front. He pictured women charging with hatpins at him and his collaborators. He spoke of fights in the auditorium after the curtain fell, of a female who tried to put out his eyes with a hatpin, and of the man who said to his wife: "If I'd known it was going to be so silly I'd have brought the children." A bayonet charge in Flanders, he declared, was as nothing compared with that unruly scene.

Though Cocteau over-dramatised the incident, there is no doubt that the audience was shocked and confused. It is unlikely that before the performance started they had had time to absorb the contents of the programme book to which Guillaume Apollinaire contributed a lengthy note. Not only a poet but also an art critic and theorist who did much to champion modern art, he came to rehearsals and afterwards wrote the newspaper article on *Parade* which was reproduced in the programme.

Definitions of *Parade*, he wrote lyrically, were flowering everywhere, like the lilac branches in that tardy spring:

The innovating composer Erik Satie has turned this stage poem into astonishingly expressive music, so clear and simple that you can see in it the wonderfully lucid spirit of France itself.

The cubist painter Picasso and Léonide Massine, that most daring of choreographers, have brought it to the stage, so consummating for the first time a union between painting and the dance – between plastic and mime – which heralds the arrival of a more complete art . . .

From this new alliance – for up to now scenery and costumes on the one hand and choreography on the other had only a very superficial link – there emerges in *Parade* a kind of *surréalisme*. This I see as the starting point in a series of revelations of that New Spirit [a favourite topic in Apollinaire's theoretical writings] which, finding today an opportunity to show itself, will not fail to attract the enlightened and will look forward to transforming arts and manners from top to bottom amid universal rejoicing. For it is logical to wish art and manners to keep up with industrial and scientific progress . . .

There followed much praise for Picasso and Massine but little mention of Cocteau. (Feeling between Cocteau and Apollinaire was shadowed and ambiguous.) Then Apollinaire concluded:

In short, *Parade* will upset quite a few people in the audience. They will be surprised, assuredly, but in the pleasantest way. They will be charmed and able to appreciate the grace of modern movement – something they had never suspected.

A magnificent music hall Chinaman will give full scope to the play of their imagination. By turning the handle of an imaginary car the American Girl will express the magic of their everyday life, and the acrobat in blue and white tights fulfils its mute ceremonies with an agility that is exquisite and surprising.

The scenario outlined by Apollinaire in his last paragraph is quite different from what Cocteau imagined at the very beginning. He had conceived of an acrobat performing outside a booth while a megaphone exhorted the crowd to enter and see David battling with Goliath. Stravinsky's uninterested reaction and Diaghilev's lack of enthusiasm had urged him to modify the notion still further. In the end, especially after Picasso and Massine had contributed their own ideas, the work became very much of a collaboration. Satie himself, although he took part in discussions, usually on Picasso's side and in opposition to the extravagances put forward by Cocteau, was only really interested in his music. He held out firmly against the suggestion of an amplified voice and other extraneous sounds. He made his point.

The ballet opened with a short chorale, dry and sparse in the style of the one that prefaces *Sports et divertissements*, though the acerbity is sweetened by soft touches on the harp at the ends of phrases. This is followed by the "Prélude du rideau rouge". Satie was rather pleased with what he had written. "It's a fugal exposition, very *contemplative*, very *serious*, and even rather 'stuffed-shirt', but *short*," he told Valentine Hugo. He added, impishly translating into "Japanese" a familiar piece of vulgar French slang: "I like this slightly conventional, pseudo naïf sort of thing – quite 'Kono' as the Japanese say."

Picasso's drop curtain, a romantic circus picture, now rose on the set proper. This showed, at the centre, the façade of a side-show crowned with a lyre and, on both sides, tall modern buildings. The music changed gear into the fast bustling rhythm of a fairground. The first of the Managers was on the stage dressed in a tall Cubist structure with a house attached to his back. Like his other colleagues, one habited in Wild West style and the other presented as a comic pantomime horse, he was supposed to be a representative of the commercial spirit as opposed to the "art" of the performers themselves.

"Number 1" clicked up on a card as in music-halls when a turn was announced. The Chinese Conjurer appeared. He materialised an egg from his shoe and juggled with it before engulfing it in his mouth. He breathed fire, set himself alight and scuffled to put out the sparks – all to music that reached its climax with a pounding three-note phrase mercilessly repeated on trumpet and trombone. Here occurred some of the incongruous sounds the composer allowed himself, either at Cocteau's urging or simply because he fancied them: the noises of siren and lottery wheel. By contrast the next section introduced a gentle tune on the horns while the strings pursued their determined ostinato pattern.

The next turn was provided by the American Girl, one of the few Cocteau inspirations that emerged reasonably intact. He had an obsession with early American silent films – his ballet *Le Boeuf sur le toit* showed it even more clearly – and especially with the long-running serial depicting "The Perils of Pauline". He wanted his American Girl to swim, box, dance, and leap perilously on to moving trains. In *Parade* she rushed on stage to a swirling figure played by woodwind and strings. The brave little creature in her white skirt and blazer mounted a race-horse, jumped on a bi-cycle, imitated the jerky motion of silent films, zig-zagged like Charlie Chaplin, and chased a thief brandishing a revolver. A typewriter and pistol shots accompanied her adventures. Then she danced a ragtime in which the tuba's mournful note lived up to Satie's direction in the score which read "triste".

The acrobats who succeeded her began with a flourish on the "bouteillophone" and xylophone. They cavorted to the rhythm of a clumping waltz that expressed all the vulgarity yet all the nostalgia as well of the fairground. This dissolved into a new version of the Manager's theme complete with siren, heavy and thunderous. The Managers danced themselves into exhausted despair, the music drove relentlessly on, and the ballet ended with a pianissimo conclusion to the earlier fugal prelude.

"Ballet réaliste" was Cocteau's definition of *Parade*. Apollinaire's adjective "sur-réaliste", which for the first time gained common currency, emphasises the realism of the ballet as compared with stage conventions so far which had not progressed much beyond the "verismo" of a Mascagni or a Charpentier. *Parade* is as far removed from the traditional ballet as it would be possible to imagine. Even after more than half a century the music still sounds uncompromising in its modernity. With his large orchestra, the largest he ever wrote for, Satie caught the harshness of contemporary life. He mixed ragtime and music-hall in a blend which expressed both the ugliness of a mechanical, commercialised age, and the spirituality that is crushed beneath it.*

The "New Spirit" invoked by Apollinaire had been convincingly translated into music. The score, Satie's most ambitious in terms of size, was built up of many small phrases carefully woven together. He used jazz techniques not only for reasons of effect but because they appealed to him. "Jazz," he said, "tells us its sorrow – and we couldn't care less . . . that's why it's *beautiful* . . . *real* . . ." Jazz amused him with its grotesquerie, and he adopted it, as he'd adopted the café-concert, with an affection that was half mocking, half genuine.

For more than a year he had worked in his usual way, noting down scraps of music in the little exercise-books, recording ideas that occurred to him and adjusting them as time went on, and pencilling in reminders about keys and tempi. Unity was achieved by the fugue that opens and closes the work and by the Managers' theme that dominates the music with its wiry insistence. A great deal of *Parade* was written in a café in the place Denfert-Rochereau, that busy crossroad near the Montparnasse cemetery. There, fortified throughout the evening by a succession of beers

---

* In 1974 the Festival Ballet staged a revival of *Parade* under the personal supervision of the ageless Massine. No longer capable of shocking an audience, it had been rendered merely charming and nostalgic by the passage of time. The greatest success of the evening, to judge from the delighted applause that greeted it, was the prancing of the pantomime horse. Only the music remained aloof and uncompromising.

alternating with Calvados, he pared and polished the stark little phrases. Although he modestly described the result as "a background to certain noises which Cocteau thought necessary to define the atmosphere of his characters", the music he had written gave him intense satisfaction. As he later observed to Poulenc, "it showed that I can orchestrate no worse than the next man. For many people the work only sounded well on the piano. Pure legend!!!"

XXI

Cock and Harlequin

The scandal caused by *Parade* made Satie notorious. The obscure musician, once the hero of a small clique, was suddenly transmuted into a personality who dominated newspaper headlines. For those who wished to keep up to date it was indispensable to have seen *Parade*. Marcel Proust was very taken with the scenery by the artist he called "the great and admirable Picasso". (Over fifty years later, at an auction of scenery and costumes from the Ballets Russes, the back legs of the circus horse in *Parade* went for a modest £160.) André Gide, a conservative in music, and one, moreover, who disapproved of Cocteau, did not like what he saw of the ballet at one of its later performances: "You don't know which you ought to admire more: its pretentiousness or its poverty of invention. Cocteau was strolling backstage, where I went to see him; he looked aged, drawn, in pain. He's well aware that Picasso created the scenery and costumes and Satie the music, but he doubts whether he himself created Picasso and Satie."

The liveliest and most public of all the disagreements caused by *Parade* was that between Satie and the critic Jean Poueigh.* The

* In his book *Picasso: Theatre* (Weidenfeld & Nicolson, 1968) Douglas Cooper has, however, put forward the theory that the critic's name was Voueigh.

latter was a not unfamiliar type: the composer who, unable to get a hearing for his own work, is forced to earn his living by criticising the music of others. Poueigh had studied under Fauré and d'Indy. Although his music was occasionally performed – an extract from a symphonic poem was heard briefly in Paris and Toulouse, and a few chamber works appeared on the programmes of "advanced" music societies – his masterpieces were rarely published. His ballet *Frivolant* trickled on to the stage of the Paris Opéra where it survived thirteen performances, though another venture in the same genre with the uninviting title of *Fünn* had to be turned by its despairing composer into an orchestral suite. Resignedly, he devoted himself to the editing and publication of Pyrenean folk songs for which, it seemed, there was a larger audience than he could charm with *Fünn*. His book *Musiciens français d'aujourd'hui*, a useful compilation which he wrote under the name of Octave Séré, enabled him to feature with more generosity than allowed elsewhere the achievements of "the young musician M. Jean Poueigh".

Of course, the press in general was not kind to *Parade*. Simone de Caillavet, the future wife of André Maurois, tore it to tatters in her article. Pierre Lalo, whose father was the composer Edouard, took a notably harsh tone. What, though, especially angered Satie about Poueigh's hostile remarks was the fact that, at curtain-call, the critic had gone out of his way to congratulate him. Next week his review attacked Satie and denied him any credit at all for craftsmanship or invention.

Satie was thunderstruck at this abrupt turnabout. In his impulsive rage and hurt he took up a pen and traced in his elaborate handwriting on a postcard the following riposte:

Monsieur et cher ami,
Vous n'êtes qu'un cul, mais un cul sans musique.

It was, perhaps, the stinging afterthought – "un cul sans musique" – that wounded Poueigh most deeply. He sued for libel. At the court hearing Poueigh's counsel argued that the postcard, naked and unashamed, could have been read by everyone, postman, concierge, the whole street. His client had been exposed to public ridicule and contempt. And then, with that passion and eloquence for which the French bar is noted, he enlarged his plea into a colourful assault on "modern" art and dismissed its practitioners with the supreme insult of the time: they were "Boches".

Satie appeared in the witness-box, trembling with emotion and outraged by the injustice, gloved hands clasping his bowler hat to his chest with, crooked over his arm, the eternal umbrella. He turned towards his friends who jammed the public gallery and, as the judge pronounced sentence, begged them with a silent glance to still their shouts of indignation. For Poueigh had won his action. The author of the postcard was condemned to a week in prison, a fine of a hundred francs and damages of one thousand.

Outside the courtroom Satie's friends talked and gestured angrily, among them Cocteau, Fargue and Viñes. Poueigh's counsel stalked past them. Cocteau darted forward, beside himself with anger. He waved his cane and slapped the lawyer's face. The police immediately grasped the furious poet and hustled him downstairs whence he returned, some time later, bruised and dishevelled. Satie, much distressed, pleaded with the guardians of order, apologised for his supporter's rashness and humbly took all the fault to himself. He walked to the railway station with a friend, talking as they went of the day's incidents and trying to smooth over the unpleasantness. From time to time he would stop, head thrown back, hand on hip and left arm supported by his umbrella. As he reached the end of a phrase his index finger would reach up and point to the sky with an emphatic flourish.

At about this time he made the acquaintance of the poet Max Jacob. A creature of fantasy, a Jew turned Catholic who lived in eternal dread of punishment for the sins he could not help committing with child-like pleasure, Max was known to everyone in Montparnasse. Picasso was his godfather at his baptism into the Catholic faith. He himself painted – views of his native Brittany, of well-known Paris scenes – and made a sparse living from selling the results to tourists. Gossip he adored, and he retailed it with malicious enjoyment. But he had a strange and unspoilt innocence, and however much people were annoyed with him they soon forgot their irritation in sympathetic laughter. He was a clever mime, a welcome dinner guest who could be relied on to provide sly entertainment. His poetry is a moving blend of lyricism and knockabout humour, of deep mystical feeling and sarcasm. This picturesque genius, bald-headed and bright-eyed, was murdered by the Germans in 1944. He welcomed his martyrdom.

Roland-Manuel had set one of his prose poems to music, and it seemed a good idea to bring Max and Satie together. Satie would not, or could not, come to dinner, but he promised to arrive in the afternoon at Jane Bathori's house where the music was to be played over. It was a "temple of music", so Max described the place afterwards, with photographs of composers everywhere, the walls covered with mock trellis as in a winter-garden, and windowpanes made of bottle ends. Jane Bathori was a hostess without airs. She dressed so unpretentiously that she might have at first been taken for the maid. Her septuagenarian husband, the tenor Emile Engels, was a serene and pink-cheeked figure.

Satie arrived that afternoon in a worried state, fresh from his ordeal in the courtroom. He was full of woe. His publisher, he reported, would not give him any money because it was feared that all the rights in his music would be distrained upon. Poueigh was entitled to seize everything Satie possessed, including his scores. The composer of *Parade* saw himself with a criminal record. He would be unable to travel, America would be forbidden him, his works would never be played in any State theatre . . . (A journey to America and a Satie production at the Opéra are events impossible in any case to imagine.) If he were to appeal he would need a barrister and two thousand francs. The poor man was crushed, overwhelmed. Max tried to calm him – in the most tactless way by quoting examples of great artists who had gone to prison and emerged unscathed. This delightfully inane attempt at comfort, so typical of the well-intentioned but clumsy Max, made Satie bristle. He rushed from the house scarcely pausing to take his leave, and for some time afterwards he looked the other way whenever he chanced to see his Job's comforter.

Satie decided after all to appeal. Fortunately the Prefect of Police was amenable because his son happened to be a friend of the artist Juan Gris who belonged to the same milieu as Satie. Another source of support was the rich dress-maker Jacques Doucet, patron of Max Jacob and so many other poets and artists. Influential sympathisers were not lacking, and Satie once again appeared in court. This time he was successful. He did not go to prison and the judgement for damages against him was reversed. His old spirits returned. He wrote gaily to Pierre Bertin: "Paris is happy. I'm enjoying myself as if I were a very young man. I am going to the ball with my wife and children. I dance all the Bach fugues."

Some of his gaiety was due to new friendships with the young for whom he always had a tenderness. *Parade* was to become a rallying-point for one group of musicians in particular. It included Georges Auric, a prodigy who at the age of fifteen had already set verse by Satie's friend René Chalupt. Like Satie, he had studied under Vincent d'Indy at the Schola Cantorum. Another was Germaine Tailleferre, a beautiful Norman girl who wrote Schumannesque piano music when she was five years old. Her exact contemporary was the Swiss Arthur Honegger. They were soon to be joined by Darius Milhaud who, at the time, was in Brazil acting as secretary to the poet Claudel, then a career diplomatist. The oldest member of the group was Louis Durey, an early but discreet follower of Schoenberg. The second youngest (after Auric, with just over a month's difference) was Francis Poulenc, son of a rich upper-middle-class family and a pupil of Ricardo Viñes.

In June 1917 there was a concert in the rue Huyghens to celebrate the advent of *Parade*. The programme featured new music by Durey, Auric and Honegger, and at the end Satie himself took part in a two-piano version of his ballet. This was the first of a number of concerts given by the young musicians with Satie's connivance and encouragement. At these functions, often organised by the tireless Jane Bathori, he gave little talks and introduced the music. He christened the group "les Nouveaux Jeunes" and became their spiritual godfather. "We have neither a President, nor a Treasurer, nor an archivist, nor a bursar," he remarked. "We haven't any treasure, any way. That suits us very well."

The "Nouveaux Jeunes" soon made themselves known. At one of their recitals the critic Henri Collet, inspired by memories of that famous group of five Russian composers which included Balakirev, Borodin, Cui, Mussorgsky and Rimsky-Korsakov, nicknamed them "les Six". His review, which he called "Les Cinq Russes, les Six Français et Satie", gave them the title by which they were known throughout the Twenties. A second article, "Les Six Français", confirmed it.

Thus linked together by a journalist's whim, they decided to accept the situation, though all they really had in common were youth and friendship. If Milhaud was a Southerner with a lyrical bias, Honegger had an attachment to German romanticism and Durey found his models in Schoenberg, Debussy and Ravel. Auric and Poulenc, perhaps because they were the youngest, showed the most sympathy towards the ideas which other people tended to bestow on "les Six". For Cocteau saw in the group an opportunity to publicise theories which he had already been formulating. As time went on the young composers found, with surprise and elation, that Cocteau's inventive brilliance often forecast their experiments and summed them up in language of striking originality.

His pamphlet, *Le Coq et l'Arlequin*, set the stage for the new movement. In epigram, paradox and aphorism, he exhorted the young to be daring – the essential tact, he pointed out, was to know to what extent you could go too far. The young should not invest in gilt-edged securities. They should react positively against harmful influences. Among the latter was music both German and Russian. The siren charms of Wagner and Stravinsky were to be resisted. Even Debussy, with his mistiness and imprecision, set a bad example.*

Music needed to be purged. French music, in particular, must rid itself of the cloudy colouring injected by foreign influences. The call was for down-to-earth music, everyday music. Bareness and simplicity were all. Cocteau found his ideal in the work of Erik Satie, who had dared to be simple. He had rejected the treacherous lure of the Impressionists and evolved a style that was admirably lucid. The score of *Parade* was a masterpiece of architecture unflawed by rhetoric.

Cocteau made his analogy with the music-hall, where the technique of the acrobat is reduced down to its essentials. Superfluous gesture is eliminated, flourishes are not allowed. Everything is subordinated to a dominant concept which is followed with

* But not all of Cocteau's gems were original. The famous one quoted above – about knowing how to go too far – was pilfered, of all unlikely sources, from Charles Péguy. Cocteau blandly confessed this to the American composer Ned Rorem in 1952. (*The Paris and New York Diaries of Ned Rorem*, Discus Avon, 1970.)

single-minded austerity. This, he argued, was Satie's technique, pure and objective.

Le Coq et l'Arlequin had a powerful effect. It was read and discussed with admiration for the wit and intellectual dexterity – or with disapproval for its advocacy of the vulgar music-hall and its tilting against Debussy and Wagner. It quickly sold out.

Now, more than ever, Satie was consecrated as father-figure of the Six. He contributed to a short-lived periodical devised by Cocteau and printed on brightly coloured poster paper. More of a broadsheet than a magazine, *Le Coq* appeared at irregular intervals and crowed its way through a number of issues. Other members of the Six wrote for it, and so did the young Raymond Radiguet, Cocteau's sensational new prodigy. "M. Ravel," Satie observed acidly, "has refused the Légion d'honneur but all his music accepts it." (Ravel was now very much in disfavour, along with Debussy. "He is the leader of the sub-Debussyists," Satie wrote in his notebooks. "In cold blood he has just – *again* – refused the Cross of the Légion d'honneur . . . What *does* he want? . . . He must be doing it for a bet." And, presumably in a gibe at Ravel's war service, he scribbled: "Of course . . . During the next war Ravel will *still* be an airman – on a lorry.")

In another article for *Le Coq* he divided musicians into poets and pedants. The poets included Chopin, Liszt, Schubert and Mussorgsky. In the ranks of the pedants was Rimsky-Korsakov. Mozart and Beethoven belonged to the poets, the first with a style that was light, the second with one that was heavy. Debussy, a poet himself, nonetheless had pedants among his followers. Their orchestration was thick, clouded, and not really orchestration at all but merely piano writing translated into orchestral terms. While not wishing to criticise Debussy, Satie deplored the hangers-on who gathered in his wake. There could, he rightly declared, be no such thing as a "School of Satie" or a "Satiste" movement. He opposed the notion. There must be no slavery in art. He had always tried to throw his followers off the scent and kept them guessing about the nature of every new work of his. That was the only way to avoid the fate of becoming a "chef d'école" or pedant.

Caught up in the excitement so shrewdly stimulated by Cocteau, pleased and flattered by the youthful admiration of the Six, delighted with the notoriety that had come his way at last, Satie broke with his old friends Debussy and Ravel. Jealousy tainted his feeling, and resentment, and a certain malicious jubilation in the fact that he, for so long the poor relation, was now enjoying some of the limelight that they had monopolised. He also felt, genuinely, that their music was inappropriate to the age and had been overtaken by his own work:

It is certain – alas! – that I have neither taste nor talent [he wrote ironically, now that his music seemed to be coming into its own]. I've been told so enough times . . . And so I'd like, with your permission, to speak about a matter that is not at all personal and has not the slightest interest.

Allow me to address myself politely to the following question: what is the Prix de Thingummy, please? A superior creature, outstanding, of the highest quality, exceptional, out of print and extremely rare . . .

When I think that Debussy himself was on matey terms with that lot! . . . [i.e. the winners of the Grand Prix de Rome].

So it was that he had the weakness to let himself be nominated to the Conseil Supérieur of the Conservatoire. He was a true victim of the early teaching he'd had, although, so far as he could, he repaired the damage it did with the greatest of energy.

At the time of Satie's new-found celebrity the composer of *Pelléas et Mélisande* lay desperately ill and in the throes of the malady that was finally to destroy him after a long and painful siege. Overwhelmed by the tragedies of war and by the awareness of his own doom, he could not appreciate the turn his old friend's career had taken. When he heard of concerts devoted to Satie's music and of lectures being given about him, he was mystified. He could not attend because he was already confined to his room, and he was tempted to dismiss as practical jokery the reports he heard of their success. Or perhaps they were the result of yet another among the interminable conspiracies and intrigues that made up the life of musical Paris?

Satie knew of his attitude and was extremely annoyed at what he took for a jealous refusal to acknowledge his achievements. He wrote a brutal letter which Debussy received a few weeks before he died. The invalid's trembling hand crumpled it against the blanket of his bed and, suddenly, the paper tore.

"Forgive me!" he murmured, tears in his eyes, like a scolded child.

It was, perhaps, Debussy's approval that Satie had wanted above all. Circumstances forbade it. Too late, after Debussy's death, he realised the truth. "How I must have made Debussy suffer when he was ill," he lamented.

XXII

Socrates

Miss Winnaretta Singer, who hailed from Yonkers, was the elder
daughter of Isaac, the sewing-machine millionaire. She journeyed
to Europe for her education and became an accomplished painter,
organist and pianist. The unwary tended to mistake one of her
paintings for a Manet. The enterprises which had the support of
her immense fortune attested to the variety of her benevolence.
The Ballets Russes were an obvious target for her subsidies. Less
spectacular were archaeological work in Greece and the Salvation
Army.

   She also collected pictures. At an auction she battled hard
to acquire one of Monet's loveliest paintings, a view of a tulip
field near Haarlem. The rival bidder, dizzied at last by the vertig-
inous sums announced from the rostrum, gave up regretfully.
He was the prince Edmond de Polignac. "How maddened I
was!" he said. "That picture was snatched away from me by an
American woman whose name I vowed to eternal damnation."
A few years later she changed that name for his and became
the princesse de Polignac. The Monet at last entered into
his possession and hung on the wall of his mansion in the rue
Cortambert.

Winnaretta's sister also married into the French nobility. As the duchesse Decazes she was, so Marcel Proust reminds us with delight, related to the la Rochefoucaulds, the Croys, the Luynes and the Gontaut-Birons. Through this link Winnaretta blossomed into the aunt and great-aunt of many a duchess and many a count. But her salon was not remarkable alone for the impeccable quarterings of her guests. The prince de Polignac, son of a famous minister to King Charles X, was himself a skilled musician. The woods and forest scenes around his country home at Fontainebleau inspired him to write songs. These he had performed at his town house against a background provided by photographs of wood-land views projected on to a large screen. He arranged produc-tions of Rameau's *Dardanus* at his home in the rue Cortambert, and Bach sonatas and Fauré songs were often heard at elegant little recitals in the music-room. In the closing years of his life the prince spent much time in Amsterdam and Venice, his pain-ter's eye revelling in the qualities of light there. He bought a handsome Palazzo in Venice. It was, he said, the only town where you could talk by an open window without having to raise your voice.

He died in 1901 after eight years of a civilised and happy marriage with the former Miss Singer. His widow continued the tradition of art and music which they cultivated together. Their only disharmony had been caused by the temperature of the studio in the rue Cortambert. Winnaretta always felt too warm. He, very susceptible to cold, always suffered from the incessant draughts that froze the atmosphere. So he was permanently wrapped up in rugs and travelling blankets. When friends teased him about his bulky appearance, he replied: "What do you expect? Anaxagoras said that the whole of life is a journey!"

The receptions in the rue Cortambert, at Fontainebleau and in the Venetian palazzo went on with a luxury undimmed. The princesse de Polignac entertained generously. She was a hospitable patron to Fauré, whom she commissioned to write music for her. Like many other composers, he spent agreeable holidays at her home in Venice. Ravel and Stravinsky received commissions from her. At her salon Milhaud introduced to her Cole Porter, and the result was the jazz ballet *Within The Quota*. She sponsored also Milhaud's opera *Les Malheurs d'Orphée*.

She was the dedicatee of Poulenc's two-piano concerto and

organ concerto. At the outbreak of war in 1939 she wrote to him from England where she was staying:

I deserve none of the nice things you say to me – I'm the one who owes you a great debt of gratitude for so many hours of lovely music, and for having written for me the Venice concerto and the Paris one, whose deep beauty haunts me.

My family have asked me to stay in England for the time being – and I shall be living near a niece in the country to which the 1870 war led me in my early years.

The wheel had come full circle. Her last years were spent in Torquay. She died in 1943 at the age of seventy-eight.

The sardonic eye and the well-clipped beard of the Republican Erik Satie often appeared at the salon in the rue Cortambert. Like so many others, he shared in the princess' bounty. Did he appreciate the irony? He, the left-wing socialist, frequented the drawing-room of this rich and aristocratic lady and gratefully accepted the favours she showed him. There he spoke with a grave and classic courtesy to dukes and counts and duchesses. His manner was formal, his deportment irreproachable. The paradox was that nowhere else could he have found support and sympathy for his avant-garde music. All the official establishments were closed to him. The old tradition still persisted in Paris whereby a handful of big public concerts was supplemented by many smaller functions and recitals given in private houses or at the headquarters of struggling societies. New music was more often heard through the efforts of the latter than of the former, and it depended a great deal on private patronage. Satie had no choice. His aristocratic patrons were readier to hear his music than were the proletariat with whom he identified. But he could not resist the temptation of an occasional deadpan reference to the "Arcueil Soviet" which he dropped in to tease.*

* Marcel Proust had heard of Satie as early as 1894, the presumed date of his essay "Mélomanie" in *Les Plaisirs et les jours*. Satie was very little known at this time and certainly had not yet begun to visit the great houses frequented by the novelist. Perhaps his association with the Rosicrucians and Péladan had brought him to Proust's attention. In "Mélomanie" his name is mentioned in the course of argument, simply as a modern composer, and not as a particular result of knowledge of his music. This opinion is strengthened by the evidence of the manuscript, where Proust had originally written the name of the composer Ernest Chausson before replacing it with Satie's.

At the time of his legal entanglement with Jean Poueigh the princesse de Polignac gave him eleven hundred francs to help with expenses. After he had met his commitments there remained a large sum still. As a result of the war, he told her, he found himself "destitute of *sols*, ducats and other articles of that kind". Might he keep this remainder? Might he look on it as an "advance"? No doubt the open-handed princess agreed.

His mention of an advance presumably referred to the work he had already begun on *Socrate* as a commission from the princess, to whom he subsequently dedicated it. He started composing it almost as soon as *Parade* was finished and may, in fact, have been working on both pieces at the same time. The two works are wholly different in their nature and conception. They illustrate most vividly his belief in constantly seeking fresh fields, in renewing himself by means of ceaseless experiment. Repetition meant artistic death.

Why Socrates? As a schoolboy Satie always did well in classics and history. At a superficial level he himself, as an avuncular companion to the Six and other young musicians, presented a Socratic figure. More to the point, he must have felt a special sympathy for the old Greek philosopher's character. Socrates was judged and condemned for bringing in alien gods and corrupting youth. Had not Satie been violently criticised for introducing strange music and gathering around him a band of unruly young who came under his subversive influence? Socrates lived a plain and simple life. He refused luxury and riches. They left him indifferent. He was the sort of man whom admirers describe as uncompromising in his ideals and whom enemies attack as quixotically stubborn. With all this he had a sharp sense of humour. These traits were to be found in Satie. The hermit of Arcueil lived near to poverty. He despised wealth and material goods. He preached – and practised – an obstinate independence. He loved the young. His humour was unique. And in Socrates' unfortunate marriage to Xanthippe there could be seen a strong argument for Satie's own lifelong bachelorhood.

His idea was to write a sort of chamber oratorio. He based his text on Victor Cousin's translation of the Platonic dialogues. Cousin was a disciple of that great metaphysician Maine de Biron. In the early nineteenth century he proved to be an eloquent professor of philosophy and later a government minister. He wrote and lectured fluently on the history of his subject, was an early propagandist for Hegel, and brought out a pioneering edition of Descartes. His philosophical system was attractive and undemanding. It was based on the idea of God and took much of its stimulus from the bland affirmations of Rousseau. It was known as eclecticism, for it chose all those ideas in past philosophies that seemed most apposite and rejected those which rang false. The method is at once appealing and treacherously frail.

On 6 January 1917 Satie wrote to Valentine Hugo. She was then not well, exhausted by recent stormy arguments with him and depressed by her engagement to a rich but not very congenial young man. (This was not, of course, the delightful Jean Hugo whom she eventually married.) He enquired anxiously after her health:

Are you seeing a doctor? Above all, do nothing rash.

I've got a very heavy cold. I shan't go to Mme Garrett's tomorrow. I've written to her about it and asked her to excuse me. I'd like to have gone to that dinner, but – *really* – I'm too tired and ill.

I'm busy with *La Vie de Socrate*. I'm frightened to death of bungling this work. I want it to be as white and pure as antiquity.

I'm all of a dither about it and don't know where to put myself. What a splendid piece there is to be written on this idea. It's *fantastic* . . .

He mentioned incidents with Diaghilev, who was about to go to Rome for rehearsals of *Parade*, and apologised for troubling her with his worries. "You, dear friend, are an exquisite magical person, worthy of reverence," he ended. "Yes. Good morning from Erik Satie."

She began to see that her prospective marriage was ill-advised and not worth the sacrifice of her liberty. She wanted to get away from her problems and take a holiday in the warm South. But she did not feel she could go until Satie was in a happier mood and better able to deal with the gestation of his new work. That winter, "the coldest, the cruellest of the war", she took refuge in a hotel. Then another letter arrived from Satie.

"What am I doing?" he wrote. "I'm working on the *Vie de Socrate*. I've found a fine translation: the one by Victor Cousin.

Plato is a perfect collaborator, very gentle and never importunate. A dream, eh! I've written about this to the good Princess. I'm swimming in happiness. At last I'm free, free as air, free as water, as the wild sheep. Long live Plato! Long live Victor Cousin! I'm free! so very free! What happiness! I send you a great big hug. You're my beloved big girl. Your grandfather, E.S."

All was well. She knew that she could safely leave him on his own in Paris. At Cannes each week she received a letter from her "grandfather". "Are you having fine weather?" he enquired. "The sun is as cold as ice here. He must be short of coal too."

Victor Cousin's translation is a scholarly one – a version, that is to say, which aims more at the precise rendering of content than at felicities of style. This was all to Satie's purpose. The simpler the text the better. He did not want fine language that distracted attention from the subject or elegant phrases that demanded admiration and obscured the issue. The three dialogues he chose were from the "Symposium", "Phaedrus" and "Phaedo". These he shortened considerably, eliding what seemed to be unnecessary phrases, cutting out whole passages, and censoring pages where even Cousin's modest lyricism allowed itself a poetic flight. There is little philosophy, technically speaking, in the compact wordage that Satie distilled. It gives, rather, a concise picture of Socrates the man as seen through the eyes of those who admired him most.

In the first section, "Portrait de Socrate", Alcibiades praises the charm of the philosopher. He compares him with the satyr flute player Marsyas. (Is not Socrates, he remarks, like those figures of Silenus which you see, flute in hand, in sculptors' studios, and which, on being opened, are seen to conceal statues of the gods inside?) Marsyas cast a spell upon men with the lovely melodies his mouth drew from the instrument. So, too, does Socrates, except that he makes his effect not with reed pipes but with his speech alone. When listening to him, says Alcibiades, I feel my heart beat more strongly than if I were impelled by the dancing frenzy of the Corybants. His words cause my tears to flow, and I see many other people experiencing the same emotions.

"You have praised me," replies Socrates, gently deflecting the ardent words of his follower, "and now it is my turn to do the same for the neighbour who sits on my right . . ."

The next section, "The banks of the Ilyssus", is a conversation between Socrates and Phaedrus as they walk by the riverside. They find a tall plane-tree that will give them shade and coolness, and beside it thick grass to sit on. The water here flows bright and limpid. Socrates tells the legend of Boreas.

The "Mort de Socrate" concludes the work. Phaedo recounts how each day after Socrates had been sentenced his followers assembled to visit him in prison. There they found him, recently liberated of his chains, together with Xanthippe and one of their children. Socrates rubbed his freed leg. What a strange thing, he said, is the feeling men call pleasure – and what wonderful links it has with the pain which they claim to be its opposite! Is it not by way of enjoyment and suffering that the body overcomes and tames the soul? It is all the more difficult for him to persuade other men that he does not regard his present condition as a misfortune, since he knows he cannot even persuade his own disciples of it. So he tells the story of the dying swan, which, aware that it is fated to meet the god it serves, sings on its last day of existence more beautifully than ever before.

An envoy announces that the time is near. "Socrates," he says, "I hope I shall not have to make the same reproach to you as I have to others: as soon as I come to tell them by order of the magistrates that the poison must be drunk, they rage at me and curse me; but you I have always found to be the bravest, gentlest and best of those who have ever entered this prison, and at the moment I know you are not angry with me but with those who are the cause of your misfortune. Now that you know I have come to say farewell, try to bear with resignation what is unavoidable." He turns away in tears.

Socrates orders the poison to be prepared and brought in. A slave carries it to him and the condemned man asks instruction of an official. "Very good, my friend, but what must I do? It's up to you to tell me."

"There is nothing to do," is the reply, "but to walk about after you have drunk until you feel your legs becoming heavy. Then you must lie on your bed and the poison will act of itself."

The cup is proffered and Socrates drinks it calmly while his disciples weep. "In spite of all my efforts," says Phaedo, "my tears escaped in such abundance that I covered myself with my cloak to weep for myself; for it wasn't Socrates' misfortune that

I bewailed, but my own, in thinking what a friend I was about to lose . . ."

The philosopher's legs take on the heaviness predicted. He lies face upwards on his couch as he has been told. The man who administered the poison grasps his foot firmly and asks if he feels anything. He answers no. Then the legs go numb, the upper part of the body freezes and stiffens. As soon as the cold reaches Socrates' heart, says the man, he will be gone.

"Crito", murmurs Socrates, "we owe a cock to Aesculapius; do not forget to settle the debt."

A convulsive movement shakes his body. His look becomes fixed. Crito closes his mouth and eyes. "Such, Echecrates, was the end of our friend . . . of the wisest and justest of all men."

Socrate is the composer's longest work. He called it a "drame symphonique". This is misleading, for its dimensions are small. The score asks only for flute, oboe, English and French horns, clarinet, bassoon, trumpet, harp, kettle-drums and strings. Like Racine, who drew his magical effects from the use of a severely limited number of simple words, Satie restricts himself to a tiny vocabulary. The slim filament of sound which opens the "drame symphonique" may widen a little as time goes on, it may shift rhythm almost unnoticeably and change colour with a slight variation of nuance, but the tone remains the same throughout: cool, lucid, fluent. The choice of four sopranos to sing the vocal parts emphasises the purity of the concept. When Alcibiades traces his portrait of the philosopher, the direction instructs: "As if reading." The cadences of speech are reproduced in a free-flowing metre.

In many ways *Socrate* is the culmination of Satie's musical development and the flowering of all his experiments. At the very beginning and elsewhere come reminiscences of the Gregorian mode. The swirling run on the harp as Alcibiades is about to speak of the effect Socrates' talk had on him recalls a similar figure in *Parade* at the entry of the American Girl. Socrates, on the banks of the Ilyssus, speaks in a gentle, rocking waltz tempo with touches of the *Trois Valses distinguées du précieux dégoûté*. At one point there is even a discreet cake-walk passage. But never do these elements seem incongruous. They are refined and transmuted. This is music without a seam or visible join.

Violence and melodrama are absent. The most dramatic incident is a sudden leap of an octave in the voice or a sometime accidental. The continuous melody embraces a number of small independent phrases and keeps up the line unbroken. It floats serenely onward in the timeless fashion of the *Gymnopédies*. Satie's own sketches for *Socrate* show his preoccupation with melody. He saw it not only as the basic idea but also as the contour of a work, quite as much as form and content. Harmony he viewed as "lighting".

Yet although there is no conventional "development" in *Socrate*, no obvious climax and no easy use of accepted musical techniques to create and then dissolve excitement, the emotion is there. Because he so rigorously disciplined himself to employ the barest of elements, when Satie wishes to darken feeling or express tragedy he has only to deviate a little from the narrow path to gain his effect. Poignancy hinges on the steady repetition of a simple chord. Drama arises from a soft succession of ostinato phrases. If one looks at the whole span of *Socrate*, the layout shows that, while denying himself all the familiar tricks for arousing musical excitement, Satie has plotted a graph which rises with remorseless drive and perfect gradation until it reaches those last bleak pages of Socrates' death, where the suggestion of a bell tolling on a pedal chord is repeated until it vanishes into eternity.

With *Socrate* he achieved a sort of "Greek" perfection which is his most notable contribution to music. It has not grown old or wrinkled, as so much of Romantic music tends to do with time. There is no period charm about it. Reticent, austere, dignified in its rejection of the obvious, *Socrate* keeps its colouring untarnished and its clear lines unmuddled.

The preface to *Socrate* observes: "This method of drawing with a precise and severe line is rather as if Ingres had illustrated these passages from Plato at the request of Victor Cousin." It remarks that Satie had wanted to pare down his music, to show it as modest in its nudity. The commentator was René Chalupt whom Satie had asked to write a few words introducing it. He deliberately avoided calling on Jean Cocteau, who, he knew, would have been delighted to oblige. This time, he determined, Cocteau would not be allowed to lay his greedy hands on the work. Satie had had enough of this over *Parade*. *Socrate*, he resolved, would be his own and no one else's. (At later revivals of *Parade* he was to complain bitterly to Valentine Hugo that Cocteau had not changed since the time of the original production: he was still hogging everything. In that case, Satie enquired, why hadn't he designed the sets and costumes and written the music as well?)

Socrate had an early performance on 24 June 1918, at the home of Jane Bathori. A handful of friends heard the soprano sing it to the composer's accompaniment. They were moved by its strange beauty. Another hearing followed soon after at the home of comte Etienne de Beaumont. He, like the princesse de Polignac, was to prove a sympathetic patron of Satie. The composer had shown the manuscript to Pierre Bertin and his pianist wife Marcelle Meyer. Beaumont got to hear of it. "You must sing it in my house," he declared. "Will you, please, Bertin?"

The resourceful Bertin, an actor who happened to have a pleasing voice, though daunted by high passages in the work, accepted the challenge. Beaumont had his way, as he usually did.

Etienne de Beaumont lived near the boulevard des Invalides in an eighteenth-century mansion at No. 2 rue Duroc. He belonged to the Bonnins de la Bonninière de Beaumont, an old Catholic family from Touraine. His interests lay in jewellery, which he designed for Cartiers, in art, and in the ballet which he loved with passion. For several ballets he himself designed sets or costumes. *Le Beau Danube* and *Gaîté parisienne* were among them.

His wife came of an even more distinguished and wealthy family. Their marriage was an affectionate one. The comtesse de Beaumont's quieter tastes did not prevent her from joining loyally in the social life her husband enjoyed. He adored dressing up and giving lavish entertainment to his aristocratic friends and the artists whom he supported. She did not even seem to mind his attachments to the handsome young men who passed regularly through his life. It is pleasant to know that the elegant but erudite comtesse was happiest when immersed in Greek poetry. Was there a hint of malice, a suggestion of getting her own back, when she eventually published, with illustrations by Marie Laurencin, a translation of Sappho?

She exercised a discreet authority over her husband. Though she gave an impression of vagueness, of dreaminess even, she was full of commonsense. Her husband, wrapped in fantasy, depended heavily on her. He could not do without her, and their existence together relied on a subtle balance between that side of his nature which needed Madame de Beaumont and the side which found its expression in his closest friendships, those with Jean Cocteau and Lucien Daudet, the dandified man about town, writer, son of Alphonse and brother of the acrimonious Léon. During the war Beaumont had organised a Red Cross ambulance unit. His abilities were much praised. He deserves credit, too, for having looked after Cocteau, who was one of the unit's auxiliaries, and for having preserved that mercurial figure among shell and shrapnel at the Front.

Socrate was given at the Beaumont home soon after the end of the war. Pierre Bertin acquitted himself honourably before an audience which had taken up again the pre-war habit of wearing evening dress. It may have been at this or at another private hearing that Stravinsky first made acquaintance with *Socrate*. Although, like others, he found it a little boring in its regularity, he thought the music for Socrates' death to be "touching and dignifying in a unique way". At the end of it Satie, who accompanied, turned to his hearers and said, in mock bourgeois style: "Voilà, messieurs, dames."

By the following year Cocteau had inserted himself into the framework. On 21 March *Socrate* was heard at Sylvia Beach's bookshop in the rue de l'Odéon. Suzanne Balguerie was the singer and the composer assisted at the piano. The programme announced: "Préface par Jean Cocteau." Literature was represented by André Gide and the poets Claudel and Jammes, drawn there probably by Cocteau's persuasion. Gide does not seem to have been impressed. Claudel, who surprisingly had sympathy for modern music and was to collaborate with Milhaud, is likely to have been more favourable to what he heard.

The first "official" performance of *Socrate* does not seem to have taken place until January 1920. Satie asked the composer Gustave Samazeuilh, then secretary of the Société Nationale de Musique, if it could be given at one of their concerts. This was done and the work began to find a wider audience.

Naturally it aroused argument. Its defenders waxed as hot as those who disliked it. There were hisses and scornful laughter. One opinion claimed that Satie had merely imitated the techniques of *Pelléas et Mélisande*, although, in fact, his cool sobriety is totally different from Debussy's misty romanticism. It is true that Satie did not help matters by his public declarations. "Those who do not understand are requested by me to assume an attitude of submission and inferiority," he wrote defiantly. To a critic he observed: "You can see what I wanted to achieve: originality by way of platitude."

But when he heard the boos and hisses that greeted *Socrate*, he simply remarked: "Odd, isn't it?" For despite the mocking appearance he thought himself obliged to keep up, he must have felt that with *Socrate* he had written his masterpiece.

XXIII

Eccentric Belle

The war years were difficult for Satie, particularly towards the end. There was talk that he had joined the militia as an NCO and was engaged in mysterious war work. He could be relied upon to embellish the enigma with oracular humour that confused the issue. The writer Blaise Cendrars found him during a heavy air raid ensconced at the foot of the obelisk in the place de la Concorde. Cendrars leaned forward, thinking him dead. The body stirred and Satie's eye twinkled faintly. He felt, he explained, protected by the obelisk towering over him. And besides, he was composing some music for the Pharaoh's wife who lay buried underneath. "Nobody ever thinks about her. It took this filthy bombardment to make me come here for the first time. Not bad, eh?" His hand spread out over his beard and he looked up mischievously at the monument.

He is reported also to have entered an air raid shelter at a time when Parisians' nerves were badly alarmed by attacks on the capital. "Good evening. I have come to die with you," he announced equably.

In private his humour failed to alleviate a sense of despair. On 4 October 1917 he wrote to his publisher Alexandre Rouart of the

Rouart–Lerolle firm: "I'm in the most critical situation: penniless. This is all the more painful to me in that I fear I shan't be able, thanks to this stupid poverty, to finish my *Socrate* for the princesse de Polignac ... Copeau [the theatrical producer] has commissioned music from me for three of the Tabarin farces. Will you be the publisher of these things?" Rouart did not publish them and neither, in fact, does Satie appear to have written them.

He was depressed by the separation from his friends that war entailed. In August 1918, he reached the lowest and blackest depths of his misery. As usual, Valentine Hugo received his confidences:

I'm suffering too much [he wrote]. There seems to be a curse on me. This beggar's life revolts me.

I'm looking for, and want to find, a job – some sort of employment – however small it may be. I'm *fed-up to the back bloody teeth* with Art: it's brought me too many muck-ups. It's a *sucker's* craft is the artist's, if I dare say so.

Forgive me, dear friend, these true remarks – only too true.

I'm writing to everyone. No one answers me, even with a friendly note. Dash it!

You, dear friend, who have always been so kind to your old friend, will you see, I beg of you, whether it wouldn't be possible to fix him up somewhere where he could earn his bread.

Anywhere. I wouldn't be put off by the meanest sort of task, I swear to you.

See about it as quickly as you can: I'm at the end of my tether and can't wait.

Art? For a month and more I've not been able to write a note.

I've not a single idea, nor do I *want* to have one. So?

Valentine Hugo was unable to help. She asked a friend, the musician André Lebey, for aid. Not long afterwards Satie received an anonymous gift of a thousand francs.

With the end of the war things improved a little. Satie was even persuaded to go to Belgium for, among other things, performances of *Socrate* in Ghent and Brussels. He was an inveterate stay-at-home who disliked travelling and preferred the gloomy streets of Arcueil and his favourite Paris café to anything that "abroad" could offer. Pierre Bertin, deploying the maximum of charm, at last succeeded in winkling him out of his old haunts and installing him on the train. The carriage was filled with members of the Six, their friends, a dancer or two, and "a whole circus" as Bertin afterwards described it. The journey proved gay and noisy.

Satie arrived at Ghent in a very bad temper. He and his colleagues were to play at a charity gala in the opera house organised by the Francophile mayor of the city. The theatre was large and beautiful, though the intimate music-making of the Six tended to get lost in its grand open spaces. Satie came on to the vast stage grumbling and muttering. With Georges Auric he played the *Trois Morceaux en forme de poire*. Applause rang out briskly. In those immediate post-war days France and things French enjoyed great popularity in Belgium.

The party went on to Brussels. There Satie made an acquaintance whose youth and charm helped to compensate for the inconvenience of the travelling he loathed. At that time the Belgian painter E. L. T. Mesens was seventeen years old. With his friend René Magritte and others he afterwards formed the important Belgian group of Surrealists. In 1936 he helped organise the famous International Surrealist Exhibition in London. Here he lived for some thirty years and ran, with adorable eccentricity, a Cork Street art gallery stuffed with what were then almost unsaleable pictures by Ernst, Miro, Magritte . . .*

When Satie met him Mesens was a student at the Brussels Conservatoire. During the war and the German occupation, which left the young with plenty of spare time, Mesens read widely. In back-numbers of magazines he discovered Satie's "Mémoires d'un amnésique". Their humour delighted him. His enjoyment was complete when he started working through Satie's music. Already the composer of several songs, he was stimulated to further efforts.

The singer Evelyne Brélia, who helped to introduce Satie's work in Belgium, promised to put Mesens in touch with his hero. Satie was staying at the old Hôtel Britannique in the place du Trône. Even then this venerable establishment, though still trail-

* George Melly, the jazz musician and film critic, knew him well. In an affectionate obituary he described how Mesens spent three hours at his toilette every morning: this involved making a ritual choice from "an enormous pile of Gillette razor blades". He shaved three times. The blades were then carefully dried and rewrapped.

ing a shred of its old aristocratic glory, was out of date and not frequented by the truly fashionable. Mesens and Evelyne Brélia were five minutes late, and when they arrived in the place du Trône they saw, far off, an impatient Satie marching up and down on the pavement outside his hotel, his umbrella under his arm. With him was Pierre Bertin. Even before the introductions were made, Satie threw a black look at Evelyne Brélia and said sharply: "You're late, dear friend." He went on muttering complaints about the rest of the party, Georges Auric and Bertin's wife Marcelle Meyer, who were also unpunctual. When they turned up they were tartly greeted.

Then Satie's mood changed. Putting on his most genial smile he inspected Mesens from head to foot. The young man wore long hair, a nascent beard, a velvet jacket, a floppy bow tie and rust-coloured trousers. (Soon afterwards, like Satie himself, he was to reject these arty raiments, and from then on to sport the neatest bourgeois suits and well-polished shoes.) The group set off to the concert, Satie and his new friend bringing up the rear.

"This hotel is very chic, dear friend . . . much too chic for a poo-er man like me," observed Satie in amiable tones. He devoted the rest of the day to Mesens, asked his friends to keep him for lunch, talked with him all the afternoon and obtained an invitation for him to a party that evening. "They'll probably play music there," he bantered, "but we'll manage to chat a bit in a corner."

Their friendship never faltered. When Mesens came to Paris Satie would send him a telegram fixing a meeting outside some café or other. It was Satie who arranged for him a trip up the Eiffel Tower and who carefully detailed all the beauties of Paris laid out below. Though poor, Mesens recalled, he was very generous. One day, after meeting as usual at a café, Satie asked him to come to the office of the Société des Auteurs. One of his works had been played abroad and there were a few hundred francs in performing rights to be collected. Satie emerged full of bustle. "Now," he said, "I'm inviting you to lunch in one of the finest places in Paris. You'll remember it." And the meal was, indeed, unforgettable. He took, Mesens said, an obvious and childish delight in doing this good turn.

To Mesens he showed odd streaks of Anglomania. "Do you know the worthy Leigh Henry?" he would ask. "He's a fine old fellow." (Leigh Henry? The name sounds like those fictions with which he decorated his music. Mesens thought it referred to one of his English friends.) The young Belgian took his cue and mentioned the British composer Lord Berners, whose choice of titles – *Petite marche funèbre pour une tante à héritage*, for example – reminded him of Satie. The composer's reaction was curious. He showed irritation and snapped: "He's a professional amateur. He hasn't understood." When in a better humour he would explain to Mesens the reason for his third baptismal name of Leslie. "It's a Scottish name from my mother's family," he pointed out, adding with mock surprise, "What! Don't you know the Leslie clan?"

Towards the end of his life he travelled again to Belgium and delivered lectures in Brussels and Antwerp. He gave to Mesens, as a souvenir, his lecture notes which had first been ornately inscribed in pencil and then traced over with ink on the pages of a school exercise book. The final leaves contained a meticulous plan of the main centres of Brussels with careful directions on how to reach them.

On occasion Mesens would show him his compositions. Satie examined them with interest and passed judgement that was discreet and tactful. He gave novel advice and avoided always a pedantic tone. Their discussions strayed on to the subject of painting. More often they talked about poetry: poems that deserved to be set to music, poems not to be touched at any price . . . In that respect they very rarely found themselves in agreement. But, however hot their arguments, they remained close friends. For the interest Satie took in young people, Mesens recalled, was "genuine and very lively".

The Belgian trip of 1919 and the acquaintance of Mesens seem to have restored Satie's musical inspiration. Between August and November of that year he wrote the five *Nocturnes*. These, together with the *Sonatine bureaucratique* which he composed in July 1917, are his last works for piano. The *Sonatine bureaucratique* is a straightforward pastiche of Clementi set in a humorous verbal framework. The civil servant is described setting off for work and arriving at the office. He sits comfortably in his chair and dreams of promotion while he hums "an old Peruvian air collected from a deaf-mute in Brittany". A touch of the *Trois Valses distinguées du précieux dégoûté* is slipped in towards the middle of the third movement, but otherwise the piece is an amusing skit on the neo-classic style. It is the sort of exercise that the Six took up with gusto, notably Auric in *Les Fâcheux* and Tailleferre with her piano concerto and the ballet *Marchand d'oiseaux*.

More important from a purely musical point of view are the five *Nocturnes* and a *Premier Menuet*. There is no humour here and no wish to entertain. The music is written in conventionally barred notation. The objective tone is entirely alien to the world of John Field or Chopin, those traditional masters of the form, and yet the emotion, though strictly controlled, is no less deep. If, in the *Sonatine bureaucratique*, Satie skilfully adopted the outer trappings of classicism, in the *Nocturnes* he captured its spirit. The mood of *Socrate* is perpetuated, and the monochrome sound of the piano flows evenly in a manner that is described as "Doux et calme". This is, in a way, a return to his earlier manner. It is as if he had to purge himself by means of the jocular whimsicalities of his middle period before evolving the austerity which runs like a silver seam through the *Nocturnes*. Among the dedicatees of his grave farewell to the piano were Marcelle Meyer, Valentine Hugo, the comtesse Etienne de Beaumont and Jean Cocteau's mother.

A year later, on 21 February, his *Trois petites pièces montées* were given at a concert organised by the ubiquitous Cocteau and financed by Etienne de Beaumont. This was the famous occasion when *Le Boeuf sur le toit* made its first appearance. Yet another example of Cocteau's impresario gifts, the ballet introduced clowns, ideas inspired by American silent films, and many other of his preoccupations at the time.* The Six were well represented. Milhaud provided the light-hearted music for the ballet. The overture was by Poulenc, who also furnished the song cycle *Cocardes* to words by Cocteau. Auric's piece was *Adieu, New York!*, a foxtrot in the same style as Satie's "Ragtime du Paquebot" from *Parade*. Satie's own *Trois petites pièces montées* illustrated Rabelais. The first, "De l'enfance de Pantagruel", was an orchestration of a piano piece, dreamy but punctuated by a murmurous bassoon. The second, "Marche de Cocagne", typically sub-titled "Démarche", strutted boldly on its way led by a hectoring trumpet. The concluding "Jeux de Gargantua" danced in polka tempo, crisp, sharp, dry.

* A fuller discussion will be found in the present author's *The Ox on The Roof*, Macdonald, 1972.

A similar piece of music was *La Belle Excentrique*, a variety number in four sections called "Grande Ritournelle", "Marche Franco-Lunaire", "Valse du Mystérieux Baiser dans l'Oeil", and "Cancan Grand-Mondain". This was written for the dancer known as Caryathis. Bakst designed a famous poster of her. It shows her, arms and hands elegantly curved, body at right angles to the floor and poised on her right leg while an immense coloured chiffon drifts in the air. She had fierce black hair and a smouldering sexuality in her dark eyes. Even in old age, when illness prevented her from going beyond her garden, when she sat carefully on her veranda wearing a shawl, heavy horn-rimmed glasses, a thick dressing-gown and massive wellington boots that protruded incongruously below, it was possible still to trace remnants of the passionate creature she had once been. For she enchanted many men. Her explosive affair with Charles Dullin, the famous producer and actor, cast the most lurid light of all her entanglements.

Dear Elise! (She had been christened Elizabeth Toulemon). She was maddening and she was adorable. She arrived in Montmartre round about 1910. A friend – he was an unfrocked priest, naturally – introduced her to the maître de ballet at the Opéra. On the latter's advice she trained in classical and character dancing. Soon she was appearing in Ravel's *Ma Mère l'oye* and other ballets. At the Théâtre des Arts she met Charles Dullin, who was just then scoring his first triumph as Smerdiakov in an adaptation of Dostoevsky's *The Brothers Karamazov*. One day he asked her to visit him so that he could help her plan some dances she had to perform. As she mounted the stairs of his cheap and shabby hotel, she could hear him running through his part. She entered a poverty-stricken room furnished only with a bed and a table on which stood a flask of cod liver oil and a bottle of port. Seeing her hesitation, he locked the door and threw the key out of the window.

"I only left that room next morning," Elise used to say with dramatic relish. It was the beginning of a *grand amour* that lasted for ten years.

They lived in the rue Lamarck, opposite the rue Bonne where Berlioz had once owned a house. She planned, with Dullin's aid, to turn several movements from the *Symphonie fantastique* into a ballet. To his annoyance, she did not wish to act. Her memory was poor and she suffered from stage-fright. Dancing was her chosen art. Georges Auric was a near neighbour in the rue Lamarck and for her he wrote *La Danse d'aujourd'hui*. Through him she met artists, writers, musicians. She inspired Poulenc to compose a dance for her called *Le Jongleur*, an extremely difficult number in which – as she always told it – she both juggled and danced intricate steps wearing an elaborate but hampering costume designed by Goncharova.

One morning Dullin came back and found her with an acquaintance. He burst out jealously: "I'm going. You'll weep tears of blood! I shall never see you again." He went.

Nearly twenty years later they met in his dressing-room. He was famous then, director of the Théâtre Sarah-Bernhardt, a distinguished figure whose protégés included Jean-Louis Barrault and Jean Vilar. (But after disagreements with authority he was thrown out. At the age of sixty he was on the street, as poor as he had been in his early youth.) He asked Elise to live with him once more. She refused, though she still had tenderness for him. Or at least, that is her account of the incident.

Jean Cocteau became what she called her "prince charmant". He delighted in her fantasy, her wildness, and always attended her first nights. By now she had a large house in the rue du Commandant Marchand where Cocteau organised parties and receptions. There was a masked ball at which he appeared as Mercury, and Max Jacob, fulfilling an old ambition, paraded in a monk's robe and cowl. Rose trees bloomed in the dining-room and exotic plants flowered on the balconies. On Saturdays she met Cocteau and his friends for lunch in the place de la Madeleine and afterwards they would go to her house. Her "prince charmant" mixed the cocktails. Once he used as ingredients a selection of the perfumes and essences he found in her bathroom. The taste was memorable. No one died.

The artist Marie Laurencin, Apollinaire's one-time mistress, was responsible for introducing Elise to her future husband. Marcel Jouhandeau, the writer, taught Latin and French to the first form in a boys' Catholic school. Each morning he would get up at four or five o'clock to work on his current book. Then he went to the school for the day's work that guaranteed his living. He was a good teacher and popular with the boys. "Writing, for me," he once said, "is breathing." Now in his late eighties, he has written more than a hundred books which range from the frankest revelations about his private life to philosophical disquisitions on the nature of evil. Gide thought him to be the finest contemporary writer of French prose. Many would agree.

Marie Laurencin and Jean Cocteau, who both had a fatal weakness for stage-managing the lives of their friends, hustled Elise and Marcel into marriage. The union was catastrophic. For a few years they observed the conjugal formalities. Then, though living in the same house, they kept apart. Jouhandeau's emotional tastes lay elsewhere. But his unfortunate marriage had provided him with an incomparable advantage as a writer. The capricious and overbearing Elise gave him an inexhaustible source of inspiration. He wrote many books in which he depicted their life together. His picture of this unforgettable woman is cruel, comic, often terrifying. True, he "arranged" his impressions with artistic licence. Often one felt, when at their home, that both of them were living up to the image he had created in his novels, and even that Marcel would deliberately provoke Elise in order to bring on the incident he hoped would supply the material for his next chapter.

Elise was a clever businesswoman, for all her talk about art. She bought and sold property. She had a hand in all sorts of commercial deals. Her mania for architecture was such that she continually disturbed Marcel by building on to the house, which she owned, or continually altering the layout. Plumbers and labourers were hardly ever out of the place. In the nineteen-fifties, tired of what she considered to be the libels her husband published about her, she answered back with a series of autobiographical volumes that gave her side of the story. Alas, she was not equal to Marcel as a writer. In 1971 a mortal illness confined her to her bedroom among the erotic Chinese prints that adorn the wall. She was no longer the supple and graceful Caryathis in the Bakst poster which hangs in a downstairs corridor of their Malmaison home. An unfair destiny enabled Marcel to have the last word. What, thought his friends, would he find to write about now that Elise had died? The answer was simple. He started work immediately on his next book, which was to be entitled *La mort d'Elise*.

Elise/Caryathis probably met Satie through Auric. A sympathy grew between them. He was amused by her notion of giving a masked ball – it was the one where Cocteau dressed as Mercury and Max Jacob as a monk – and although he did not go to it himself, he had plenty of ideas for it.

"Chère grande Artiste," he wrote, "exquisite friend, you're a good sort! Of course I enjoy your company. On Thursday I'll come, if it suits you, to lunch under the great oak in your garden. The fountain will be obligatory. In this terrible heat my skin is so sensitive!"

The "fountain" was a hose-pipe which, hooked to the tree, directed a jet of water against the wall. Satie, bloated with the many apéritifs and champagne taken at his meal, liked to sit at ease in front of the splashing coolth. His plan for the masked ball was to broadcast through a loudspeaker what an announcer would describe as quotations from the greatest artists of all time. Such would be the effect on the touchy writers and painters among the guests that, not to be outdone, they too would vie with each other in citing their own pearls. In the squabbles that followed, Satie mischievously imagined, the masks would fall off and glorious disorder would break out. His suggestion was appreciated but not taken up.

Many times he came to lunch in the rue du Commandant Marchand. He called Elise "Belle Dame", the name musicians had given her, and encouraged her when she was depressed by practical problems. "Belle Dame," he would tell her, "it's a mistake to prefer oneself to one's art. You should serve it with self-denial."

She found that Satie, who appeared so careless about other people, had a tender heart. On occasion she thought him surly to the point of stupidity. His saving grace was irony. She admired the way he subordinated his whole existence to music. With a woman's curiosity she tried to sound him out about his love life. Instantly the shutter came down. His visage went blank, impenetrable.

Neither he nor Elise could make up their minds about the costume she was to wear as La Belle Excentrique. They went to see the painter van Dongen, then at the beginning of his vogue and conscious of the fact. Satie was repelled by his commercial approach. They called on the dressmaker Paul Poiret who took his inspiration from Eastern fashions and exotic colour schemes. Scarcely had they seen three dresses before Satie turned to Elise and hissed: "Oh no, not odalisques! Be damned to the harem!"

Marie Laurencin, the specialist in drawing pretty little foals and angelic does, created a heavily plumed costume with a horse's mane. "For Heaven's sake!" groaned Satie, "I'd rather see you as a zebra."

In despair Elise turned to Cocteau. "You know, Jean, Satie is clarity, order, reason itself. He knows how I ought to be dressed, extravagantly, of course, but deliberately absurd." Her prince charming did not let her down. "Give me, Carya, some paper and pencils." As she watched him draw, the costume appeared as by magic: a black velvet corsage, long sleeves, a skirt with panels of multi-coloured tulle, diamond-studded shoes, a heart-shaped morsel of black velvet in a strategic position . . . The face was entirely hidden by a mask except for a pair of wicked, heavily made-up eyes, and above it, rising from the hip, there quavered a white ostrich feather in the shape of a question mark. Satie was content at last.

In June 1920, *La Belle Excentrique* danced her grotesque way across the stage of the Théâtre des Champs-Elysées. Her version of Poulenc's *Le Jongleur* was applauded by a noisy house. Auric's *La Danse d'aujourd'hui*, representing a newspaper seller, earned less enthusiasm. After some orchestral pieces by Milhaud and Poulenc, Caryathis danced the *Rhapsodie espagnole* of Ravel, evoking, as a critic said afterwards, the spirit of Edgar Allen Poe and Baudelaire. She took her bow before an excited audience. A piercing shout emerged from the back of the theatre. "What a pity the costume looks like a public lavatory!" She learned afterwards that the heckler was the artist André Derain.

Satie's music for *La Belle Excentrique* may in one way be described as parodistic. The instruction for the "Valse du Mystérieux Baiser dans l'Oeil" runs: "Very exaggerated." So it is possible to see it as a skit on music-hall numbers of the time. Yet the satirist often loves, despite himself, the things he mocks. Noël Coward's satires on the British Empire and other national institutions were basically affectionate. So, it could be, are Satie's tilts at popular music. The "Grande Ritournelle" opens with a pitter-patter "vamp-till-ready" that includes much bustling interchange between clarinet and bassoon. It is impossible to hear or play without a smile. The waltz, though it moves in exaggerated swoops, has something of the genuine café-concert nostalgia. A simple nursery tune is heard through the badinage of the "Marche

Franco-Lunaire", and there is an innocent vigour about the bois-terous galop "Cancan Grand-Mondain" with which the little suite ends. The sub-title "Fantaisie Sérieuse" defines the mix of naïveté and knowingness which Satie adopted in his music-hall diversions. For a long time afterwards Elise was known as "La Belle Excentrique". Then she gave up dancing. She destroyed most of the copies of Bakst's famous poster, so increasing the value of the one she kept, and devoted herself to dabbling in business and out-raging her husband. She never forgot her youth of art and the dance. Her three volumes of autobiography were to be called *Joies et douleurs d'une Belle Excentrique*, a title that stirred memories for those who had been young with her. And she was convinced that she alone had understood Satie, "that exceptional man, so different from all who surrounded him".

XXIV

Furnishing Music

Often the painter Fernand Léger would accompany Satie on his long walks across Paris to Arcueil. They talked endlessly. On occasion some remark or another, some passing comment, would make Léger think he was about to be admitted to the composer's hidden domain. Then he would realise that, like everyone else, he was fated never to penetrate Satie's watchful guard.

He lunched with Satie and some friends in a restaurant. The music played during meals by the resident orchestra was so noisy that they were obliged to leave. Mused Satie: "There's a need to create furnishing music, in other words music that would be a part of the surrounding noises and would take them into account. I imagine it to be melodious; softening the clatter of knives and forks without dominating them, without imposing itself. It would fill up the awkward silence that occasionally descends on guests. It would spare them the usual commonplaces. At the same time it would neutralise the street noises that tactlessly force themselves into the picture." It would, he said, fill a need.

The idea of *musique d'ameublement* had floated in the recess of his mind for some time. It can even be traced back to the static and purely decorative incidental music he composed during the Rosicrucian period. Now he saw *musique d'ameublement* as satisfying "useful needs". Art, he was quick to point out, had nothing to do with it. Furnishing music played the same part as heating and lighting, as comfort in all its forms. It should be supplied in public buildings, in lawyers' offices, in banks. No marriage ceremony would be complete without furnishing music. The concept pleased him. He went so far as to analyse *Socrate* in terms of *musique d'ameublement*. One section would fit an inner room. Another suited the vestibule with its colonnades and bas-reliefs. Yet another would do for a glass cabinet.

On 8 March 1920, a few months before *La Belle Excentrique*, he had put his idea into practice. At the Galerie Barbazanges in the Faubourg Saint-Honoré he devised a performance of furnishing music. This took place during the interval of a play by Max Jacob which was followed with music by the Six and by Stravinsky. Unlike his five colleagues, Darius Milhaud was interested in Satie's new venture and himself contributed to it.

Pierre Bertin was master of ceremonies and addressed the puzzled audience:

> We present to you for the first time, under the supervision of Messieurs Erik Satie and Darius Milhaud and directed by M. Delgrange, furnishing music which will be played during the intervals. We earnestly beg of you not to attach any importance to it and to behave throughout the interval as if it did not exist. This music, specially written for the play by Max Jacob (a ruffian always, never the tramp), claims to contribute to life in the same way as a private conversation, as a picture in the gallery, or the chair on which you may or may not be sitting. You can test it out for yourself. Messieurs Erik Satie and Darius Milhaud are at your orders for all information and commissions.

From various parts of the room came the sound of a piano, three clarinets and a trombone. They played, over and again, scraps of music from Ambroise Thomas' opera *Mignon*, from Saint-Saëns' *Danse macabre* and from anything else which had caught the fancy of Messieurs Satie and Milhaud. The audience, uncertainly, began to take their seats again. Satie bustled among them. "Talk, go on talking," he commanded. "Keep moving. Whatever you do, don't listen!" The instruments honked and

197

squeaked their disjointed phrases while people looked at each other in puzzled alarm.

Matisse had had a similar idea when he visualised a neutral form of art, unobtrusive and akin to a comfortable chair. Satie was the first to put it in music. He never published anything strictly labelled *musique d'ameublement*, and, quite clearly, it was just another of his fantasies, a passing whim like the brass dirigible or the cast-iron sixteenth-century house which he drew in elaborate pen-and-ink detail. His comment that art had nothing to do with "useful needs" is significant. Yet furnishing music is important in that a few years later he applied the principle in his score for René Clair's film *Entr'acte*.

In a rather chilling way, though, his original idea has since been realised to the full. Muzak conquers all. In the USA children are born to it, cats and dogs are neutered to it, people are buried to it, and astronauts conquered the moon to it. Eighty million pairs of ears are assaulted by it each day. A farmer who drenched his cornfields with an accompaniment of Muzak jubilated that yield went up threefold. A slaughterhouse reported that until Muzak was installed the animals' blood kept clotting. Now, the blood flowed more freely because Muzak helped to relax them.

Muzak has been called "sound you inhale". In mental hospitals and knitting mills, in soap factories and airline offices, its treacly murmur has increased output and hypnotised workers. Intricate charts plot the forward movement that irons out fatigue, monotony and boredom. An upward trend is remorselessly induced by choice of tempo and orchestration. Muzak is like air-conditioning, like a colour scheme. It emphasises, claim its promoters, the quality of good food and surroundings. It banishes, they observe, echoing Satie, those heavy pauses that arise in the most congenial of company.

How would he have viewed this complete realisation of his idea, this whole-hearted and logical conclusion to the dilettante experiment he launched? His reaction might have been horror. On the other hand, one cannot help an uncomfortable suspicion that the use of Muzak in mental hospitals and slaughterhouses would have pleased his macabre sense of humour.

For some time after his adventure into *musique d'ameublement* Satie lay fallow. He toyed with a number of projects. Among them was a ballet to be called *La Naissance de Vénus* with scenery by André Derain. Another was an opera based on the novel *Paul et Virginie*. The Satie family had a weakness for Bernardin de Saint-Pierre. Grandfather Jules, it will be remembered, was accustomed to read, surreptitiously, that author's *Harmonies de la nature* during Mass. Perhaps Satie himself had at one time or another been encouraged to write his chamber oratorio by Bernardin's *La Mort de Socrate*. The sentimental tale of Paul and Virginia, those two idyllic young persons, and of their adventures on the exotic isle of Mauritius, has moved generations of readers. It must be, as its latest editor has declared, "one of the worst and most widely read books in French literature."

Several operas had already been taken from it, one of them by the Rodolphe Kreutzer to whom Beethoven dedicated his sonata. "The overture, in C, begins with a very simple and rather monotonous tune . . ." remarks a commentator, suggesting that the true flavour of this lachrymose novel has been captured. Others are by the late eighteenth-century Lesueur and by the English William Reeve. The latter, a versatile gentleman, doubled up as church organist and part owner of Sadler's Wells Theatre. It is good to know that, besides *Paul and Virginia* and some thirty other stage works, he wrote the music for a Sadler's Wells pantomime called *Bang Up* which included the clown Grimaldi's famous song "Tippity-witchet".

A libretto for *Paul et Virginie* was written by Cocteau and Raymond Radiguet, the young, very young genius whom Jean had discovered and sponsored. The manuscript has prose dialogue in Cocteau's handwriting and arias in Radiguet's. There would have been many opportunities for Satie. Among them are slave songs, a bamboula, and a number where a Negro maid smokes a pipe and dances in time to other servants beating their brooms on the floor. Satie would have been able to try his hand at love duets, a sailors' chorus, banjo music, and a funeral march for Virginie. The plot is given what one suspects to be a Coctelian twist. When Virginie and her mother and Paul have died, they all meet together among the other living characters. They can see and talk with themselves, but of course the living are unaware of them. "We're dead, all three of us," says Paul happily, "and nothing can separate us."

Satie let it be understood that he had completed the music. Of course he had not, and after his death no trace of it was discovered. In August 1921 he had told Poulenc he was working on the opera "as much as I can". Cocteau was hoping for what he called "a genuine opéra-comique in the style of *Lakmé* (though I don't know *Lakmé* very well)" he wrote to his mother. "For the last act I've imagined something which I think is very fine. Radiguet sends me charming couplets. I'd like him to join me here [at Le Piquey] and complete this nice surprise for Satie . . ."

Obviously Satie did his best. A faux-naïf remoulding of this ancient tear-jerker would probably have resulted in another *Geneviève de Brabant*, enriched by the experience of the twenty years which had passed since that charming little work. It would have been something less than *Parade*, something more than a sophisticated giggle. But Satie could not do it. He secretly renounced the idea. All that remain are two bits of prose he jotted down in his notebooks. The first is called "Paul et Virginie". It runs: "Virginie sang like a very sweet little potato. Then Paul danced, on one foot so as not to disturb his parents. Virginie liked to watch him dance. Virginie's song made the monkeys weep." The second, entitled "Robinson Crusoe", is in similar vein:

> In the evening they ate their soup and went to smoke their pipes at the sea's edge. The smell of tobacco made the fishes cough. Robinson Crusoe didn't enjoy himself on his desert island. "It's really too deserted," said he. His Negro Friday was of the same opinion. He said to his good master: "Yes, mister: a desert island is really too deserted." And he shook his great black head.

Though Satie never musicked the arias Radiguet contributed to *Paul et Virginie,* he did set a little poem the young man had written. It is the fourth of the *Quatre petites mélodies* of 1920. This "Adieu", a bright and ironical flourish, pirouettes in waltz tempo. Other songs included Lamartine's "Elégie", labelled "in memory of thirty years' admiring and tender friendship" with Debussy, which is a strangely bleak and abrupt homage. "Danseuse", by Cocteau, and an eighteenth-century drinking song complete the quartet. With Fargue's *Ludions,* which have been discussed earlier, they represent Satie's last works for voice.

In 1921 there came, at last, a public performance of his surrealistic *Piège de Méduse.* First given in 1913 at Roland-Manuel's home, it had lain half-forgotten until the wilder post-war years brought about a climate more sympathetic to its dotty conceit. The piece was included on a programme of "Spectacle de théâtre bouffe" presented at the Théâtre Michel in May. Its companions were Max Jacob's "drame lyrique" *La Femme fatale* and a two-act play by Radiguet called *Le Pélican*. Radiguet's hero wants to be a poet. But, says his father, he will have to change his name from the odd-sounding "Pélican". Why? says the ambitious poet. It's no sillier than Corneille (crow) or Racine (root). There were also a jazz-band shimmy by Milhaud, *Caramel mou*, and *Le Gendarme incompris*, a "critique bouffe" by Cocteau and Radiguet. This hilarious anecdote included a prose-poem by Mallarmé which none of the critics recognised in their annoyance with the piece.

Milhaud conducted the ensemble for *Le Piège de Méduse*, Satie having had a characteristic tiff with the musician originally engaged for the task. A further source of annoyance was revealed as soon as the curtain rose. Pierre Bertin in the leading rôle had made himself up to look like Satie, complete with pince-nez and beard. The composer was not amused.

During the creative lull that descended on him early in the nineteen-twenties, he turned to giving lectures and writing articles. His experience of music critics over the past few years had, he felt, provided him with plenty of material. What were his views on the Paynes and Crichtons of his time? "Physically," he wrote, "the critic is serious in appearance. He's the sort of fellow who reminds you of a c —." Or such, at least, was the sentence Ravel claimed to have come across in a newspaper. "Are we going to have another Poueigh–Satie court action?" Ravel joked. In fact, whether or no this was a case of misreporting or of Ravel's impish misinterpretation, what Satie actually wrote was that the critic reminds you of a "contre-basson", and not of the three-letter monosyllable which begins that word. Although, of course, he would secretly have approved the gloss:

There are three kinds of critic [he observed]. The ones who are important; the ones who are less so; and those who aren't important at all. The last two kinds don't exist; all critics are important . . .

Mediocrity and incompetence are not to be found in critics. A mediocre or incapable critic would be the laughing-stock of his

colleagues; it would be impossible for him to exercise his profession, his priestly vocation I mean, for he would have to
leave the country of his birth, and all doors would be closed to
him; his life would be nothing but a long-drawn-out agony,
terrible in its monotony.

The Artist is but a dreamer, in short; the critic, on the other
hand, is conscious of reality . . . An artist can be imitated; the
critic is inimitable, and priceless. How could you imitate a
critic, I wonder? In any case, the attempt would be pointless.
We have the original, and THAT IS ENOUGH FOR US. The
man who said criticism was easy said nothing very remarkable.
It's shameful even to have said such a thing: he ought to be
chased, for at least a mile or two.

The man who wrote such a comment will regret it perhaps.
It's possible, it's what one would wish, IT'S CERTAIN.

The critic's brain is like a shop, a big department store. You
can find everything there: surgical footwear, the sciences,
bedding, the arts, travelling rugs, a wide range of furniture,
writing paper both French and foreign, smokers' requisites,
gloves, umbrellas, woollen goods, hats, sports items, walking
sticks, optical instruments, perfumery, etc. . . . The critic knows
everything, says everything, hears everything, dabbles in
everything, stirs everything, eats everything, mixes up everything, and goes on meditating just the same. What a man! Let
no one forget it!! All our articles are guaranteed!! During hot
weather goods are kept inside!!! INSIDE THE CRITIC!!
Look!! Examine but don't touch!!! It's unique, unbelievable . . .

The true critical sense doesn't lie in criticising oneself but in
criticising others; and the beam you have in your own eye doesn't
in the slightest prevent you from seeing the mote in your
neighbour's: in which case your beam becomes a telescope, a
powerful one, that enlarges the mote out of all proportion . . .

It is only proper that Artists should be guided by critics. I
have never understood the former's ultrasensitiveness when
faced with critics' warnings. I believe this to be an instance of
pride, a misplaced pride that is unwelcome. Artists would
profit from revering critics more; from listening to them
respectfully; from loving them, even; from inviting them often
to sit at the family table between uncle and grandfather. Let
them follow my example, my good example: I am dazzled by

the presence of a critic, his light shines so brightly that I have to blink for over an hour; I kiss the imprint of his slippers on the ground; through politeness I drink his words in a tall long-stemmed glass . . .

We need a discipline of iron, or of any other metal. Only the critics can impose it and, from a distance, see that it is observed. All they ask is to inculcate in us the excellent principles of obedience. He who disobeys is much to be pitied, for not to obey is very sad. But we should not obey our evil passions, even if they themselves command us to do so. How can we recognize that passions are evil, as evil as the itch? Yes, how?

By the pleasure we take in giving way to them, in surrendering to them, and BY THE FACT THAT THEY DISPLEASE THE CRITICS.

They don't have evil passions. How should they, brave fellows? They have no passions at all, *none*. Always calm, they think only of their duty, which is to correct the defaults of this poor world and thereby make a decent income, enough to buy their little bit of baccy.

For the rest of his life he kept up a steady fusillade against critics. Irony was his chief weapon. Critics, he would point out, were much more intelligent than was generally believed. That was why he'd like to be a critic himself – not a great one, of course, but only a very tiny one. He reproved those who showed no respect for critics. Such people could only be of no account.

But there were times when he found it impossible to contain his feelings within a jocular wrapping of irony. Goaded by the hostility that greeted his music, he burst out: "The critic called 'musical' is a putrid secretion of the Art to which he claims to belong . . . I believe that the critic known as 'literary' is in the same boat . . . The 'art' critic must of necessity belong with them. What do you think, Dear Friend?"

XXV

Doing a Gounod

"Dear old chap," wrote Satie to Poulenc on 11 September 1923, "how lucky you are to have completed your thingummyjig. I'm just finishing the second act. Yes.

"I've had two charming letters from your exquisite Director. Unfortunately my third act won't be ready for 1 October. I'm weeping like Croesus about it. Yes.

"Come back quickly: there's nothing to see in the country . . ."

It had been one of Diaghilev's neatest inspirations to revive some lesser-known Gounod operas. These were *Le Médecin malgré lui*, *La Colombe* and *Philémon et Baucis*, the first based on Molière and the second two on La Fontaine. Unlike such "grandes machines" as *Faust* or *Roméo et Juliette*, the smaller works are the purest expression of Gounod's genius. He was a cultured man and responded gratefully to these adaptations from the French classics. They were far superior to the usual fodder turned out by Scribe and others. So stern a critic as Bernard Shaw praised "the irresistible flavour of Molière" which pervades Gounod's version of *Le Médecin malgré lui*. It captures the very spirit of France's greatest comic writer in a way that is consistently delicate and sure. No less charming are *La Colombe* and *Philémon et Baucis*, whose worldly wisdom and elegant craftsmanship do honour to La Fontaine. Berlioz described the second of these as "one of the most graceful" the composer had written.

Diaghilev commissioned Poulenc to turn the spoken dialogue of *La Colombe* into recitatives and charged Auric to do the same for *Philémon et Baucis*. *Le Médecin malgré lui* he entrusted to Satie. The latter set about the job with his usual punctiliousness, as his notebooks show. On the right-hand page he copied out the dialogue that was to be set. On the left he sketched a musical analysis, breaking down the syllables into note values and dividing the words into bars for each line of dialogue. It was slow work.

On 28 September, a fortnight or so after the letter to Poulenc, Satie wrote to Diaghilev:

Cher Exquis Directeur – I shan't have finished *Le Médecin malgré lui* by 1 October. Alas! I hope you'll kindly allow me to cash the little cheque. I beg you with clasped hands. Yes.

I must talk to you about Scene VII (page 42 in the libretto) and page 174 of the score. What's to be done about the Andantino? and how shall we handle the flute and bassoon gimmicks? I'd like to see you about this. Yes. Couldn't the "spoken to music" bit go with the *Andantino*? Think about it, I entreat you. I'll call at the "Savoy" [the Hôtel Savoy in the rue de Rivoli] on Monday morning at 11 (eleven o'clock.) This scene VII is giving me a bit of trouble: you can enlighten me about it. Yes.

The worthy *Octet* will be allright. Nothing could be simpler, in fact, and you've convinced me about it. You'll have the whole of the *3rd Act* by Thursday at the latest.

Je vous embrasse fort.

Satie kept his word. *Le Médecin malgré lui* was given at Monte Carlo early in January 1924. Alexandre Benois designed the scenery and Nijinska arranged the dances that add so much to this exquisite work. It was the last commission Benois carried out for Diaghilev. The restless tyrant of the Ballets Russes now considered Benois to be out of date, and gratitude for past glories did not prevent him from dropping the puzzled artist. On the other hand, *Le Médecin malgré lui* also marked an important "first": it was the opportunity for Serge Lifar to make an impression with his dancing, his fine body, his handsome features, that ravishing tip-tilted nose.

This Monte Carlo season was extremely important for French music. In addition to the Gounod operas Diaghilev, at Satie's prompting, had engaged Milhaud to do the recitatives for his revival of Chabrier's *Une Education manquée*. A few days after *Le Médecin malgré lui* came the triumphant première of Poulenc's *Les Biches*. This was quickly followed by Auric's *Les Fâcheux*.

One might have expected Gounod to be beyond the pale so far as modernists of the time were concerned. Diaghilev showed good sense in ignoring this tendency. Was not Stravinsky himself later to champion the much-abused composer? Writing to Stravinsky in the course of his labours on *Le Médecin malgré lui*, Satie adopted a rather defensive tone – and also inserted a quick gibe at Florent Schmitt, that composer of huge and ambitious works on the grand scale. "I'm doing a Gounod, which can't be any sillier than doing a Ravel. Perhaps it would be better to do a Schmitt . . . Yes. For that I'd have to write a piano part on eight staves. Alas! I can't: I'm not intelligent enough!"

Even more memorable than the works presented at Monte Carlo that month was the fact that Satie had been tempted to make one of his rare excursions outside the capital. He set off in good spirits, remarking amiably to the ticket collector: "I congratulate you. You have a very beautiful train." On arrival his mood darkened. Poulenc and Auric had both overlooked the time he was expected and neither was at the station to meet him. At first he seems to have shrugged off his irritation at the imagined affront. Poulenc was able to write about him to Marie Laurencin, designer of *Les Biches*: "I think he was very pleased if I can judge from his excellent mood during his short stay."

Other accounts tell a different story. They report that he lavished "incredible abuse" on his friends Poulenc, Auric and Cocteau. After which he cut short his trip and jumped on the train back to Paris. He stood all the way in the corridor of his sleeping car.

What had happened? The presence of Louis Laloy in Monte Carlo was, it seems, the catalyst which provoked this reaction. Laloy, a man of wide and curious learning, fluent in Greek, Russian and Chinese, had studied like Satie under Vincent d'Indy.

He wrote a book on Chinese music, followed Romain Rolland as a professor at the Sorbonne, and later taught at the Conservatoire. He provided Roussel with the libretto for *Padmâvati*. His studies of ancient music, of Rameau and of Debussy retain their usefulness. But he was also a practising critic who had spoken ill of *Parade* and of works written by the Six. In Satie's eyes he was an implacable enemy.

Something about *Les Biches* and *Les Fâcheux* which he saw in Monte Carlo inspired Laloy to revise his opinions. He gave warm reviews to Poulenc and Auric. A personal friendship even bloomed, and Cocteau joined in the new-found atmosphere of amity. Their meetings together were celebrated with the pleasures of opium, and daily the four men retired to a discreet hotel room for a tranquil smoking party. Had not Laloy written a standard handbook on the subject?

Satie watched, fuming, on the sidelines. Whenever he saw any members of the quartet he would cut them dead. Auric and Poulenc, the youngest of the Six to whom he had given a special affection, were traitors. They consorted with the enemy. They compromised the ideals of the gospel handed down by Satie.

Back in Paris he wrote a sharp article about the goings-on in Monte Carlo. He spoke of *Les Biches* and *Les Fâcheux* as "musical lemonade" and "syrups". Diaghilev, he reported, was as sympathetic and conscientious as ever. Alas, though, "the horrible Laloy" was also there ("what an abomination . . . sly as a monkey"), and he had written fulsome reviews of their "lollipop music". Satie even injected a reference to the opium sessions.

Perhaps, in a calmer mood, he might have liked the ballets by his former protégés. As it was, his ire prevented him from making an objective appraisal. The events in Monte Carlo signalled an end to his patronage of the Six. Several members had already in fact been excommunicated. The first to go was Honegger, who was never very keen on Satie and offended him by not following his advice. Then it was Durey's turn. He opened the door to Satie one day and was confronted with a face of stone. A letter was handed over in silence and the caller departed. Durey opened the letter and read: "Monsieur Durey no longer belongs to the Six." He never knew what sin he had committed.

One rainy day the Six met for lunch at a friend's house. The occasion was light-hearted and Satie enjoyed himself teasing

Isadora Duncan who arrived late. After the meal he went to collect his umbrella from the stand where others, damp and unfurled, dripped in a wet mass. He perceived that someone had carelessly jabbed an umbrella through his own. The culprit was Auric. Satie hurtled away slamming the door behind him and ignoring the hostess. His resentment simmered for months.

The umbrella incident and the Monte Carlo episode added fuel to Satie's annoyance. Auric made it worse by criticising Satie's music in an article. The riposte was quick: "Very good, my little friend. Let him carry on; let him 're-Laloy' himself from head to toe. Oh yes. What was my crime? I didn't like his faked-up, re-jigged *Fâcheux*. Those who say my late friend is nothing but a fathead exaggerate, he is, very simply, just an Auric (Georges) – which is already more than enough for one man (?) alone."

Then Poulenc happened to see a child's rattle in a shop. The face daubed on it reminded him irrevocably of the sage of Arcueil. He told Auric who promptly bought it. They posted it with a jolly letter to Satie. He never spoke to them again. In an article he wrote: "ACKNOWLEDGEMENT OF RECEIPT. My dear Auric. I have received your bauble safely (showing the noble head of an old man) ... Yes ... It was coupled with an amusing letter, politely ribald and, above all, very pornographic ... Ho! ... Great scamp ... Nasty? If only your Daddy knew! ... What a beating you'd get! ..."

Elsewhere he returned, rather pathetically, to the subject: "INVOCATION. If my adversaries don't respect my age, let them at least have some regard for my modesty (don't you agree, Auric – and you, great booby of a Poulenc?)"

Even on his deathbed he was to exclude them. "What's the point of my seeing them once more?" he muttered. "Debussy died without my seeing *him* again, didn't he?"

Except for Milhaud, too genial a man to quarrel with anyone, Satie broke off all connection with the Six. He turned now to another group of young musicians who, under his patronage, were briefly known as the "école d'Arcueil". This included Henri Cliquet-Pleyel, who wrote chamber works and film music. Another was Roger Désormière, who achieved fame as a conductor until a serious accident shortened a distinguished career in his fifties. Maxime Jacob was later to enter the Catholic faith. As Dom Clément Jacob of the Benedictine order he composed songs and liturgical music. Henri Poupard, under the name of Henri Sauguet, is the best known of them, a graceful and witty composer of stage-works.

Sauguet never forgot an agitated evening he spent with Satie. The composer had been asked to accompany a performance of *Socrate* on the same night as a revival of *Parade*. Never at his best when he had to play in public, Satie was even more panicky than usual. If only he could cut himself in half and attend both performances!

The young man was deputed to turn the pages for Satie as he crouched, pallid and wild-eyed, over the keyboard. After playing only a few bars he asked Sauguet to turn the page. Hesitantly, Sauguet reached over. "Not yet, though – wait a bit!" hissed Satie. Then: "Turn, will you, turn!" This went on throughout the whole of the performance: frenzied commands to turn, followed by rebukes for acting too fast and then, finally: "Turn, will you, turn!" The last note was played and they went off stage. The singer, behind whose back the drama had passed, watched them in astonishment. "You dumb cluck!" the composer raged at Sauguet.

There was, of course, no question of Sauguet accompanying his mentor to the performance of *Parade* that evening. He wrote to Satie apologising. The reply came: "Let's not talk about it. But seeing the way you set about things frightened me to death . . ."

A long silence fell. Then another telegram arrived. It was an invitation to lunch with Satie "and my good friend Diaghilev. I've spoken to him about you and he wants to meet you . . ."

The whole incident, as Sauguet realised, threw light on Satie's character. Satie was unaware of his tendency to bad temper and gave way to it as much through a natural vivacity as through a wish to tease. Having put himself as a result in a difficult position, he went on to make it untenable because of his excessive reaction. The only way for him to extricate himself was by means of some startling gesture. Hence the invitation to lunch with Diaghilev which eventually prepared the way for Sauguet's ballet *La Chatte*. It is easy to imagine the effect of such an invitation on a twenty-three-year-old composer but lately arrived from the provinces.

XXVI

The Adventures of Mercury

In the May and June of 1924 an elegant poster by Marie Laurencin announced a season of "Soirées de Paris" at the Théâtre de la Cigale in the boulevard Rochechouart. This was sponsored by Etienne de Beaumont and designed to raise funds for war widows and Russian refugees. Distinguished persons – the President of the Republic, the Prime Minister, Marshal Foch – allowed their names to be quoted as patrons. The main reason, though, for Beaumont's enterprise was a wish to help the dancer and choreographer Massine, who, having left Diaghilev's company, had had little success in attempting to launch his own productions.

During this season Milhaud's ballet *Salade* received its first performance. Inspired by an episode in the Commedia dell'Arte, it offered a lively and complicated entertainment with Massine dancing the rôle of Punchinello and with scenery by Braque. (Milhaud later turned it into a suite for piano and orchestra as *Le Carnaval d'Aix*.) Sauguet wrote the music for *Les Roses* and Derain provided the setting for *Gigue* which drew from Scarlatti, Bach and Handel the accompaniment played by Pierre Bertin's wife Marcelle Meyer. There were also a version by Jean Cocteau of *Romeo et Juliette* – which, notably lacking in feminine charm, earned the name of *Roméo et Jules* from Parisian wits – and a Dadaist play called *Mouchoir de nuages* by Tristan Tzara. Satie's contribution was the ballet *Mercure*.

The conditions under which the season was rehearsed and mounted were characterised by wild disorder. If the dancers were plied with champagne and exquisite cold collations as they practised in the elegant rooms of Beaumont's house, they were utterly confused by the vagueness which their impresario favoured as a method of organisation. It was typical that on one evening the audience in the theatre should consist solely of Beaumont's mother and a handful of friends. In a praiseworthy effort to help her son she had bought every ticket available ... and then forgotten to pass them on.

Beaumont seems to have inherited this maternal absentmindedness. It is not known who had the original idea for *Mercure* nor who put together the scenario. Satie, ever meticulous in his composing habits, became more and more anxious to have the precise details that were necessary before he could start work. He went to see Beaumont and pleaded with him for the scenario.

"Ah, mon cher ami, that's very difficult," came the maddening answer, "because it's a surprise."

It may be that, as with *Parade*, a number of different people contributed ideas. Massine himself was to dance the part of Mercury. Picasso designed the scenery and costumes. A plot finally emerged. "Les aventures de Mercure" opened with Night preparing for the "Danse de tendresse" between Apollo and Venus. The signs of the Zodiac surrounded them. Jealous Mercury entered, cut the vital thread of Apollo's life and, with his magic power, revived him again immediately. The three Graces danced and took their bath. While they were doing so Mercury stole their pearls and fled pursued by Cerberus. In the third tableau Bacchus led the celebrations. Mercury invented new dances to charm the guests. Among the latter was Proserpine. The final scene depicted her abduction by Pluto with the aid of Chaos.

By April Satie had completed much of the score. In friendly letters to Beaumont and his wife he kept them informed of his progress. The comtesse de Beaumont's name appeared on the title page as dedicatee of the work. The finished product followed closely his original sketch. The short-score, with each bar numbered, carried notes for the orchestration – second trumpet at bar nine with violins and violas, at bar eleven second violins and violas, first horn, cellos, bassoon and double bassoon, and so forth. He jotted down the keys for the different items: F major for "Polka des Lettres" and A major for the "Nouvelle Danse".

The Mercury of legend has only a tenuous link with the ballet which Satie, Massine and Picasso created. The characters were, as Satie told a journalist, "simply fairground characters and the music, naturally, is fairground music . . . I think the music will convey very closely what we sought to express. I wanted it to be not the music-hall type of harmony, but, rather, made up of the rhythms so very particular to shows at a fair."

Mercure was given at the Théâtre de la Cigale on 15 June. At one point after the curtain had risen Massine heard what sounded like muffled hissing in the audience. This grew into noisy shouts. The box where Picasso and his wife sat was invaded by men bawling "Vieux pompier!" at the artist. Beaumont called the police and the rioters were expelled. The demonstrators, it later appeared, were Surrealists. They had been annoyed that Picasso, whom they admired, should have lent himself to an undertaking patronised by ornaments of a society they despised, for among the audience were high-ranking diplomatists and government figureheads with their ladies.

A few days later the militants explained themselves. Their statement, illustrated by a witty Touchagues drawing, was headed "Homage to Picasso". In view of the mediocrity and compromise that had recently tended to obscure the true purpose of art and thought, noted the signatories, they wished to show their "deep and total admiration for Picasso, who, disdaining acceptance by the conventional, has never ceased to explore the anxiety of our time and to express it in terms of the highest value. And now, with *Mercure*, while giving the full measure of his daring and genius, he has once more come up against a general lack of understanding. In the light of this event, which assumes an exceptional character, Picasso, *far more than those around him*, appears today as the eternal personification of youth and undisputed master of the situation." Among those who signed the statement were the poets Louis Aragon and André Breton, and the painter Max Ernst. Two other names appearing with them, names likely to cause Satie a flicker of wry annoyance, were those of Auric and Poulenc.

In a country such as France, where in those times, if less so today, the classical tradition still meant something, the ballet's novel presentation of the inventor of the lyre, messenger of the gods, escort of dead souls to the infernal regions, must have caused an initial shock. What was to be made of the three Graces who were represented as having what Massine describes as "plaited necks like telephone extension wires which stretched and contracted as their heads bobbed up and down"? How was the dignity of the classics upheld by a scene where "three male dancers, dressed in raffia wigs, swam in an inclined wooden bathtub"? And how could one accept that Proserpine was abducted to the ebullient strains of a café-concert march? History has drawn a veil over what was thought by the President of the Republic, the Prime Minister, Marshal Foch and their consorts.

Even, however, if this unconventional approach were accepted, there remained disparities. The most obvious of these was between Picasso's designs and Satie's music. The visual aspect was elegant and sophisticated. The musical accompaniment followed its own brash and independent line. Stubborn as ever, Satie was determined to use the fairground techniques he had spoken of to journalists.

Mercure is prefaced with a jaunty "Marche-Ouverture" that neatly combines two themes of contrasting natures, the one gentle, the other truculent. In "La Nuit", which opens the first tableau, there is, contrary to Satie's declaration, no hint of the fairground. It is a calm and sustained evocation of the night played by strings with mysterious interjections from the clarinet. The "Danse de tendresse" between Apollo and Venus burgeons into a lilting café-concert waltz containing passages in the manner of the *Trois Valses distinguées du précieux dégoûté*. It is marked to be played very expressively and caressingly. Though the origin of its style is plebeian the melody and treatment are refined. It is followed by what must be one of Satie's finest inspirations. A tuba, grotesque but lovable, picks out the tune of "Signes du zodiaque" in a descending figure which recalls Geoffrey Grigson's remark about Satie's work: "Then I thought of Erik Satie," he wrote, "who drops slow simple drops of music into music." Whereupon Mercury makes his entrance to a rumbustious measure which ends in a repeat of a leading theme from the overture.

The second tableau begins with the "Danse des Grâces", hollow, white, inscrutable. The mood is prolonged in the "Bain des Grâces", a tranquil section, plaintively moving, for strings alone. Abruptly, Mercury's flight and the anger of Cerberus bring the tableau to a noisy end.

A "Polka des Lettres" inaugurates the final tableau. Here an impudent trumpet plays a pop-style tune with silvery elegance. The "Nouvelle Danse", grave and beautiful, sketches harmonies as poignant in their reticence as those of "La Nuit". The trumpet returns, again in polka time, to represent "Chaos". The triumphantly objective quality of this number is achieved by mixing together, on brass and woodwind, themes from the "Polka des Lettres" and, on strings, from the "Nouvelle Danse". The "Rapt de Proserpine" reaches a finale which is repeated several times in an almost irritable burst of energy.

Fairground music? Admittedly in this ballet Satie uses the techniques and rhythms and cut of melody usually associated with it. But he also here attains to passages of beauty and tenderness which are as fine as anything else in his work.

XXVII

Closed

Already for some years a fully paid up member of the Socialist Party, in 1920 he joined the Communists. His membership card is stamped "Arcueil-Cachan branch".

As his first biographer points out, he was totally ignorant of Marxist doctrines. At that time the epithet "Bolshevist", which he liked to apply to himself, had picturesque undertones. It carried a romantic hint of oppressed freedom fighters. His adherence to the Communist cause was an emotional reaction. He sympathised with the poor. He detested militarism, profiteering and the race for material success. The bourgeois mentality revolted him. Yet the nonconformism which attracted him to the party was the very factor which would have ensured his doom under a Communist régime. As a political innocent with a mocking tongue he would have found himself confined, at best, in one of those mental hospitals thoughtfully maintained for the benefit of eccentrics who have shown irreverence towards authority.

A movement to which he also adhered at this time, and one far more amusing though shorter-lived than Communism, was Dada. This anarchic impulse to subversion sprang up first in Zurich at the height of the war. There, in 1916, it was launched by the

215

Romanian poet Tristan Tzara, handsome, elegant, monocled. The name, meaning hobby-horse or gee-gee, was chosen haphazardly at the page where a dictionary fell open. "Dada was born," said Tzara, "of a rebellion common to all adolescence and demanding the individual's complete submission to the deepest needs of his nature without regard for history, logic or parochial morality . . . As the motto for our publications we used that phrase of Descartes: 'I don't even want to know that there have been men before me.'"

Depressed and nauseated by the war, the Dadaists wanted to make a clean sweep, to destroy existing patterns and to start afresh. The movement spread from Zurich to Berlin and Cologne and Hanover. In Paris, wrote Tzara. "Dada was anti-philosophical, nihilistic, universal and polemical, but the anti-bourgeois and anti-academic spirit was everywhere expressed with equal virulence."

A famous document was Tzara's advice on how to write a Dadaist poem. "Take a newspaper," he counselled. "Take a pair of scissors. Choose in this newspaper an article of the length you intend your poem to be. Cut out the article. Then snip out with care each of the words that make it up and put them in a bag. Shake gently. Then take out each cutting one after another in the order in which they have emerged from the bag. Copy conscientiously. The poem will resemble you. And there you are, 'an infinitely original writer gifted with a charming sensibility, though not understood by the common herd.'"

Wit, humour, satire and a steely impertinence were the arms of the Dadaists. The movement was rich in personalities. An early pioneer was Arthur Cravan who always billed himself as "the nephew of Oscar Wilde". He edited a little review called *Maintenant* which he sold from a barrow in the street. It shocked with cynicism and originality. In 1914 he gave a riotous and memorable lecture. The proceedings began with a few pistol shots loosed off by the speaker. Then he delivered a wild eulogium of sportsmen as being superior to artists, of homosexuals, of thieves, of madmen. From time to time he assailed the audience with energetic insults and threw things at them. He concluded his performance by dancing, boxing and lecturing at the same time. Such was "the Mysterious Sir Arthur Cravan, the poet with the shortest hair in the world, grandson of the Lord Chancellor, naturally, Oscar

Wilde's nephew (naturally again), and great-nephew of Lord Alfred Tennyson (naturally for a third time)."

Dada reached its peak soon after the war. It specialised in organising sensational events. One of these was the trial of the novelist Maurice Barrès. In the eighteen-nineties his writing had been hailed by young Frenchmen as a triumphant affirmation of individuality. Later generations dismissed him as a Fascist. He was to earn derision for his attitude over the Dreyfus affair and for his jingoistic declarations in wartime. At his "trial" the accused was symbolised by a stuffed figure. André Breton presided. The defence (led by Louis Aragon) wore red caps, the prosecution black ones. The good faith of the affair was rather damaged by the fact, subsequently disclosed, that Breton, once an admirer of Barrès, had earlier asked him to write a preface to one of his books. Barrès refused. And the rancorous Breton did not forget. Whence the trial.

Dada might have been made for Satie. The mouthpiece of the movement, a review called *Littérature*, allotted marks to personalities of the day. Satie came high in the estimation of Breton and Aragon, and he was awarded (a great honour) more or less the same ranking as the mass-murderer Landru. Debussy, Anatole France and Marshal Foch were relegated to the bottom of the league table.

The Dadaists quoted with approval the bizarre titles Satie gave to his music. They revelled in the fantastic directions and elaborate texts that accompanied the *Véritables préludes flasques* (*pour un chien*), the *Embryons desséchés*, the *Sports et divertissements* and the *Croquis et agaceries d'un gros bonhomme en bois*. A particular favourite was the "Marche du grand escalier" in the *Enfantillages pittoresques*, where the King, in love with a beautiful stairway that is never used for fear of its being spoiled, decides to have it stuffed. Besides, claimed the Dadaists, was not "furniture music" the purest affirmation of the Dada spirit? He had shown himself to be one of their own.

Soon he was caught up in all the dramas and adventures the movement created daily. *Littérature* published very superior writings by Paul Valéry, André Gide, Fargue and Stravinsky. There were poetry by Raymond Radiguet and music criticism by Auric. The editors were Breton, Aragon and their fellow poet Philippe Soupault. In January 1920, with the aid of Tristan Tzara, the magazine organised the *Premier Vendredi Littérature*. This meeting took place in the Palais des Fêtes. Marcelle Meyer played music by Satie in a programme that included works by the Six (Milhaud, Auric, Poulenc) and by Henri Cliquet-Pleyel of the "école d'Arcueil". Poems by Max Jacob and Apollinaire were recited. The opening lecture billed as "La crise du change" had attracted many local tradesmen who looked forward to hearing a talk on the crises of economic change. They heard, instead, a discourse on revolution in the arts.

A worse disillusionment followed when André Breton delivered a commentary on pictures by Gris, Léger and Chirico that were on display. Tristan Tzara appeared and read an article from a newspaper while bells and rattles provided a strident background of noise. The audience was furious. The "first Friday" of *Littérature* turned out to be the last.

Another lively incident was provoked by Breton's idea of arranging a congress to explain and defend the modern spirit in art. Tzara was invited to join the organising committee. He declined. The committee, which consisted for all intents and purposes of Breton himself, replied in a vexed tone and referred haughtily to "the promoter of a movement originating in Zurich". Now the bulletins flew thick and fast. The Dadaists, annoyed by the xenophobic slight on their leader, summoned Breton to explain himself on a given date at the Closerie des Lilas. (Known, to the ribald, as the "Connerie des Lilas".) Satie was among those who signed this command. He was also present when Breton duly attended and admitted responsibility for the disobliging remarks about Tzara. The congress, declared Satie and his friends, would not take place. In *Le Coeur à barbe*, a Dada publication, Satie announced grandly that the congress wasn't a meeting of domestic servants.

André Breton was too forceful a personality, too original a thinker to stay long among the Dadaists. Tzara, compared with him, was little more than a playboy, an amusing wit who had propagated a single idea brilliantly. Once you have proclaimed that all art is idiocy, that life itself is pointless, there is not much else to be said. Dada was self-destructive. Once its shock value had worn off it had nothing to propose. The gap it breached was filled by the Surrealism of which Breton made himself the high priest.

In the meantime Satie had gained several friends among the Dadaists. The American photographer Man Ray was one of them. Obeying Tzara's call to renounce oil painting and similar traditional methods, he made pictures with the aid of a spray gun. He is celebrated for the "rayograph" technique which he invented and displayed in Paris soon after his arrival there in 1921. The method was to place some object or other, a key, a pencil, a handkerchief, in the dark on a sheet of sensitive paper and then expose it briefly to the light. The resulting image was mysterious and often poetic. He also took many portrait photographs, one of them a very good representation of his friend Satie. These sold far better than his pictures. From then on he specialised with the camera.

Satie helped him in the preparations for his first exhibition at Philippe Soupault's gallery and bookshop. They went shopping together and bought a flat-iron, a box of nails and a tube of gum. Then Ray stuck a single line of nails on the underside of the iron, up-ended it and called it "Cadeau". The item figured prominently at the exhibition. The photographer was introduced as having been "a coal merchant, a millionaire several times over and chairman of the Chewing Gum Trust". Guests who came to the private view found the room obscured with toy balloons. Suddenly cheering Dadaists burst the skins with lighted cigarettes and the exhibition was declared open.

Another artist who befriended Satie was the strange and little-known Georges Malkine. He had travelled in the South Seas and worked his way back to France as a dish-washer. His past was ideally surrealistic and included the jobs of proof-reader, actor, fairground employee, street-seller, photographer and violinist. In 1966, remembering old acquaintance, he painted "La maison d'Erik Satie". It is a perfectly normal, almost picturesque view of a quaint house ... except that it defies with fascinating nonchalance the laws of gravity and architecture in a way impossible to describe with words. In visual terms it counterpoints the straight-faced absurdity of Satie's verbal fantasies.

Closest of all to Satie among the Dadaists was Francis Picabia. Painter, poet and a fellow of infinite jest, he for many years lightened the Paris art scene with his intermittent flamboyance. His mother was French, his father Cuban. He began his career as an orthodox Impressionist. After a visit to America he took up the abstract style. An intimate was Marcel Duchamp who became notorious for his "Tableau Dada", where he drew a moustache on the Mona Lisa and added the legend L H O O Q, which, when spoken with the French pronunciation, turns out as a schoolboy rudery.

During the 1914–18 war, taken under the patronage of a friendly general who made him his chauffeur, Picabia was sent under some pretext or other to Cuba, his father's homeland. He never got there. Having had to change boats in New York he remained in that town for a year or so and indulged to such an extent in the pleasures it offered that he became seriously ill. His wife arranged for him to convalesce in Spain. There he founded the magazine that played a large part in his activities. While in New York he had contributed to a famous review called *291* after the address in Fifth Avenue where it was published. So he called his own publication *391*.

After another brief stay in New York he returned eventually to Paris. An obliging mistress called Germaine Everling nursed him through illness and hallucinations caused by drugs. He made the acquaintance of Tristan Tzara and designed a cover for the magazine *Dada*. Meanwhile *391* had become a prominent weapon in the battle waged by Dada. Apollinaire had written for it, and so had Max Jacob. With humour and a joyful anarchy Picabia shared in all the fun that was going. "Dada is the biggest confidence trick of the century," he genially declared.

His poetry and his pictures (which included paintings in enamel and collages built up with matchsticks) he did not take seriously. They were expressions of his joie de vivre. In *391* he juggled with typography and amused himself with experiments in layout. When André Breton wrote a letter reproaching him about one of their eternal disagreements, Picabia featured it with the heading: "A letter from my grandfather." Underneath he printed his reply: "When I've smoked cigarettes it's not my habit to keep the dog-ends."

Stuffed with poems, drawings, epigrams and esoteric puns, every page of *391* carried the mark of the editor's ebullient personality. "Erik est Satierik" claimed a line referring to one of the contributors who was, of course, Erik Satie. In the "Cahiers d'un mammifère" Satie carried on his private vendettas against those who had offended him. "Cocteau adores me," he wrote. "I know it (only too well, indeed) ... But why does he kick me under the table?" He elaborated: "The author of *Parade* (J. Cocteau) was explaining (*for the thousandth time*) the miseries that overwhelmed him, carved him to pieces, burned him up, cast him down, scraped him raw, while he was writing that work – three lines long ... Everyone wept (*with laughter – even Laloy and Auric*) ... Suddenly, without warning – Monsieur X (*so well known for his perspicacity*) rose and said coldly: 'Down with Satie!' ... The effect was marvellous ... Yes ..." But Cocteau's offence – that of stealing Satie's thunder – was mild compared with Auric's and for the latter Satie reserved his deadliest thrusts.

When he was not attacking his enemies he threw off witticisms. "Don't breathe without having had your air boiled in advance ... If you want to live a long time live to a ripe old age ..." Or in the Rabelaisian mood popular with *391*: "J'aimerais jouer avec un piano qui aurait une grosse queue."

Besides giving him a regular platform in the magazine Picabia often invited him to his country home. (For the creator of *391* was rich, and this perhaps accounted for the gaiety and total lack of pompousness with which he faced life.) He never stayed long in one place and soon tired of the elegant Paris flat where he entertained Tristan Tzara, a thick lock of hair obscuring one eye and his monocle the other; the American poet Ezra Pound, some of whose *Cantos* first appeared in *391*; the dress-maker Paul Poiret; and others of fame or notoriety. At Tremblay, near Montfort-l'Amaury where Ravel lived, he bought a house, converted it and called it "la maison rose". A troupe of dogs lived there with the master and his mistress.

Satie was invited to lunch. As a precaution a mutual friend and his wife accompanied him. The composer was on his best behaviour. Picabia met them at the nearest railway station and drove them to Tremblay. Satie greeted Germaine Everling in high good humour, saluting her as "la bonne dame". Then he quickly shot out of the house and a little way down the road. At last he found what he sought: a convenient tree. A pressing need had made him too shy to enquire of his hostess the whereabouts of the bathroom.

Then everyone retired to the village's unique *bistrot*. Satie engulfed quantities of Pernod alternating with beer and Calvados. Rarely at ease with women, on this occasion he was particularly attentive to his friend's wife. Not only did she share his Scottish ancestry, she won his admiration by keeping slightly ahead of him in the drinking stakes.

They walked through the village and came to a monument which commemorated those who had fallen in the war. Satie read the list of names carefully. His hand spread out over his face. "What, my dear old mates! It's scandalous. Is that all the dead they have around here!"

Another acquaintance of Picabia was Blaise Cendrars. (Explorer, novelist, poet and adventurer, Cendrars looked and certainly lived the part of a congenital tough guy. Yet his private life was oddly at variance with the public figure. His conjugal arrangements must be delicately described as a "mariage blanc".) He had recently collaborated with Milhaud on *La Création du monde* which Rolf de Maré commissioned for his Ballets Suédois. Cendrars was anxious to bring Picabia and de Maré together. "You're made to understand each other," he told Picabia. Before going off to Brazil on one of his many journeys, Cendrars gave Picabia a plan for a ballet. The artist was to get in touch with de Maré, the idea being that he would design the scenery.

Picabia did as proposed. The result was that both he and de Maré agreed in disliking Cendrars' idea. They dropped it. Picabia outlined some of his own notions, humorous, illogical, fantastic. He offered to write the scenario and design costumes and scenery. Impressed by his enthusiasm, de Maré accepted. They confirmed Cendrars' choice of Satie to compose the music. The night the contract was signed he drank glass after glass of quetsche, remarking over and again: "Ah, mon vieux! C'est chic! Ça va être épatant!"

Rolf de Maré was a Swede, rich and the owner of large estates. Apart from his domain at Hildesborg in the south of his native country he had houses in France and Kenya. Ballet, folklore and agriculture were his interests. He sometimes described himself as a farmer. When the dancer Michel Fokine quarrelled with Diaghilev and came to Stockholm, he frequently stayed with de Maré. They thought of founding a ballet company. Though Swedish by origin it was to be French in style. The Ballets Suédois made their début on 24 March 1920 at the Théâtre des Champs-Elysées. Between then and the melancholy evening of 17 March 1925, when de Maré was forced gloomily to announce the disbandment of his company, two thousand seven hundred and eighty-six performances had been given of twenty-four ballets. For these the impresario had commissioned designs from Léger, Chirico and Bonnard. His composers had included Ravel, Poulenc, Milhaud, Auric, Honegger and Cole Porter. At certain moments in their brief career the Ballets Suédois equalled Diaghilev's own creation and sometimes went beyond it.

The principal of the Ballets Suédois was Jean Börlin. He was a dancer at the Stockholm Opera when Fokine discerned his outstanding talent. "His brief life was like a flame," said Fokine, "a sustained creative process. He went from one style to another, from one form to a new one. He did much to broaden the concept of ballet. He showed that it can be a serious art form." His brilliance depended more on inspiration than on technique. Painting deeply interested him. He believed that creative stimulus could just as well arise from another art. In fact, he stated that so far as choreography was involved "painting can be the departure point for the initial inspiration". He died at the age of thirty-seven, a suicide. Fokine paid him the supreme tribute: "Börlin was the one who most resembled me."

At a time when Cendrars was still supposed to be the author of the new ballet, Satie wrote to de Maré: "Future productions. Personally, I am very fond of you; and I'm convinced that with Jean Börlin and you, we shall, Cendrars and I, do good work."

With Cendrars safely out of the country and his ideas rejected, Picabia set to work on his own plan. He wanted a title that would symbolise the break between what had been once and what he dreamed of doing. The single word he chose was *relâche*, the expression which, on theatre bills or shop windows, means that the establishment is closed. *Relâche* was to signify that the old ideas were shut up and out of business. Another of the new elements he wanted to introduce was film. Like Man Ray, who produced several films, Picabia was attracted to the cinema. It was, as Germaine Dulac, Dali, Cocteau and Buñuel were to prove, an ideal surrealist medium. A close friend of his was Marcel Levesque who played a leading rôle in that series of silent crime epics titled *Judex* which enchanted the surrealists. He saw film as a help towards renewing dramatic art. *Relâche* would be an essay in "cinéchoreography".

"*Relâche*," he explained, "like infinity, has no friends. In order to have friends you need to be very ill, so ill that you can no longer keep them away. If Satie liked *Relâche* he probably liked it in the way he liked Kirsch, roast mutton or his umbrella. *Relâche* has no meaning. It is the pollen of our age. A little dust on our finger-tips and the drawing fades . . . We must think about it at a distance and not try to touch it . . ." As the frontispiece to the score he made a sketch of a naked man, clad only in a top hat and a wristwatch, exhorting a gentleman in evening dress. The latter, bearded, one eye shut and the other glaringly open, has just written, after several crossings-out on a large piece of paper: "When will people get out of the habit of explaining everything?"

This motto is particularly suited to *Relâche*. The first act opens with the Woman's entrance. She stops in the middle of the stage and examines the scenery. She sits down and smokes a cigarette while listening to the orchestra. Then she performs a "dance without music". The Man enters and executes with her a "dance of the revolving door". Men come in and dance. The Woman dances. Finale. In Act II everyone comes back again. The Men take off their evening dress to emerge clothed in spangled tights. They go back to their place and get their overcoats. There follow a wheelbarrow dance and a "danse de la couronne". The Woman places a laurel wreath on the brow of the most beautiful female member of the audience. (At the first performance the statuesque opera singer Marthe Chenal was selected for this attention.) After which this deliberately inexplicable Dada entertainment ends with a "Chanson mimée".

Between the acts there was to be a film which Picabia entitled, with a logic rare for him, *Entr'acte*. He asked René Clair to make it. That greatest of all French directors was then twenty-six years old. He had written poetry, worked as a newspaper journalist and put together songs for a music-hall star. As an actor he had played in a film made by the dancer Loïe Fuller and in another by Louis Feuillade, creator of *Judex*, a cinéaste whom, with Chaplin, the young man was to acknowledge as his master. The year before *Entr'acte* he had directed his first film, *Paris qui dort*, which revealed already his gifts of delicate invention.

Rolf de Maré took over the Théâtre des Champs-Elysées for a period and made Jacques Hébertot his manager. During that

224

time the Ballets Suédois were not the only distinguished company to appear there. Stanislavsky's troupe, Diaghilev's Ballets Russes, the Vienna Opera, and leading actors such as Louis Jouvet played in the theatre. As if all this activity were not enough for him, Hébertot also published three magazines. One of them carried a film supplement for which René Clair was responsible. When Picabia started looking for someone to make his film, Clair explained modestly, "since I was the only person about the place to have anything to do with films, I was the one they called on."

One evening at Maxim's Picabia scribbled a scenario on the restaurant's headed notepaper. The film was to open with Satie and himself loading a cannon which should explode "with as much noise as possible". Marcel Duchamp and Man Ray were to play a game of chess and Picabia was to clear the board with a jet of water from a hosepipe. A huntsman aimed at an ostrich egg balanced on a spray. A second huntsman aimed at a bird and shot his colleague. A scene showed twenty-one people lying on their backs presenting the soles of their feet to the camera. A woman dancer was viewed from below through transparent glass. The longest scene was a funeral procession involving a hearse pulled by a camel.

Since the prologue to *Entr'acte* seems to be the only occasion when Satie was pictured by the ciné-camera, it is worth describing the episode. The view shows a perspective of Paris rooftops seen from a high building. A cannon wheels itself in and, without human assistance, finally positions itself in front of the camera lens. Two men enter. The one who comes from the right is Satie, his beard freshly trimmed, his wing-collar and dark suit faultless. He wears a bowler and carries the famous umbrella. From the left comes Picabia, hair and shirt-sleeves billowing in the wind. The two conspirators hop in slow motion towards the cannon and admire it.

They argue. Satie, very dignified, puts his point of view. Picabia outlines his own. The composer lifts his umbrella and points at the audience. Picabia registers astonishment and dissent. Satie shrugs his shoulders as if in resignation. Finally, Picabia agrees and opens the breech of the cannon. Satie hands him a shell. The two men jump for joy. The shell is loaded into the gun while Satie and Picabia continue their rejoicing. The mouth of the cannon looms up and fills the screen. The shell zooms forth and the screen explodes into blackness. *Entr'acte* is ready to begin.

"I gave René Clair a tiny little scenario made out of nothing at all," wrote Picabia. "He turned it into a masterpiece: *Entr'acte*. The entr'acte in *Relâche* is a film that expresses our dreams and the unmaterialised events that occur in our minds; why recount what everyone can see every day?"

Entr'acte lasts for twenty-two minutes. After the prologue it assaults the eye with unexpected images. Jean Börlin is the huntsman who aims at ostrich eggs and is eventually shot by accident. Man Ray and Marcel Duchamp, posed on the edge of a rooftop, play chess as directed by the scenario. Others who appear from time to time include the playwright Marcel Achard, the artist Louis Touchagues, and Rolf de Maré himself. The ballerina, who revolves tirelessly on her glass pedestal, is seen in close-up to be wearing pince-nez and a black beard. A reminiscence of Satie?

The climax of the film and its longest sequence is the funeral procession. This releases all Clair's humour and ingenuity. The mourners assemble in line behind the hearse which is drawn by a camel. The driver, habited in three-cornered hat and ceremonial uniform with breeches, carries a brief-case under his arm. The hearse is decorated with a monogram constructed from the initials of E. Satie and F. Picabia. Among the wreaths hang bunches of sausages and hams which the mourners nibble at from time to time.

The procession moves slowly off and into the open road. It comes to the fairground of Luna Park. Here, unperceived, the camel slips its traces and goes in one direction while the hearse rolls in another. The vehicle gains speed and the mourners start trotting to keep up. Now, with brilliant editing of long-shot, close-up and angle-shot, comes the funniest episode in the film. The hearse, continually increasing the pace while the exhausted mourners struggle behind to keep up, lurches round narrow corners and down steep hills at terrifying speed. Once it drives straight onto a switchback and hurtles up and down at a dizzy rate. Released from the switchback it bumps along country roads. The coffin is shaken out and drops into a field. A handful of mourners who have stayed the course run up to it. The coffin opens and Jean Börlin jumps out dressed as a conjurer. He waves his magic wand and the coffin vanishes. Another wave and the mourners disappear. He turns the wand on himself and evaporates also.

While shooting progressed – and there were many problems, not least of which was how to find a suitable garage at night for the hearse and the camel – Satie fussed and fidgeted. "And the film?" he wrote to Clair. "When? . . . Time passes (*and doesn't pass again*). Am in a tizzy at the thought of being forgotten by you. Yes . . . Send me quickly the details of that wonderful work of yours. Warmest thanks. Ever yours, I am . . ."

When the film was complete he viewed it with anxious attention. Each episode he timed to the second and matched it against appropriate lengths of music. This, of course, is the usual technique nowadays, but Satie was the first to approach the writing of film music in a professional manner. As early as 1908 Saint-Saëns had composed an accompaniment for the historical film *L'Assassinat du duc de Guise*. Unlike *Entr'acte*, which used the modern procedure of quick cutting from shot to shot, *L'Assassinat du duc de Guise* was more of a photographed play than an original film. If Saint-Saëns deserves credit as the earliest important composer to write film music, Satie must be honoured for recognising the technical demands of the medium and pioneering the craft.

The basic unit is a theme of eight bars which is first heard during the opening sequences that pan over chimneys and exploding balloons. It returns, completely unchanged by variation or development, again and again throughout the film. The terse little tune accompanies the scene where boxing-gloves dance across the screen and where matches strike against each other before catching fire. When the funeral procession starts this is the theme which is played. It makes its last bow in the final episode when Jean Börlin leaps through a paper screen.

In between there have been other motifs, each as short and abrupt as the main one. The bearded ballerina twirls round to a theme with the faintest suggestion of a café-concert waltz, though it is sternly truncated before it can develop. A distorted version of the Chopin Funeral March makes its appearance as the hearse covers the first lap of its journey. The accompaniment to go with scenes where mourners run after the speeding hearse is anything but conventional "chase" music. Yet its very refusal to extra-illustrate the film, its prim, steadfast reserve strike just the right note of incongruity.

As with all good film music, the *Entr'acte* score refuses to draw attention to itself. It is purely functional. The aim is to point the action of the film without the audience being aware of it. Sound and vision fuse into a whole. One need only compare *Entr'acte* with the lush Hollywood scores written by a Max Steiner or an Erich Korngold to realise the concise perfection of Satie's work – though it is true that neither of these composers ever had the privilege of collaborating with a film-maker so original or inspired as René Clair. What Satie produced is, in effect, the supreme example of "musique d'ameublement". With *Entr'acte* he had found the ideal application for it.

After its first performance in 1924 *Entr'acte* was screened two years later at an avant-garde Paris cinema in a double bill with Pabst's *Joyless Street*. In 1968 it was reissued with a sound-track containing Satie's complete original score conducted by Henri Sauguet. (Milhaud's four-handed arrangement for two pianos, which he called *Cinéma*, "Entr'acte symphonique", dated from 1926 and may have been prepared for the showing with the Pabst film.) In between, of course, it has been projected a number of times at the National Film Theatre in London and at other cinémathèques in France and the u.s.a.

The score of the ballet for which Clair provided *Entr'acte* is almost as unassertive as the film music. After the overture, a march of awkward innocence, comes "Projection", an item which accompanied the prologue to *Entr'acte* where Satie and Picabia fired the cannon on the roof. Like the other film music, it is broken up into short phrases, though here Satie does allow himself a little more room for elaboration. The ballet proper starts with the Woman's entrance, a very slow and caressing number imbued with a charming hesitance. The same tenderness is shown in the Dance of the Revolving Door, a simple restatement of the café-concert waltz mood, and, indeed, in all the Woman's solo numbers and those which she dances with the Man. These are to be set against the nervous truculence that flavours the music associated with the Men at their entrances and exits. Snatches of popular tunes are blandly worked into the score. "Cadet Roussel" is heard when the Men take off their evening dress, and other pop morsels include "As-tu vu la cantinière?" and "Retire tes pieds, Tu n'vois pas que tu m'ennuies". Satie knew there would be objections. "Timid people and conventional thinkers blame me for using these tunes. I'm not interested in the opinions of such folk . . . Reactionary fatheads will thunder . . . Pooh! – I only admit to one judge: the public. They'll recognise the tunes and won't be at all shocked to hear them. Isn't the public human? . . . I wouldn't want to make a lobster blush, or even an egg . . ."

The music of *Relâche* has a notable symmetry. The gentleness, the almost wistful quality of the episodes for the Woman are paired with the rough vigour of the dances of the Men. This taste for pairing extends also to individual numbers. The theme of the first item, "Projection", is echoed in one of the last scenes where a laurel wreath is placed on the head of a woman in the audience. The melody of the Woman's entry recurs in her final solo. As you work inwards, with the beginning and the end of the ballet marking the outer edges, you find that each number is mirrored by another placed at a given point. Each act could be played backward as well as forward. Nothing would be lost. Like the trinitarian piano pieces, *Relâche* is a well-made artifact. No stitching can be detected. No join shows.

He worked hard on the score of *Relâche*, assembling each detail, choosing, rejecting, constructing the total framework only after he had subjected it to exacting criticism. On Thursday 15 May 1924, six months before the scheduled performance, he wrote to de Maré:

> Cher Exquis Directeur – I'm working for you: it's falling into place a bit, but I still haven't found the true direction. It'll come, sharply and surely, let's not doubt it. As for the Beaumont seats, you'll receive two for the dress rehearsal [of *Mercure*] which – something very unexpected – will take place on the following day (Sunday) after the "première"! . . . I shan't be at the performance. Casella [the Italian composer] is in Paris. I told him to write to you: he would be good company in our work. All best wishes to Börlin, please. Let him be very sure that I'm working seriously *for him*.

By 23 October, in a letter to Roger Désormière who was to conduct the first performance, Satie disclosed that he still had seven pages to orchestrate. On Saturday, he promised, he'd be giving the second act to the copyist. Désormière would have the complete score early in November, "towards the 10th". This would give a fortnight or so in which to rehearse the music.

Picabia in the meantime was launching the sort of campaign at which he, an alert publicist, excelled. In the pages of *391*, in newspaper puffs, on posters, in manifestoes, he spread sensational word about the ballet to come. The Ballets Suédois, he announced, were the only representatives of contemporary life, the only opposers of academicism, the only group capable of pleasing the international public. They did not seek to be ancient or modern. They furthered revolution by means of a new movement which every day destroyed convention and replaced it with invention.

Relâche was trumpeted as an "Instantaneist ballet in two acts and a cinematographic entr'acte and the Tail of the dog". (Tail of the dog? As René Clair points out, no one ever saw a shadow of it. He was not even quite sure what "instantaneist" meant. . . .)* Picabia teased his readers with elaborate riddles about men in evening dress, camels, dogs' tails. "Bring black glasses and something to plug your ears with," suggested advertisements for *Relâche*. "Ex-members of Dada are requested to come and demonstrate and shout: 'DOWN WITH SATIE! DOWN WITH PICABIA! LONG LIVE THE *Nouvelle Revue Française*!'"

An article in the programme for *Relâche* expounded its creator's views:

> *Relâche* is life, life as I love it, life without a tomorrow, the life of today, everything for today, nothing for yesterday, nothing for tomorrow. Car lights, pearl necklaces, the delicate round contours of women, advertising, music, the car, a few men in evening dress, movement, noise, action, clear transparent water, the pleasure of laughter, that's *Relâche* . . . *Relâche* is movement without a direction, neither forward nor back, neither to left nor right. *Relâche* doesn't turn and yet it doesn't go straight ahead; *Relâche* ambles through life with a great burst of laughter; Erik Satie, Börlin, Rolf de Maré, René Clair, Prieur and I created *Relâche* rather in the way God created life. There's no

* Perhaps something to do with snapshots (instantanés) which Kodak had made a part of the language. Satie himself had written the *Heures séculaires et instantanées*.

scenery, no costumes, no nudes, only space, the space our imagination loves to survey; *Relâche* is the happiness of moments without reflection; why reflect, why have a convention of beauty or joy? You have to risk indigestion if you want to eat! Why not ruin yourself? Why not work forty-eight hours straight off if we like? Why not have fifteen women; and why shouldn't a woman have fifty-two men if it can give her pleasure? *Relâche* advises you to live it up, for life will always be longer in the school of pleasure than in the school of morality, the school of art, the school of religion, the school of social conventions.

During the preparations for *Relâche* Picabia established headquarters at the Hôtel Istria in Montparnasse. He had, anyway, tired of the country and wanted an excuse to live in Paris. All the guests at this rambling hotel were artists or intellectuals or models or their lovers. None of the rooms possessed a key, each was open to any passer-by in the corridor, and life there had a pleasing quality of unexpectedness. It was an ideal setting in which to bring *Relâche* to life.

As the day of the first performance drew near (it had been set for 17 November) the atmosphere in the Hôtel Istria became frenzied. There were rehearsals throughout the afternoon of the 17th. Picabia came back to his room exhausted but full of confidence. The telephone rang. In a broken voice, Rolf de Maré reported that Jean Börlin had succumbed to an attack of nerves and would not be able to dance. He asked Picabia to join him immediately. Picabia himself was too agitated and sent his companion Germaine Everling as his deputy.

She found all access to the Théâtre des Champs-Elysées jammed with cars. Crowds of first-nighters pressed angrily against closed doors while a helpless manager repeated that Börlin was ill and the performance postponed. Whipped up to a pitch of expectation by Picabia's campaign, they refused to believe him and insisted on waiting. "It's a joke by Picabia," they said, ". . . not bad as publicity." Until eleven o'clock that night the frustrated audience kept vigil. Then reluctantly they trickled away. Custom at the *Boeuf sur le toit* night-club increased visibly as people filed in to assuage their disappointment. Circumstance had played a greater joke than any released by Picabia so far: the word

Relâche displayed on the theatre's façade meant exactly what it said.

When Börlin had recovered *Relâche* made its postponed début on the 27th. The audience, now, was ready for anything. A drop curtain embellished with provocative slogans met their eye. The set dazzled them with the reflected light of hundreds of bright metallic discs arranged in geometrical form. Jean Börlin came on in an invalid carriage. His partner Edith Bonsdorff, dressed in white and covered with diamonds, inspired him to recover the power of movement. He left the carriage and went towards her. This illustrated one of Picabia's favourite ideas, that of the man who is "paralysed" through auto-suggestion until a source from outside sets him free.

The film of *Entr'acte* turned indignant murmurs into laughter. Then the mood changed. Whistles were heard, and clamorous protest. Picabia was delighted. The bearded ballerina and the camel-drawn hearse were received with hoots. The dizzy ride on the switchback stimulated groans and uproar. As many boos as cheers were heard at the film's conclusion.

By now the audience was as lively as Picabia had hoped. The second act of *Relâche* unfolded amid noisy disapproval. The scenery included posters declaring: "Those who aren't satisfied are authorised to — off", and, "There are people who prefer the ballets at the Opéra, poor idiots". Throughout the whole of the act a uniformed fireman poured water ceaselessly from one bucket into another while the dancers gyrated around him. At the tumultuous curtain call Satie and Picabia squeezed into a tiny Citroën car and puttered around the stage waving at the audience.

As Fernand Léger wrote, the ballet delivered "a lot of kicks up a lot of bottoms, sacred or otherwise". It made its sensation and had twelve consecutive performances. Like "the pollen of our age", in Picabia's phrase, *Relâche* vanished and left not a wrack behind. The music lingers. There were many who did not agree that Satie, in the words of a slogan on the drop curtain, was "the greatest musician in the world". Even some of his friends were repelled by his association with Dadaist extravagance. Georges Auric was the most belligerent. He jeered at his former idol as "a Norman notary", "a suburban chemist", as "Citizen Satie (of the Arcueil Soviet)". After *Relâche* he brought out an article entitled

"Adieu, Satie" in which he deplored the music and explained why he could no longer sympathise with the composer. Satie was caught in a merciless crossfire that emanated from both the outraged supporters of tradition and from the avant-garde musicians upon whom he might have relied for support.

XXVIII

Last Communion

One evening he invited friends to dinner before taking them on to a performance of *Relâche*. Normally blessed with a good appetite, he ate, they were surprised to note, but little and drank only Vittel water.

At the beginning of 1925 he wrote to Rolf de Maré. The message sounded a valedictory note:

> Arcueil, 10 January 1924 (25, I mean).
>
> Mon Cher Directeur,
> Forgive me for not having thanked you earlier for your kind invitation of 31 December. I was too tired to see you that evening to give you in person my New Year greetings and my best wishes for a good journey . . . I would, too, have told you what a charming impresario you have been to me. Good day, my dear Director: all my good wishes to Börlin, please; and believe me, your most devoted Erik Satie.

After the first night of *Relâche* he had fallen seriously ill. The diagnosis reported cirrhosis of the liver. This did not surprise his friends. At the age of fifty-nine he had behind him close on forty years of solid drinking in the bars of Montmartre. His capacity never ceased to astonish. He could easily imbibe half a bottle of cognac followed by several glasses of beer without showing the slightest effect, his speech unflurried as always and his manner perfectly steady.

Now he was so weak that he found it difficult to hoist himself up into buses or trains. At the beginning of 1925 he would travel into Paris each day from Arcueil and lunch at the home of friends – Derain, Braque, Milhaud. Once inside the house he kept on his coat and the bowler, which he pulled firmly down to his eyes. He clung pathetically to his umbrella, a fetish, a comfort, a support. Until the time came for him to catch his train back to Arcueil, he sat motionless and silent. He was persuaded to take a room at a hotel in order to avoid tedious journeys back and forth.

In the hotel room, still wearing coat and bowler, he sprawled in a chair contemplating the reflection that gazed fixedly back at him from the mirror. The hours passed in silent stillness. He contrived an elaborate arrangement of strings that enabled him to open the door to callers without stirring from his chair, or to work the light-switch. The telephone he had always loathed – when visiting friends he would take the receiver off so that conversation would not be interrupted – but in his present state he was ready to acknowledge its existence. Sometimes he would ring people for a chat, though the vagaries of the system and the pertness of the operators drove him often to a frenzy.

He pined for the livelier surroundings of the Hôtel Istria where Picabia had held court. There he installed himself and his doctor promptly ordered him to bed. On one floor lived Marcel Duchamp in the throes of a dying love affair with the wife of a well-known artist. They slept together on the express condition that their bodies did not touch. The frustrated lady would erupt into hysterics and seek comfort from other tenants, usually at an early hour of the morning. In the middle of the night there would be thumps and bangs as some artist pursued a fleeing nymph up and down the stairs. The magnificent Kiki de Montparnasse, the famous model and beauty who lived on the first floor, had the habit of addressing acquaintances in a stentorian voice from one landing to another.

For once in his life Satie needed human company, the presence and the chatter of fellow artists. He lay on his bed growing thinner every day. Pleurisy supervened. Etienne de Beaumont obtained for him a private room at the Hôpital Saint-Joseph. Milhaud's cousin Madeleine, whom Milhaud was soon to marry, came and packed Satie's case for him, the case he had bought to go on his journey to Monte Carlo in 1923. An ambulance took him to the hospital. With astonishment a helpful nun laid out the articles of his toilette: a couch-grass toothbrush and a pumice stone.

His compulsive neuroses multiplied. The gifts visitors brought him – and they were received with genuine pleasure – had to be arranged in a particular formation so that he could contemplate them from his bed. The pieces of string, the bric-à-brac he hoarded with jealous care, were subject to the most scrupulous rules of order. Each item had its place and must be put exactly where habit demanded. The money his publisher brought him as an advance payment for *Relâche* was stowed away, note by note, inside the pages of old newspapers.

He refused steadily to see Poulenc and Auric. His closest friends, apart from Milhaud, were now the sculptor Brancusi, the young composers Jean Wiener and Roger Caby, and Roger Désormière who had conducted *Relâche*. To Valentine Hugo he remained faithful. She bought him the handkerchiefs he ordered on a whim (Madeleine Milhaud found eighty-nine of them in a bundle of washing at Arcueil) and she felt as never before that she was his "douce petite fille". With a feeble hand he rolled back the blanket and horrified her at the sight of his cadaverous, skeletal frame.

In the days of his youth people had said to him: "You'll see when you're fifty years old." Later he was to add: "I'm fifty; I've seen nothing." That was his attitude throughout life. In many ways he never grew up. He retained the vision of a child and preserved it wonderfully untainted among the raffish bars and dives where he spent his manhood. Despite the presence of a brother and a sister he had the mentality of an only child. The early death of his mother and his father's wanderings deprived him of a steady focus. His formative years were spent in an elderly household under the care of a religious grandmother and a grandfather of vague eccentricities. He passed a great deal of time in the company of whimsical Uncle Adrien, who had withdrawn from everyday life and ignored its demands in order to indulge his fantasies. At the age of ten he had submitted to the Gothic charm. By the time he was twelve years old and had joined his father once again in a settled home the basis of his character was already formed, immutable.

Obstinate he was, and contrary too. Even though he showed signs of enjoying music, the fact that his stepmother, whom he disliked, encouraged him to study it seriously, was enough for him to react against her well-meant plan. He would not be driven. The slightest threat to his independence made him shy away. He was determined to command his own fate. When, in middle age, he put himself to school again, this was to some extent an acknowledgement that he had earlier been at fault. On the other hand, had he experienced the full rigours of an academic training at the usual age, one may argue that his original gifts might have been drilled into a bland uniformity.

His life became a series of renunciations. It is true that in youth he fell to the temptation of seeking publicity with his Rosicrucian antics. But every saint needs, on at least one occasion, to have been a sinner. The bad example of Péladan betrayed him into the lapse. For the rest, he gave up fame, self-seeking, money, and all the lures that most men exhaust themselves in pursuing. His behaviour during the *Relâche* episode, which struck many people as undignified and the result of a squalid desire for notoriety, must be seen, rather, as part of the Dada pattern intended to shock torpid sensibilities into making a reappraisal of what had been numbed by tradition.

Money had no attraction for him except as a means to obtaining good food, drink, and presents for the boys and girls of Arcueil. A loan he regarded as a demeaning transaction. A gift he would accept with delight. He was content with the most trifling sums for his music, and would even feel offended when a publisher offered what, to him, was an immorally high amount.

Women were unimportant in the existence of this solitary. His youthful affair with Suzanne Valadon is the only documented adventure he is known to have had. There may have been others with less celebrated females. It is doubtful. "I am," he said, "a man whom women do not understand." He was afraid of them, timid, shy, unable to appreciate them. His irony, defensive but penetrating, was not calculated to make him popular with them. In growing older he preferred avuncular relationships, as with Valentine Hugo. There are many instances of his genuine affection for talented young men and his efforts to help them. Might this have been a sublimation? Saint-Saëns was also noted for the tendency, and he was a man, like Satie, of many repressions.

Satie claimed that he never married for fear of being cuckolded. This is significant. He was afraid of committing himself, afraid of being duped, afraid of attracting derision. He would not dare to take a first step that might reveal him without defence. So he lived alone, choosing to meet friends under circumstances of his own making and at times when he knew his mask was well adjusted. A terrible insecurity haunted him. It drove him to furious rage over trifles. He was ultra-sensitive to imagined slights. He detected insult in the lightest remark and denigration in a passing phrase. Something had happened long ago to cause this. The early death of his mother, his unsettled infancy, the strain of being an elder child, the disappointment with Suzanne Valadon, are all among the things which could have nurtured this trait.

Like Alphonse Allais, he concealed his shyness beneath a façade of elaborate mockery. In his life, as in his work, the deepest feelings were encased by a protective covering of humour and jest. His adoption of the very uniform – bowler, umbrella, dark suit – of those whose conventions he laughed at was the supreme joke. Yet if he sometimes appeared to be a clown, he was a clown with a secret that verged on the tragic. And again like Allais, he sought in alcoholism an escape from it, a way of dulling the despair he felt at the shock to his sensitivity of a hostile world and at his distress with a humanity that was brutal and uncaring.

His refusal to commit himself, which in practical matters was a drawback, emerged as one of the great strengths in the artist. He was able to stand back and coolly appraise. Accepted enthusiasms passed him by. Reactions hallowed by unthinking custom were foreign to him. His gaze was cool and fresh. He looked at music anew and put a bomb under it. The incongruous verbal decoration he gave to his derisive piano pieces, the purely musical techniques of parody and satire, were a healthy counterblast to Romantic excess. Having emphasised in this way the absurdities of an outdated style no longer capable of useful exploitation, he evolved an idiom to replace it.

The bizarre humour in which he draped the wrecking job he undertook has sometimes been misunderstood. There are those who believe him to be little more than an eccentric, a poseur even.

Irony, that most French of characteristics, is a dangerous weapon. It can so easily deceive the unwary. The composer of *Socrate* was not a practical joker. Nor was the musician who slaved grimly and long over each bar he wrote, who with every new work sought a fresh beginning.

There never was, there could never be, as he said himself, a Satie school. His solution to the problem of filling the gap caused by his subversion was unique and entirely his own. The music he wrote was inimitable and self-contained. Other composers would have to work out their own salvation. His imitators could only follow him on the most superficial level by playing the sedulous ape to the café-concert forms and music-hall styles he adapted to his own purpose. Attempts to discern an identifiable system by which he worked have not succeeded. A contemporary avant-garde musician became very excited when he found, in Satie's notebooks, what appeared to be arcane sequences of numbers. Were these the formulae that governed his compositions and techniques? Milhaud explained that they referred to the composer's shopping lists.

Satie's literary style has also been reproduced. The rows of dots, the jerky exclamations, the disconnected phrases, have been adopted by those who have little to say but who believe that they are thus conferring a novel profundity upon their writings. In a piece he wrote on Ambroise Thomas there recurs from time to time the banal refrain: "Now where did I put my umbrella?" The repetitions are amusing – once. When the mannerism is taken up and elevated into a system, as it has been by imitators, it becomes merely a tiresome camouflage for poverty of thought.

Imitation of Satie the musician and Satie the writer is doomed to barrenness. This is an indication of his achievement. He stands entirely alone, unapproachable. He had always said that an artist should give up everything for the sake of his art. Fiercely, despite torments of depression and self-questioning, he clung to his ideal. There was no compromise. His failures were the result of the technical inadequacies often associated with an original creator. At his best he succeeded in evolving that true and classic simplicity which can flow only from intense concentration and thorough use of material.

"I have never written a note I didn't mean," he remarked to Robert Caby as he lay in the Hôpital Saint-Joseph. In those last months Caby looked after him devotedly and with patience sustained the rages the sufferer flew into at the routine of an invalid existence. Satie had never been ill before. He disliked the parade of thermometers and pills and diets.

His old enemy the sun shone very brightly. The weather was hot. He had little strength left and could take only liquids. By the end of June he was very weak. Elise Jouhandeau went to see him. Though his body was only a shadow, a furious will to live expressed itself on his face. A bell tinkled outside in the corridor and the sound of hurried footsteps was heard: the viaticum was being taken to a dying person. Satie struggled up on his bed. "*That* one's beaten me to it," he said.

Shortly before his last illness he had seen Stravinsky. Fresh from church he remarked: "I've taken a bit of Communion this morning." There was no doubt that he'd gone back to the religion of his Norman ancestors. He had long conversations with the nuns at the hospital. Before he died the last sacrament was administered in due form.

By the end of June his speech had turned incoherent. A visitor, used to his precise and pointed talk, sat with pitying alarm as he rambled for several hours. On Wednesday 1 July he fell into a coma. Flies crawled over his motionless face and did not wake him. Next day Valentine Hugo arrived carrying red roses for him. She met Roger Désormière who had also come to visit. They heard that he had died the previous evening. Together they went into a cold, bare, clean little room. Satie lay in a cheap wooden coffin touched up to look like mahogany. His mouth hung open. He looked, said Valentine Hugo, like a dead bird. She put the roses over his heart and arranged some of them to conceal the desperate gaping mouth. He was fifty-nine years old.

His brother Conrad, long since estranged over some trifling quarrel, heard the news by chance. The watchman at the factory where he worked asked him if he happened to be related to the Erik Satie whose death was briefly announced in the paper.

The funeral took place on the following Monday at Arcueil. Jean Cocteau was there with his mother and Valentine Hugo. Satie's music-hall connections were represented by Paulette Darty. Ravel, his "disciple" and butt of his wisecracks, joined the mourners. They included his publisher and the mayor of Arcueil, P. A. Templier, president of the "Amis du vieil Arcueil" and father of Satie's first biographer. Satie's days at the Schola Cantorum were recalled by the presence of Albert Roussel. All the members of the Six attended with the exception of Louis Durey. Ricardo Viñes and Pierre Bertin came also to pay their tribute. Others were Francis Picabia, Jean Börlin, Henri Sauguet and Robert Caby. The family numbered Conrad Satie, nephews and nieces.

The hearse was decorated with bunches of roses and hortensias. A wreath of violets, about twenty-five francs' worth, carried an inscription: "To M. Satie from his fellow tenants". The local mourners outnumbered the folk who had come over from Paris. They esteemed Satie as a man but knew little of his music. "As the hearse went down to the church through the streets of Arcueil," Cocteau remembered, "it was as if we were going down to the sea, at Honfleur, his native town. Below, instead of the sea, there stretched a lugubrious suburb." Two simple wreaths added a sparse decoration to the church. Behind the altar hung a scrap of black cloth. There were no speeches by the graveside.

Even at Satie's funeral there were mysteries. Who was the melancholy septuagenarian who joined the mourners? Somebody identified him as a composer named Alexandre Georges. Milhaud and his young friends tended to forget that Satie's career extended back into the previous century and covered the generations of Debussy, of the Sâr Péladan and the Rosicrucians, of Ravel. He had always seemed so much a part of the contemporary age. And now here was a living reminder of that distant time they never knew. Georges probably belonged to the religious period of Satie's life. His works included an oratorio for Our Lady of Lourdes, a mystery on the Passion, a Requiem, a De Profundis and a mass to the glory of Our Lady of the sea. His friendship with Satie must have been close, his affection deep, for the sad-faced mourner to have taken the trouble to come all the way to Arcueil.

Satie's married sister Olga lived now in Buenos Aires and her address was unknown. In such cases the law demanded that his home be sealed off and his belongings disposed of by public sale. Conrad obtained permission to keep his brother's letters, manuscripts and notebooks. These he confided to Milhaud who was able to arrange for posthumous publication.

The moment came when the flat at 22 rue Cauchy had to be opened up. Conrad Satie asked Milhaud, Roger Désormière, Jean

Wiener and Roger Caby to go with him. They unlocked the door and found themselves in a narrow passage that led past a tiny wash-place into Satie's room. For twenty-seven years no one had ever penetrated this inner temple. The intruders, moved as it was by their temerity, were overwhelmed at the sight that met them.

They could not believe that the neat and impeccable Satie had lived in such desolate penury. The room contained a wretched bed, a table heaped with various things, a chair, and a half-empty cupboard on which were piled half a dozen unworn and by now unfashionable velvet suits. In every corner lay strewn old hats, newspapers, walking-sticks. An ancient battered piano, its pedals held together with string, was the resting place of a postal packet. Satie had torn it open at the corner a little to see what it contained and then put it aside. Its companions were first editions of Debussy carrying affectionate inscriptions from the composer. Wedged down behind the piano were the scores of *Jack in the Box* and *Geneviève de Brabant* which Satie had long since given up for lost. An old cigar box contained thousands of bits of paper on which he had inscribed his exquisite calligraphy and inked in with maniacal precision fantastic little drawings and plans. A thick pall of dust covered everything. The windows were filthy and the curtains faded, rotten with age.

At the auction Etienne de Beaumont secured a portrait by Antoine de la Rochefoucauld showing Satie at the organ in Rosicrucian days. Another souvenir of that period was the picture by Desboutin which Braque obtained, together with the old piano. Milhaud became the possessor of many walking-sticks, drawings, medievalesque designs and a Zuloaga portrait of Satie.

A year after his death Satie was remembered with a performance organised by Diaghilev of *Parade, Mercure* and *Jack in the Box*. Etienne de Beaumont arranged an evening when Désormière conducted the first hearing of *Geneviève de Brabant* complete with puppets.

On 30 June 1928, there was a "journée Erik Satie" in Arcueil. P. A. Templier and a group of friends sponsored the unveiling of a plaque on the wall of the composer's old home. A concert in the town hall included piano works played by Ricardo Viñes and *Socrate* with an accompaniment by Milhaud. The twenty-fifth anniversary of Satie's death was marked in similar fashion on

242

25 June 1950. On this occasion Templier's son, the biographer, joined the speech-makers.

Apotheosis came in 1966. On 14 and 15 May Arcueil commemorated the centenary of its adopted townsman's birth. Another concert and an exhibition under the auspices of the Bibliothèque Nationale were among the events. The Parc des Irlandais turned overnight into the Parc Erik Satie. The mayor and Darius Milhaud unveiled the bust of Satie which today, a little weather-beaten and defiant, contemplates the children who play there.

He lies in Arcueil cemetery not far from the noisy main road. Brancusi helped design the tomb that marks his grave. What would Satie have thought about the tributes Arcueil paid him? He, one feels, would have enjoyed these remembrances offered by the little community where he spent so much of his humble and very private life. Though there was one element capable of giving him a peculiarly malicious pleasure. At the ceremony inaugurating the plaque in the rue Cauchy, the town councillor who delivered an oration was a prominent member of the Communist branch to which Satie once belonged.

List of Works

The list of works that follows is based, by kind permission of Kenneth Thompson, on the catalogue he established for his *Dictionary of Twentieth-Century Composers (1911–1971)*, Faber & Faber, 1973

1 *Elégie* (J. P. Contamine de Latour). For voice and piano. 1886. Ded. Mlle Céleste Le Prédour. Pub. 1887, Alfred Satie; 1968, Salabert, as *Trois Mélodies de 1886*, No. 2.
2 *Les Anges* (J. P. Contamine de Latour). For voice and piano. 1886. Ded. Charles Levadé. Pub. 1887, Alfred Satie, as *Trois Mélodies* No. 1; 1968, Salabert, as *Trois Mélodies de 1886*, No. 1.
3 *Les Fleurs* (J. P. Contamine de Latour). For voice and piano. 1886. Ded. Mlle la Comtesse Gérald de Marguenat. Pub. 1887, Alfred Satie, as *Trois Mélodies* No. 2; 1968, Salabert, as *Trois Autres Mélodies* No. 3.
4 *Sylvie* (J. P. Contamine de Latour). For voice and piano. 1886. Ded. Mlle Olga Satie. Pub. 1887, Alfred Satie, as *Trois Mélodies* No. 3; 1968, Salabert, as *Trois Mélodies de 1886* No. 3.

5   *Chanson* (J. P. Contamine de Latour). For voice and piano. 1887. Ded. Mlle Valentine de Bret. Pub. ?1889, Alfred Satie; 1968, Salabert, as *Trois Autres Mélodies* No. 1.

6   *Valse Ballet.* For piano. 1885.

7   *Fantaisie Valse.* For piano. 1885.

8   *4 Ogives.* For piano. 1886. Pub. Alfred Satie.

9   *Trois Sarabandes.* For piano. September 1887. No. 2 ded. Maurice Ravel. Pub. Rouart Lerolle.

9a *Trois Sarabandes.* Orch. Robert Caby. Pub. Salabert.

10 *Trois Gymnopédies.* For piano. 1888.

    1 *Lent et douloureux.* Ded. Mlle Jeanne de Bret.

    2 *Lent et triste.* Ded. Conrad Satie.

    3 *Lent et grave.* Ded. Charles Levadé.

    Pub. Rouart Lerolle. (Alfred Satie).

10a *Gymnopédies.* Nos. 1 & 3 orch. Claude Debussy. Pub. E. Baudoux.

10b *Gymnopédie No. 2.* Orch. Herbert Murrill.

10c *Gymnopédie No. 2.* Orch. Roland-Manuel. Pub. Salabert.

11 *Trois Gnossiennes.* For piano. 1890. Nos 1 & 3 marked: *Lent.* No. 1 ded. Roland-Manuel. Pub. 1913, Rouart Lerolle.

11a *Gnossienne No. 4.* For piano. 1891. Pub. 1968, Salabert. Also version orch. R. Caby.

11b *Gnossienne No. 5.* For piano. 8 July 1889. Pub. 1968, Salabert. Also version orch. R. Caby.

11c *Gnossienne No. 6.* For piano. 1897. Pub. 1968, Salabert. Also version orch. R. Caby.

11d *Gnossiennes Nos 1–3.* Orch. Lanchberry. Pub. Salabert.

11e *Gnossienne No. 3.* Orch. Francis Poulenc. 1939. Pub. 1949, Rouart Lerolle.

12 *Première pensée Rose + Croix.* For piano. 20 January 1891. Pub. 1968, Salabert.

13 *Le Fils des Etoiles.* Incidental music (Joséphin Péladan) for flutes and harps. 1891.

13a *Trois Préludes* (from "Le Fils des Etoiles"). For piano. 1891.

    1 *Act I: La Vocation.*

    2 *Act II: L'Initiation.*

    3 *Act III: L'Incantation.*

    Pub. Rouart Lerolle.

13b *Le Fils des Etoiles: Prélude, Act I.* Reorch. Maurice Ravel. 1913.

13c Le Fils des Etoiles. Version orch. Roland-Manuel. Pub.
     Salabert.
14   Hymne au drapeau (pour le Prince de Byzance du Sâr Péladan).
     For voice and piano. 1891. Pub. 1968, Salabert as Hymne
     pour le "Salut drapeau". Also version orch. R. Caby.
15   Uspud. "Ballet chrétien" in three acts by J. P. Contamine de
     Latour. 1892. Privately printed. Version orch. R. Caby pub.
     Salabert.
16   Petite ouverture à danser. For piano. Before 1900. Pub. 1968,
     Salabert. Also version orch. R. Caby.
17   Poudre d'or. Valse for piano. c. 1900. Ded. Mlle Stéphanie
     Nantas. Pub. ?1901, Rouart Lerolle. Version for café
     orchestra pub. Salabert.
18   Tendrement (Vincent Hyspa). "Valse chantée". c. 1900. Pub.
     ?1902, E. Baudoux/Bellon Ponscarme. Version with café
     orchestra acc. pub. Salabert.
19   La Diva de l'Empire (Dominique Bonnaud & Numa Blès).
     "Marche chantée" from the revue "Dévidons la Bobine".
     "Répertoire Paulette Darty". c. 1900. Pub. 1904, Bellon
     Ponscarme. Version with orchestra pub. Salabert.
19a La Diva. "Intermezzo Américain" arr. for piano by Hans
     Ourdine. Pub. 1919, Rouart Lerolle; also arr. for café
     orchestra.
20   Je te veux (Henry Pacory). "Valse chantée". "Répertoire
     Paulette Darty". c. 1900. Pub. ?1905, Bellon Ponscarme.
20a Je te veux. Version for voice and orchestra. Pub. Salabert.
     Also version for voice and café orchestra.
20b Valse (Je te veux). For piano. Ded. Paulette Darty. Pub.
     1904, Bellon Ponscarme.
20c Je te veux. Version for small orchestra (?arr. Constant
     Lambert).
21   Sonneries de la Rose + Croix. For piano. 1892.
         1 Air de l'Ordre.
         2 Air du Grand Maître. Ded. Joséphin Péladan.
         3 Air du Grand Prieur. Ded. Le Comte Antoine de la
           Rochefoucauld.
     Pub. Rouart Lerolle.
22   Danses gothiques. For piano. 23 March 1893, 6 rue Cortot.
         1 A l'occasion d'une grande peine; 2 Dans lesquelles les Pères
         de la Très Véritable et Très Sainte Eglise sont invoqués; 3 En

faveur d'un malheureux; 4 *A propos de Saint Bernard et de Sainte Lucie*; 5 *Pour les pauvres trépassés*; 6 *Où il est question du pardon des injures reçues*; 7 *Par pitié pour les ivrognes, honteux, débauchés, imparfaits, désagréables, et faussaires en tous genres*; 8 *En le haut honneur du vénéré Saint Michel, le gracieux Archange*; 9 *Après avoir obtenu la remise de ses fautes.* Pub. 1929, Rouart Lerolle.

23   *Quatre Préludes.* For piano. 1893.
     1 *Fête donnée par des Chevaliers Normands en l'honneur d'une jeune demoiselle*; 2 *Prélude d'Eginhard*; 3 *Ière Prélude du Nazaréen*; 4 *2me Prélude du Nazaréen.*
     Pub. 1929. Rouart Lerolle.

23a *Deux Préludes.* Orch. Francis Poulenc. 1939. (Nos 1 and 3).
     Pub. 1949, Rouart Lerolle.

24   *Prélude de la Porte héroïque du ciel.* For piano. 1894. Ded. Erik Satie ("Je me dédie cette oeuvre"). Pub. 1912, Rouart Lerolle.

24a *Prélude de la Porte héroïque du ciel.* Orch. Roland-Manuel. 1912.

25   *Messe des Pauvres.* For organ or piano. 1895.
     1 *Kyrie eleison*; 2 *Dixit domine*; 3 *Prière des Orgues*; 4 *Commune qui mundi nefas*; 5 *Chant Ecclésiastique*; 6 *Prière pour les voyageurs et les marins en danger de mort, à la très bonne et très auguste Vierge Marie, mère de Jésus*; 7 *Prière pour le salut de mon âme.*
     Pub. 1929, Rouart Lerolle.

25a *Messe des pauvres.* Version orch. David Diamond. Pub. Salabert.

26   *Pièces froides.* For piano. 1897.
     1 *Airs à faire fuir.* Ded. Ricardo Viñes.
     2 *Danses de travers.* Ded. Mme J. Ecorcheville.
     Pub. 1912, Rouart Lerolle.

26a *Nouvelles pièces froides.* For piano. After 1897 but before 1910.
     1 *Sur un mur*; 2 *Sur un arbre*; 3 *Sur un pont.*
     Pub. 1968, Salabert.

27   *Geneviève de Brabant.* Miniature opera for marionettes. 1899.
     1 *Prélude*; 2 *Chorus, Act I*; 3 *Entrée des soldats*; 4 *Entr'acte, Act II*; 5 *Air de Geneviève*; 6 *Sonnerie de cor*; 7 *Entrée des soldats*; 8 *Entr'acte, Act III*; 9 *Air de Golo*; 10 *Entrée des soldats.*
     Pub. 1930, Universal-Edition; vocal score.

27a *Geneviève de Brabant.* Scored by Roger Désormière. Pub. 1930, Universal-Edition.

28 *Jack in the Box.* Pantomime. For piano. 1900. Pub. 1929, Universal-Edition.

28a *Jack in the Box.* Orch. Darius Milhaud. 1926.
    1 *Prélude.*
    2 *Entr'acte.*
    3 *Final.*
Pub. 1929, Universal-Edition.

29 *Rêverie du pauvre.* For piano. 1900. Pub. 1968, Salabert.

30 *The Dreaming Fish* (Le Poisson rêveur). Esquisse for piano. March 1901, Arcueil. Pub. 1968, Salabert. Also version for piano and orchestra by R. Caby.

31 *Trois Morceaux en forme de poire.* For piano four hands. September 1903.
    1 *Manière de commencement* (*Gnossienne from Fils des Etoiles, 1891*) – *Prolongation du même*; 2 *Lentement*; 3 *Enlevé*; 4 *Brutal*; 5 *En plus*; 6 *Redite.*
Pub. 1911, Rouart Lerolle.

31a *Trois Morceaux en forme de poire.* Version orch. Roger Désormière. Pub. Salabert.

32 *Chanson médiévale.* For voice and piano. 1906. Pub. 1968, Salabert, as *Trois Autres Mélodies* No. 2.

33 *Douze petits chorals.* For piano. *c.* 1906. Pub. 1968, Salabert.

34 *Prélude en tapisserie.* For piano. 12 October 1906, Arcueil. Pub. 1929, Rouart Lerolle.

35 *Passacaille.* For piano. July 1906. Arcueil-Cachan. Pub. 1929, Rouart Lerolle. Version orch. David Diamond, pub. Salabert.

36 *Aperçus désagréables.* For piano four hands. September 1908–October 1912.
    1 *Pastorale*; 2 *Choral*; 3 *Fugue.*
Pub. 1913, Demets.

37 *Deux rêveries nocturnes.* For piano. 1910–11.
    1 *Pas vite*; 2 *Très modérément.*
Pub. 1968, Salabert.

38 (*Carnet de croquis et d'esquisses.*) For piano. After 1895 but before 1913. Pub. 1968, Salabert.

39 *En habit de cheval.* For orchestra. 1911.

1 *Choral*; 2 *Fugue litanique*; 3 *Autre choral*; 4 *Fugue de papier*.
Pub. Salabert.

39a *En habit de cheval*. Version for piano four hands. June–August 1911. Pub. 1911, Rouart Lerolle.

40 *Véritables préludes flasques* (pour un chien). For piano. 1912.
 1 *Sévère réprimande*. 12 August 1912.
 2 *Seul à la maison*. 17 August 1912.
 3 *On joue*. 23 August 1912.
Pub. 1912, Demets; Eschig.

41 *Descriptions automatiques*. For piano. 1913.
 1 *Sur un vaisseau*. 21 April 1913. Ded. Mme Fernand Dreyfus.
 2 *Sur une lanterne*. 22 April 1913. Ded. Mme Joseph Ravel.
 3 *Sur un casque*. 26 April 1913. Ded. Mme Paulette Darty.
Pub. 1913, Demets; Eschig.

42 *Embryons desséchés*. For piano. 1913.
 1 *d'Holothurie*. 30 June 1913. Ded. Mlle Suzanne Roux.
 2 *d'Edriophthalma*. 1 July 1913. Ded. Edouard Dreyfus.
 3 *de Podophthalma*. 4 July 1913. Ded. Mme Jane Mortier.
Pub. 1913, Demets; Eschig.

43 *Croquis et agaceries d'un gros bonhomme en bois*. For piano. 1913.
 1 *Tyrolienne turque*. 28 July 1913. Ded. Mlle Elvira Viñes Soto.
 2 *Danse maigre*. 2 June 1913. Ded. Hernando Viñes Soto.
 3 *Españaña*. 25 August 1913. Ded. Mlle Claude Emma Debussy.
Pub. 1913, Demets; Eschig.

44 *Chapitres tournés en tous sens*. For piano. 1913.
 1 *Celle qui parle trop*. 23 August 1913. Ded. Robert Manuel.
 2 *Le porteur de grosses pierres*. 25 August 1913. Ded. Fernand Dreyfus.
 3 *Regrets des enfermés*. 5 September 1913. Ded. Mme Claude Debussy.
Pub. 1913, Demets; Eschig.

45 *Vieux séquins et vieilles cuirasses*. For piano. 1913.
 1 *Chez le marchand d'or*. 9 September 1913. Ded. Ricardo Viñes.
 2 *Danse cuirassée*. 17 September 1913. Ded. M.-D. Calvocoressi.

3 *La Défaite des cimbres.* 14 September 1913. Ded. Emile
Vuillermoz.
Pub. 1913, Demets; Eschig.

46 *Enfantines.* For piano. 1913.
1 *Menus propos enfantins.* 10 October 1913. Ded. Mlle
Valentine Gross.
1 Chant guerrier du roi des haricots.
2 Ce que dit la petite princesse des Tulipes.
3 Valse du Chocolat aux amandes.
2 *Enfantillages pittoresques.* 22 October 1913. Ded. Mme
Léon Verneuil.
1 Petit prélude à la journée.
2 Berceuse.
3 Marche du grand escalier.
3 *Peccadilles importunes.* 26 October 1913. Ded. Mme
Marguerite Long.
1 Etre jaloux de son camarade qui a une grosse tête.
2 Lui manger sa tartine.
3 Profiter de ce qu'il a des cors aux pieds pour lui
prendre son cerceau.
Pub. 1914, Demets; Eschig.

47 *Le Piège de Méduse.* Lyric Comedy with music. 1913. Pub.
1921, Galerie Leiris.

47a *Le Piège de Méduse.* Seven pieces for piano.
1 *Quadrille*; 2 *Valse*; 3 *Pas vite*; 4 *Mazurka*; 5 *Un peu vif*;
6 *Polka*; 7 *Quadrille*.
Pub. 1954, Salabert. Version for eight instruments pub.
1968, Salabert.

48 *Les Pantins dansent.* For piano. 16 November 1913. Pub.
1929, Rouart Lerolle.

48a *Les Pantins dansent.* Version for orchestra by the composer.
Pub. 1967, Salabert.

49 (*Musiques intimes et secrètes.*) For piano. 1906–13.
1 *Nostalgie*; 2 *Froide songerie*; 3 *Fâcheux exemple.*
Pub. 1968, Salabert.

50 (*Six Pièces de la période 1906–13.*) For piano.
1 *Désespoir agréable.* January 1908.
2 *Effronterie.* n.d.
3 *Poésie.* ?1913.

4 *Prélude canin. c.* 1910.
5 *Profondeur.* n.d.
6 *Songe-creux.* n.d.
Pub. 1968, Salabert.

51 *Choses vues à droite et à gauche (sans lunettes).* For piano and violin. 1914. Ded. Marcel Chailley.
1 *Choral hypocrite.* 17 January 1914.
2 *Fugue à tâtons.* 21 January 1914.
3 *Fantaisie musculaire.* 30 January 1915.
Pub. 1916, Rouart Lerolle.

52 *Trois Poèmes d'Amour* (Erik Satie). For voice and piano. 1914. Ded. Henri Fabert.
1 *Ne suis que grain de sable*; 2 *Suis chauve de naissance*; 3 *Ta parure est secrète.*
Pub. 1916, Rouart Lerolle.

53 *Cinq Grimaces.* Composed for an unrealised production by Jean Cocteau of "A Midsummer Night's Dream". 1914.
1 *Modéré*; 2 *Peu vite*; 3 *Modéré*; 4 *Temps de Marche*; 5 *Modéré.*
Pub. 1929, Universal-Edition.

54 *Sports et divertissements.* For piano. 1914.
1 *Choral inappétissant.* 15 May 1914.
2 *La Balançoire.* 31 March 1914.
3 *La Chasse.* 7 April 1914.
4 *La Comédie italienne.* 29 April 1914.
5 *La Mariée.* 16 May 1914.
6 *Colin-Maillard.* 27 April 1914.
7 *La Pêche.* 14 March 1914.
8 *Le Yachting,* 22 March 1914.
9 *Le Bain de mer.* 11 April 1914.
10 *Le Carnaval.* 3 April 1914.
11 *Le Golf.* 20 May 1914.
12 *La Pieuvre.* 17 March 1914.
13 *Les Courses.* 26 March 1914.
14 *Les Quatre Coins.* 24 April 1914.
15 *Le Pique-Nique.* 19 April 1914.
16 *Le Water-Chute.* 14 April 1914.
17 *Le Tango perpétuel.* 5 May 1914.
18 *Le Traîneau.* 2 May 1914.
19 *Le Flirt.* 28 March 1914.
20 *Feu d'artifice.* 6 April 1914.

21 *Le Tennis.* 21 April 1914.
Pub. Publications Lucien Vogel; drawings by Charles Martin.

55 *Heures séculaires et instantanées.* For piano. 1914.
    1 *Obstacles venimeux.* 25 June 1914.
    2 *Crépuscule matinal* (de midi). 3 July 1914.
    3 *Affolements granitiques.*
Pub. 1916, Demets.

56 *Trois Valses distinguées du précieux dégoûté.* For piano. 1914.
    1 *Sa taille.* 21 July 1914. Ded. Roland-Manuel.
    2 *Son binocle.* 22 July 1914. Ded. Mlle Linette Chalupt.
    3 *Ses jambes.* 23 July 1914. Ded. René Chalupt.
Pub. 1916, Rouart Lerolle.

56a *Trois Valses distinguées du précieux dégoûté.* Orch. Greenbaum.

57 *Avant-dernières pensées.* For piano. 1915.
    1 *Idylle.* 23 August 1915. Ded. Debussy.
    2 *Aubade.* 3 October 1915. Ded. Paul Dukas.
    3 *Méditation.* 6 October 1915. Ded. Albert Roussel.
Pub. 1916, Rouart Lerolle.

58 *Trois Mélodies.* For voice and piano. 1916.
    1 *Daphénéo* (M. God). 14 April 1916. Ded. Emile Engel.
    2 *La Statue de bronze* (Léon-Paul Fargue). 26 May 1916. Ded. Jane Bathori.
    3 *Le Chapelier* (René Chalupt). 14 April 1916. Ded. Igor Stravinsky.
Pub. 1917, Rouart Lerolle. Version orch. R. Caby, Salabert (hire).

59 *Parade.* "Ballet réaliste". 1917. Theme, Jean Cocteau. Ded. Mme Edwards (*née* M. Godebska).
    1 *Choral–Prélude du rideau rouge–Prestidigitateur chinois;*
    2 *Petite Fille américaine;* 3 *Acrobates;* 4 *Final–Suite au "Prélude du rideau rouge".*
fp. 18 May 1917, Paris, Théâtre du Châtelet, Diaghilev, cond. Ernest Ansermet; with Léonide Massine, Mlle Chabelska, Woizikovsky, Statkevitsch, Lopokova; choreography, Léonide Massine; curtain, décors and costumes, Pablo Picasso.
Pub. 1917, Rouart Lerolle; Salabert.

59a *Parade.* Ballet Suite for piano four hands. 1917.
    1 *prélude du rideau Rouge;* 2 *Prestidigitateur Chinois;* 3 *Petite*

Fille américaine; 4 *Ragtime du Paquebot*; 5 *Acrobates*;
6 *Suite au Prélude du rideau rouge.*
Pub. 1917, Rouart Lerolle. "Rag-Time Parade" arr. for
piano by Hans Ourdine pub. 1919, Rouart Lerolle.

60 *Sonatine bureaucratique.* For piano. July 1917. Ded. Juliette
Meerovitch. Pub. 1917, S. Chapelier.

61 *Cinq Nocturnes.* For piano. 1919.
> *No. 1* August 1919. Ded. Mme Marcelle Meyer.
> *No. 2* September 1919. Ded. André Salomon.
> *No. 3* October 1919. Ded. Mme Jean Hugo.
> *No. 4* October 1919. Ded. Mme la Comtesse Etienne de
> Beaumont.
> *No. 5* November 1919. Ded. Mme Georges Cocteau.

Pub. 1919 (Nos 1–3) Rouart Lerolle, 1920 (Nos 4 & 5)
Demets; Eschig.

62 *Socrate.* Symphonic Drama in three parts for four voices and
orchestra. 1919. Text: Plato, transl. Victor Cousin. Ded.
Mme la Princesse Edmond de Polignac and to the memory
of Prince Edmond de Polignac.
> 1 *Portrait de Socrate*; 2 *Les Bords de l'Ilissus*; 3 *Mort de
> Socrate.*

Pub. 1919, Editions de la Sirène: vocal score.

63 *Trois petites pièces montées.* For orchestra. 1919.
> 1 *De l'enfance de Pantagruel (Rêverie)*; 2 *Marche de Cocagne
> (Démarche)*; 3 *Jeux de Gargantua (Coin de Polka).*

fp. 21 February 1920, Paris, Théâtre des Champs-Elysées,
cond. Koubitzky. Pub. 1921, Editions de la Sirène.

63a *Trois petites pièces montées.* Version for piano four hands.
1920. Ded. Mme Julien Henriquet. Pub. 1920, Editions de
la Sirène.

64 *La Belle Excentrique.* For music-hall orchestra. 1920.
> 1 *Grande Ritournelle*; 2 *Marche "Franco-Lunaire"*; 3 *Valse du
> "mystérieux baiser dans l'oeil"*; 4 *Cancan "Grand-Mondain".*

Pub. 1922, Editions de la Sirène: reduction for piano four
hands.

65 *Premier Menuet.* For piano. June 1920. Ded. Claude Dubosq.
Pub. 1922, Editions de la Sirène.

66 *Quatre petites mélodies.* For voice and piano. 1920.
> 1 *Elégie* (Lamartine).
> 2 *Danseuse* (Jean Cocteau).

3 *Chanson.*
4 *Adieu* (Raymond Radiguet).
Pub. Eschig.
67 *Ludions.* For voice and piano. 1923. Poems: Léon-Paul Fargue.
  1 *Air du rat*; 2 *Spleen*; 3 *La Grenouille américaine*; 4 *Air du Poète*; 5 *Chanson du Chat.*
  Pub. 1926, Rouart Lerolle.
68 *Mercure.* Ballet ("Poses Plastiques"). 1924. Ded. Mme la Comtesse Etienne de Beaumont.
  1 *Marche-Ouverture. Premier Tableau*; 2 *La Nuit*; 3 *Danse de tendresse*; 4 *Signes du zodiaque*; 5 *Entrée de Mercure. Deuxième Tableau*; 6 *Danse des Grâces*; 7 *Bain des Grâces*; 8 *Fuite de Mercure*; 9 *Colère de Cerbère. Troisième Tableau*; 10 *Polka des Lettres*; 11 *Nouvelle Danse*; 12 *Le Chaos*; 13 *Rapt de Proserpine.*
  fp. 15 June 1924, Paris, Théâtre de la Cigale, Etienne de Beaumont; choreography, Léonide Massine; scenery and costumes, Picasso.
  Pub. 1930, Universal-Edition.
69 *Relâche.* "Ballet instantanéiste" in two acts and cinematographic entr'acte by René Clair. 1924.
  fp. 29 November 1924, Paris, Théâtre des Champs-Elysées, Ballets Suédois; scenario and décors, Francis Picabia.
  Pub. 1926, Rouart Lerolle: piano score.
69a *Cinéma.* "Entr'acte symphonique" from "Relâche" arr. for piano four hands by Darius Milhaud. Pub. 1926, Rouart Lerolle.

Satie's Published Writings

Cartulaire de l'Eglise Métropolitaine d'Art de Jésus Conducteur – several issues in 1895.

Occasional paragraphs and obiter dicta, in *L'Oeil de veau*, February 1912.

Mémoires d'un amnésique: Ce que je suis (fragment), *Bulletin de la SIM*, 15 April 1912.

Mémoires d'un amnésique: La journée d'un musicien (fragment), *Bulletin de la SIM*, 15 February 1913.

Mémoires d'un amnésique: L'Intelligence et la musicalité chez les animaux, *Bulletin de la SIM*, 1 February 1914.

Items in *Le Coq et l'Arlequin*, broadsheet issued irregularly in 1920.

Cahiers d'un mammifère, *Esprit nouveau*, April 1921.

Eloge des critiques, *Action*, No. 8, August 1921.

Le Piège de Méduse. Comédie lyrique en un acte. Théâtre Michel, 24 mai 1921. Ornée de gravures sur bois par M. Georges Braque. Editions de la Galérie Simon, 1921.

Cahiers d'un mammifère, and other occasional pieces in various issues of *391* between 1921 and 1924.

Les Six, *Feuilles libres*, February 1922.

L'Origine d'instruction, *Feuilles libres*, June-July 1922.

Propos à propos d'Igor Stravinsky, *Feuilles libres*, Oct./Nov. 1922.

A Table, *Almanach de Cocagne*, 1922.

Conférence, *Anbruch*, January 1923.

Les Périmés, *Feuilles libres*, No. 31, 1923.

Mémoires d'un amnésique: Recoins de ma vie (fragment), *Feuilles libres*, No. 35, January–February 1924.

L'esprit musical. Portrait de l'auteur par lui-même. Liège. P. Aelberts, 1950. (Lectures given in Brussels and Antwerp, March 1924.)

Cahiers d'un mammifère. Chez les principaux marchands de céphalophones. Liège. P. Aelberts, 1951.

Mémoires d'un amnésique. Liège. P. Aelberts, 1953.

Propos à propos. Liège. P. Aelberts, 1954.

Léger comme un oeuf. L. Broder, 1957.

Oui. Lettres d'Erik Satie. Adressées à Pierre de Massot. Précédées d'une étude de Pierre de Massot. Alès, Pab, 1960.

Chronique musicale, *L'Approdo musicale*, Nos 19–20, 1965.

Mémoires d'un amnésique, *L'Approdo musicale*, Nos 19–20, 1965.

Bibliography

UNPRINTED SOURCES:
The important series of notebooks (the gift of Darius Milhaud), together with several letters, held in the Département de la musique, Bibliothèque Nationale; autograph scores, manuscripts and other documents in the Bibliothèque-Musée de l'Opéra. The registration of birth is held in the archives of the town hall at Arcueil. Another important source is the Dumbarton Oaks Library in Washington, to which Milhaud gave quantities of manuscripts – but no reply was received from this institution when enquiry was made about them.

PRINTED SOURCES:
[Ballets Suédois], *Les Ballets Suédois dans l'art contemporain,* Editions du Trianon, 1931
Bertin, Pierre *Le Théâtre et/est ma vie,* Le Bélier, 1971
—— *Erik Satie et le groupe des Six,* Les Annales, LVIII, No. 4, 1951
Bruyère, André, *A Honfleur, au siècle dernier. Erik Satie,* Bulletin des amis du musée de Honfleur, 1970

Cage, John, *Silence,* Western University Press, Connecticut, 1961

Calvocoressi, M.-D., *Musicians' Gallery*, Faber & Faber, 1925
Cendrars, Blaise, *Blaise Cendrars vous parle*, Denoël, 1965
Chanel, Pierre, *Album Cocteau*, Tchou, 1970
Chennevière, R. de, "Erik Satie and the music of irony", in *The Musical Quarterly*, 1920
Clair, René, *Entr'acte*, Poligono Socièta editrice in Milano, 1945
—— *Entr'acte*, in L'Avant-Scène, Cinéma No. 86, November 1968
Cocteau, Jean, *Le Rappel à l'ordre* (including *Le Coq et l'harlequin*, etc.), Stock 1948
—— (with Raymond Radiguet), *Paul et Virginie*, J.-C. Lattès, 1973
Coeuroy, André, *La Musique française moderne*, Delagrave, 1922
Collaer, Paul, *La Musique moderne, 1905-1955*, Elsevier, 1955
Cortot, Alfred, *La Musique française de piano*, vol. 3, Presses Universitaires de France, 1948
Crespelle, J.-P., *Montparnasse vivant*, Hachette, 1962

Davies, Laurence, *The Gallic Muse*, Dent, 1967
Drew, David, "Modern French Music", in *European Music of the Twentieth Century*, ed. H. Hartog, Routledge, 1957
Dukas, Paul, *Correspondance de Paul Dukas*, ed. G. Favre, Editions Durand, 1971

Everling, Germaine, *L'Anneau de Saturne*, Fayard, 1970

Gérard, Yves, *Introduction à l'oeuvre d'Erik Satie*, dissertation in typescript, Conservatoire de Paris, 1958
Gowers, Patrick, *Satie's Rose + Croix Music (1891-1895)*, Proceedings of The Royal Musical Association, 92nd Session, 1965-66
Guichard, Léon, "Erik Satie et la musique Grégorienne", in *Revue Musicale*, 15 Nov., 1936
—— *La Musique et les lettres en France au temps du Wagnérisme*, Presses Universitaires de France, 1963

[Hägar, Bengt.], "Svenska Baletten/Les Ballets Suédois/1920–1925/Ur Dansmuseets samlingar", *Moderna Museet*, Stockholm 27 February–7 April, 1969
[Hägar, Bengt.], *Modern Swedish Ballet*, Victoria and Albert Museum, 1970
Harding, James, *The Ox on The Roof*, Macdonald, 1972

Hill, Edward Burlingame, *Modern French Music*, Allen & Unwin, 1924
Hugnet, Georges, *L'Aventure Dada*, Seghers, 1971

Jacob, Max, *Correspondance*, ed. F. Garnier, Vol. 1, Editions de Paris, 1953
Jean-Aubry, G., *La Musique française d'aujourd'hui*, Perrin, 1916
Jouhandeau, Elise, *Le Spleen empanaché*, Flammarion, 1960
Jourdan-Morhange, Hélène, *Mes amis musiciens*, Editeurs Français Réunis, 1955

Kostelanetz, Richard (ed.), *John Cage*, Allen Lane/The Penguin Press, 1970

Lambert, Constant, *Music Ho!*, Faber & Faber, 1934
Landormy, Paul, *La Musique française après Debussy*, Gallimard, 1943
Latour, J. P. Contamine, "Erik Satie intime", in *Comoedia*, 3, 5, 6, Paris, August 1925
[Lesure, François], *Erik Satie. Exposition. Paris et Arcueil, 1966*, Bibliothèque Nationale, 1966

Massine, Léonide, *My Life in Ballet*, Macmillan, 1968
Mellers, Wilfrid, *Studies in Contemporary Music*, Dennis Dobson, 1947
Milhaud, Darius, *Notes sans musique*, Julliard, 1963
—— *Notes sur Erik Satie*, Oeuvres nouvelles, New York, 1946
Myers, Rollo, *Erik Satie*, Dennis Dobson, 1948
—— "Erik Satie", in *Histoire de la musique*, Vol. 2, Encyclopédie de la Pléiade, 1963. (See also *Revue Musicale*)

Picabia, Francis, *391* (Reprint of the magazine, ed. M. Sanouillet), Terrain Vague, 1960
Polnay, Peter de, *The Moon and the Maribou Stork*, Paul Elek, 1973
Poulenc, Francis, *Moi et mes amis* (with S. Audel), Palatine, 1963
—— *Correspondance*, ed. H. de Wendel, Seuil, 1967
Proust, Marcel, "Pastiches et mélanges", in *Contre Sainte-Beuve*, Pléiade. 1971

Revue Musicale, "Erik Satie", special number, March 1924

Revue Musicale, "Erik Satie. Son temps et ses amis", ed. Rollo Myers, June 1952

Roland-Manuel, *Erik Satie*, H. Roberge, 1916
Roy, Jean, *Présences contemporaines*, Nouvelles éditions, Debresse, 1962

Samazeuilh, Gustave, *Musiciens de mon temps*, Marcel Daubin, 1947
Samuel, Claude, *Panorama de la musique contemporaine*, Gallimard, 1962
Shattuck, Roger, *The Banquet Years*, Faber & Faber, 1959
Steegmuller, Francis, *Cocteau: A Biography*, Macmillan, 1970
Stravinsky, Igor, *Chroniques de ma vie*, Denoël et Steele, 1935
—— *Conversations with Stravinsky* (Robert Craft), Faber & Faber, 1959

Templier, P. D., *Erik Satie*, Rieder, 1932
Thompson, Kenneth, *A Dictionary of Twentieth-Century Composers (1911–1971)*, Faber & Faber, 1973

Varèse, Louise, *Varèse. A Looking-Glass Diary*, Davis-Poynter, 1972

Willy (Henri Gauthier-Villars), *Bains de sons*, Simonis Empis, 1893
—— *Entre deux airs*, Flammarion, 1895
—— *Garçon, l'addition!*, Simonis Empis, 1901

Index

Allais, Alphonse, writer (1854–1905), 33–36, 37–38, 49, 81, 238

Andersen, Hans Christian, writer (1805–1875), 19, 125

Apollinaire, Guillaume (Wilhelm Apollinaris de Kostrowitsky), poet (1880–1918), 16, 158–159, 161, 191, 218, 220

Aragon, Louis, poet and politician (b. 1897), 212, 217

Auric, Georges, composer (b. 1899): 143, 167, 168, 186, 187, 189, 191, 194, 205, 206, 207, 208, 212, 217, 218, 221, 223, 232–233, 236; *Adieu, New York!*, 189; *La Danse d'aujourd'hui*, 191, 194; *Les Fâcheux*, 189, 206, 207

Auriol, Georges-Hugot, chansonnier (1863–1938), 80, 81

Bach, Johann Sebastian, composer (1685–1750): 12, 90, 97, 173, 210; *Art of Fugue*, 97

Barrès, Maurice, novelist (1862–1923), 217

Bathori, Jane (Jeanne Marie Berthier), singer (b. 1877), 153, 154, 166, 167, 181

Baudelaire, Charles, poet (1821–1867): 4, 67, 194; *Les Fleurs du mal*, 4

Beaumont, comtesse Etienne de, 181–182, 189, 211

Beaumont, comte Etienne de, patron, 181–182, 189, 210, 211, 212, 229, 235–236, 242

Beethoven, Ludwig van, composer (1770–1827), 90, 106, 112, 169

Berlioz, Hector, composer (1803–1869): 89, 106, 190, 205; *La Symphonie fantastique*, 190

Berners, Lord (Gerald Hugh Tyrwhitt-Wilson), composer, diplomatist, writer, artist (1883–1950): 130, 188; *Petite marche funèbre pour une tante à héritage*, 188; *Strauss, Strauss et Strauss*, 130

263

Bertin, Pierre, actor and producer (*b.* 1893), 109–110, 181, 182, 185–186, 187, 197, 201, 210, 241

Blès, Numa (Charles Bessat), chansonnier (1871–1917), 78

Bois, Jules, writer: 52, 69; *Les Noces de Sathan*, 52; *La Porte héroïque du ciel*, 52, 69

Bonnaud, Dominique Marie Jean-Baptiste, chansonnier (1864–1943), 78

Bonsdorff, Edith, dancer, 232

Bordes, Charles Marie Anne, musicologist (1863–1909), 89

Börlin, Jean, dancer and choreographer (1893–1930), 223, 226, 227, 229, 230, 231, 232, 235, 241

Brancusi, Constantin, sculptor (1876–1957), 236, 243

Braque, Georges, painter (1882–1963), 210, 235, 242

Brélia, Evelyne, singer, 186, 187

Breton, André, poet (1922–1969), 212, 217, 218, 220

Busser, Henri, composer (1872–1973), 65, 66

Caby, Roger, musician, 236, 239, 240, 241, 242

Calvocoressi, M.-D., musicologist (1877–1944), 146

Caran d'Ache (Emmanuel Poiré), artist, 37, 38

Casella, Alfredo, composer (1883–1947), 152, 229

Cendrars, Blaise (Frédéric Saussure), writer (1887–1961), 184, 222, 223

Chabrier, Alexis Emmanuel, composer (1841–1894): 30, 109, 112, 124, 206; *Le Roi malgré lui*, 30–31; *Une Education manquée*, 206

Chalupt, René, writer (1885–1957), 127, 142, 152–153, 167, 180

Chavannes, Pierre Puvis de, artist (1824–1898), 31, 43, 53, 55

Chenal, Marthe, singer, 224

Chopin, Frédéric François, composer (1810–1849): 20, 123, 154, 169, 189, 227; *Funeral March* (Sonata in B♭ minor), 123, 227

Clair, René (Chomette), film director (*b.* 1898): x, 198, 225, 226, 227, 228, 230; *Entr'acte*, 198, 224, 225–228, 232; *Paris qui dort*, 224

Claudel, Paul Louis Charles Marie, poet and businessman (1868–1955), 167, 182

Cliquet-Pleyel, Henri, composer (1894–1963), 208, 218

Cocteau, Jean Maurice, poet (1889–1963): 110, 137–138, 140, 141, 154–155, 156, 157, 158, 159, 160, 161, 162, 163; 164, 168, 180, 181, 182, 189, 191, 192, 194, 199, 200, 201, 207, 210, 220–221, 223, 240, 241; *Le Boeuf sur le toit*, 138, 160, 189; *Le Coq* (editor), 169; *Le Coq et l'Arlequin*, 168–169; *Le Gendarme incompris*, 201; *Paul et Virginie*, 199, 200

Colette, Sidonie Gabrielle, writer (1873–1954), 62, 63, 64, 145

Collet, Henri, critic and composer (1885–1951), 167

Corneille, Pierre, dramatist (1606–1684), 201

Cortot, Alfred, pianist (1877–1962), 45, 136

Courteline, Georges (Moineaux), writer (1861–1929), 39–40

Cousin, Victor, philosopher (1792–1867), 175–176

Cravan, Arthur, writer and editor, 216–217

Darty, Paulette, music-hall singer (*d.* 1940), 78–79, 104, 107, 122, 240

Debussy, Achille-Claude, composer (1862–1918): xiii, 30, 52, 59, 62, 65, 67–68, 77, 88, 91, 107, 108, 109, 112, 113, 114, 115, 136, 146, 151, 153, 168, 169, 170–171, 182, 200, 207, 217, 241, 242; *La Mer*, xiii; *Pelléas et Mélisande*, 67, 77, 107, 170, 182